Praise for this book

'Thoroughly researched and thoroughly informative on a burning issue of our time'

Ghada Karmi

'Whatever position one holds on the question of a two-state solution or of a bi-national state for Palestine/Israel, it is important to understand the arguments put forward. This collection of essays engages the reader directly and honestly, bringing many new and important angles to the debate over bi-nationalism. The arguments and facts presented here succeed in bringing the bi-nationalist position from the margins of the debate to a more central position.'

Mick Dumper, Reader in Middle East Politics, University of Exeter, and author of *The Politics of Sacred Space: The Old City of Jerusalem in the Middle East Conflict* (2004) and editor of *Palestinian Refugee* *Global Perspectives* (2006)

About this book

Where Now for Palestine? marks a turning point for the Middle East. Since 2000, the attacks of 9/11, the death of Arafat and the elections of Hamas and Kadima have meant that the Israel/Palestine 'two-state solution' now seems illusory.

This collection critically revisits the concept of the 'two-state solution' and maps the effects of local and global political changes on both Palestinian people and politics. The authors discuss the changing face of Fatah, Israeli perceptions of Palestine, and the influence of the Palestinian diaspora. The book also analyses the environmental destruction of Gaza and the West Bank, the economic viability of a Palestinian state and the impact of US foreign policy in the region. This authoritative and up-to-date guide to the impasse facing the region is required reading for anyone wishing to understand a conflict entrenched at the heart of global politics.

JAMIL HILAL | editor

Where now for Palestine?

The demise of the two-state solution

Zed Books

LONDON | NEW YORK

Where now for Palestine? The demise of the two-state solution was first
published in 2007 by Zed Books Ltd, 7 Cynthia Street, London N1 9JF, UK
and Room 400, 175 Fifth Avenue, New York, NY 10010, USA

<www.zedbooks.co.uk>

Editorial copyright © Jamil Hilal, 2007
Individual chapters copyright © individual authors, 2007

The right of Jamil Hilal to be identified as the editor of this work has been
asserted by him in accordance with the Copyright, Designs and Patents
Act, 1988.

Cover designed by Andrew Corbett
Set in Arnhem and Futura Bold by Ewan Smith, London
Index: <ed.emery@britishlibrary.net>
Printed and bound in the EU by Biddles Ltd, King's Lynn <www.biddles.co.uk>

Distributed in the USA exclusively by Palgrave Macmillan, a division of
St Martin's Press, LLC, 175 Fifth Avenue, New York, NY 10010.

A catalogue record for this book is available from the British Library.
US CIP data are available from the Library of Congress.

ISBN   1 84277 839 0 | 978 1 84277 839 5 hb
ISBN   1 84277 840 4 | 978 1 84277 840 1 pb

Contents

Tables and figures

Tables

Figures

Acknowledgements

This book is an outcome of the research co-operation between the Chr. Michelsen Institute (CMI), Bergen and Muwatin, the Palestinian Institute for the Study of Democracy, Ramallah, which has been ongoing since 1995. Both institutes wish to acknowledge the Norwegian Agency for Development Cooperation (Norad) for its support.

Contributors

Ziad Abu-Amr is a member of the Palestinian Legislative Council (PLC) representing Gaza city. He was elected in 1996, and again in 2006. He is the former chairman of the Political Committee in the Council, a former minister of culture in the Palestinian Authority, and a former professor of political science at Birzeit University. He holds a PhD from Georgetown University in Washington, DC and has written extensively on the Islamic movement in Palestine. Abu-Amr is the president of the Palestinian Council on Foreign Relations.

Sufyan Alissa is an economist specialized in Middle Eastern affairs. He has served as the project coordinator for CIVITAS – a project determining the civic needs of the Palestinian refugees outside the West Bank and Gaza – at Nuffield College, University of Oxford. He taught at the School of Oriental and African Studies (SOAS), University of London, City University, UK and Bethlehem University, West Bank. He was the research coordinator and co-author of Palestine Human Development Report 2001/2002. He worked for the International Labour Organization (office of the Arab States) as consultant on labour-market issues in Mashreq countries and youth unemployment in Syria. He received his PhD in Economics from SOAS, University of London.

Nils A. Butenschøn is associate professor of International Relations and former director at the Norwegian Centre for Human Rights, Faculty of Law, University of Oslo. He has been deputy director and director of International Relations Studies at the Department of Political Science at the same university. His recent works on the Middle East include: (edited with U. Davis and M. Hassassian) *Citizenship and the State in the Middle East: Approaches and Applications*, New York: Syracuse University Press, 2000; 'Accommodating conflicting claims to national self-determination: The intractable case of Israel/Palestine', *International Journal of Minority and Group Rights*, Vol. 13, No. 2, 2006.

Sharif S. Elmusa is an associate professor of Political Science at the American University in Cairo, Egypt. He was a senior research fellow at the Institute of Palestine Studies, Washington, DC. Elmusa was a member of the Palestinian delegation in the 1993 talks with Israel in Washington. He teaches environmental politics and is author of, among others, *Water Conflict: Economics, Politics, Law and the Palestinian-Israeli Water Resources.*

Basem Ezbidi is a political science professor at Birzeit University, Palestine, and taught previously at Najah University, Palestine. Ezbidi is currently engaged in a project on the prospects of reforming the Palestinian civil service system. He is the author of several publications on the Palestinian political situation including state-building, political Islamism, corruption and reform, and civil society.

As'ad Ghanem is the head of the Department of Government and Political Philosophy as well as senior lecturer at the School of Political Sciences, University of Haifa. He is also head of the research unit at Madar – the Palestinian Center for Israeli Studies. Ghanem's theoretical work has explored the legal, institutional and political conditions in ethnic states. In the context of Israel/Palestine, Ghanem's work has covered issues such as Palestinian political orientations, the establishment and political structure of the Palestinian Authority, and majority–minority politics in a comparative perspective.

Jamil Hilal is a sociologist and has published several books and numerous articles on Palestinian society, history and politics. His recent books (in Arabic) include: *Israel's Economic Strategy towards the Middle East* (Beirut, 1996); *The Palestinian Political System after Oslo* (Beirut and Ramallah, 1998, updated, 2006); *The Formation of the Palestinian Elite* (Ramallah, 2002); *The Palestinian Middle Class* (Beirut and Ramallah, 2006). Hilal is an associate research fellow at Muwatin, the Palestinian Institute for the Study of Democracy. He is a non-resident senior researcher at the Development Studies Programme, the Institute of Women's Studies, and the Law Institute at Birzeit University, Palestine. Hilal is a co-editor of the quarterly *Journal of Palestine Studies* (Arabic edition, published in Beirut and Jerusalem).

Jad Isaac is the director general of the Applied Research Institute–Jerusalem (ARIJ) which conducts research on agriculture, environment, land use and water. He obtained his BSc degree from Cairo University, his MSc from Rutgers University and his PhD from the University of East Anglia, UK. Isaac is the former dean of science

ix

at Bethlehem University. He has published several articles and books including an environmental profile of the West Bank and the Atlas of Palestine. He headed the Palestinian delegation for the environmental working group in the multilateral talks and was an adviser to the Palestinian negotiating team on final status issues.

Are Knudsen is a social anthropologist with more than ten years' research experience in South Asia and the Middle East. He has published articles on Palestinian refugees, Islamist movements and post-war Lebanon. Knudsen is presently with the Chr. Michelsen Institute (CMI) in Bergen as scientific coordinator for research cooperation with Muwatin, the Palestinian Institute for the Study of Democracy.

Husam A. Mohamad is an associate professor in the Department of Political Science at the University of Central Oklahoma, USA. Dr Mohamad holds a BA degree in Middle Eastern Studies from Birzeit University, West Bank, and an MA and PhD in Political Science from the University of Cincinnati, USA. He has written extensively for journals, books and book reviews.

Karma Nabulsi is a fellow in Politics at St Edmund Hall, Oxford, and university lecturer in the Department of Politics and International Relations, Oxford. She was a PLO representative from 1977 to 1990, working at the United Nations, and in Beirut, Tunis and the United Kingdom. She did her doctorate at Balliol College, Oxford. She was the specialist adviser to the UK All-party Parliamentary Commission of Inquiry on Palestinian Refugees (and its report, *Right of Return*, 2000). She is currently engaged in an EU-funded collective research project, based at Nuffield College, on Palestinian Refugee Camps and Exile Communities. She is the author of *Traditions of War: Occupation, Resistance and the Law* (Oxford University Press, 2005).

Ilan Pappé is a senior lecturer in the Department of Political Science, Haifa University. He is the chairperson of the Emil Touma Institute for Palestinian Studies, Haifa. Pappé received his PhD from Oxford University in 1984 and has taught ever since at the University of Haifa. He was the founder and head of the Institute for Peace Research at Givat Haviva, 1992–2000. His books include *The Making of the Arab-Israeli Conflict* (IB Tauris, 1992), *The Israel/Palestine Question* (Routledge, 1999) and *A History of Modern Palestine* (Cambridge University Press, 2003), and *The Modern Middle East* (Routledge, 2005).

Owen Powell is a graduate of the University of Tasmania, Australia. In 2003 he graduated with a Bachelor's degree in Arts and Science, majoring in History and Geography. In 2004, he completed Honours in Environmental Science investigating the impact of land-use change on fluvial geomorphology. After working as a volunteer for the University of An-Najah, Owen currently works as a research assistant for the Applied Research Institute – Jerusalem (ARIJ).

1 | Palestine: the last colonial issue

JAMIL HILAL

The present as an explanation of the past

Palestinian demand for a sovereign territorial state was voiced soon after the collapse of the Ottoman Empire, and the imposition of British colonial rule on Palestine. It rose with the arbitrary division of the Middle East among the dominant imperialist powers at the time (Britain and France). In 1917, Britain issued the Balfour Declaration committing itself to facilitate the establishment of a 'Jewish homeland' in Palestine, ignoring the will of the indigenous inhabitants of the country (the Palestinians) and their right to self-determination. The demand for a Palestinian national territorial state became insistent once it became clear that the Arabs would not have the unified nation-state the British had promised them would be theirs once the First World War had ended. This demand attained a special urgency once the Palestinians realized the aims of the Zionist project, and the full implications of the Balfour Declaration (see Khalidi 1997; Porath 1974; Hilal 2002). This awareness is behind the dual struggle that the Palestinians waged during the Mandate against both British imperial domination and Zionist colonization.[1] It also explains why, at the time, the Palestinians stood against the partition of their country into an Arab and a Jewish state; they saw it, rightly, as an unjust violation of their rights. Furthermore, many of the 'international' (in reality the USA and Europe) resolutions and initiatives exhibited, and still do exhibit, blatant double standards in the application of the principle of self-determination when its application concerns Palestinians (see Chapter 4 by Butenschøn).

It is important to recall that religious pluralism was *not* the cause of the conflict between Palestinians and settler Jewish Zionists (later Jewish Israelis). The Palestinian national movement during the British Mandate called for a democratic state to include the various ethnic and religious communities that made Palestine their home. For this reason it was against the establishment of a Jewish state in Palestine.

The well-organized and well-armed European Zionist movement, aided by Britain, was able to defeat the predominantly peasant Palestinian society, with its badly organized national movement led by notable families (Kimmerling and Migdal 2003).[2] The highly disorganized and badly armed military contingents sent, in 1948, by neighbouring Arab states (under British and French imperial rule at the time) to aid the Palestinians were easily defeated by the well-organized and well-equipped Zionist forces. Thus, in May 1948, the Zionist movement was able to declare the state of Israel on 78% of Mandate Palestine, much more than the 51% allotted to it by the 1947 United Nations Partition Plan. The remaining 22% of the territory – comprising what came to be known as the West Bank and the Gaza Strip – fell under Jordanian and Egyptian rule respectively. Only a fraction of Palestinians remained in the areas on which Israel was established, to become a national minority (but not acknowledged as such by the Israeli state) in their homeland.

It is ironic that British and American support and collaboration went to a movement committed to the establishment of an ethno-religious state (i.e. Israel) and not to a movement that declared its commitment to a non-religious or ethnic conception. This is ironic because both countries prided themselves on building a state based on equality of citizens, regardless of religious or ethnic affiliations. In was clear, right from the beginning, that the process of creating, empowering, and maintaining a Jewish state in Palestine would entail the indigenous people being subjected to ethnic cleansing, to systemic discrimination and, sooner or later, to a system of apartheid.

Zionism is a special offshoot of European settler colonialism that is a colonialism of an exclusivist (ethno-religious) state-building project. Like European colonialism elsewhere it faced a national liberation movement that sought self-determination, emancipation and independence. The Palestine question is a colonial question, and the last colonial question to remain unsolved in the 21st century.

Israel was created against the will of both the Palestinian people and the peoples of the region as a whole. It did so by relying heavily on the support and collaboration of the world imperialist powers (first Britain, then the United States), and by becoming a highly militarized society in constant war with the region. It is telling that Israel has found it necessary 60 years from its establishment to build a Separation Wall round itself for fear of losing an imagined essentialist character.

A majority of Palestinians, as Israeli new historians (see for example

Morris 1987; Pappé 1994) came to acknowledge decades later, was forced to flee the invading Zionist forces (Masalha 1992). These became refugees, and a United Nations agency (UNRWA) was established to administer their affairs in some 60 camps that it established for the most destitute of the Palestinian refugees in the countries surrounding what became Israel. Palestinians who did not flee were given Israeli nationality but were looked upon with suspicion, treated as second-class citizens and as non-Jewish minorities, and not as a national group with collective rights. This is consistent with the self-definition of Israel as combining Jewishness and democracy (see Rouhana 2006), and of confining full democratic and equal rights to Israeli Jews only.[3]

The remaining 22% of Palestine, i.e. the West Bank and Gaza Strip, came under Jordanian and Egyptian rule respectively. The 1948 Nakba (catastrophe – as Palestinians called it) devastated the Palestinian national movement completely, and it took nearly two decades and another two wars – the Suez invasion when Israel occupied the Gaza Strip and the 1967 six-day war when Israel occupied the West Bank and Gaza Strip as well as Sinai and the Golan Heights – for it fully to re-invent itself as a Palestinian resistance movement under the name of the Palestine Liberation Organization (PLO).

The Palestinian national movement: from a one-state to a two-state solution

The vision of establishing a secular democratic Palestinian state for all its citizens, irrespective of religion or ethnicity, was proposed by the PLO in the late 1960s, but was ignored by Israel and the West. In 1974 (following the Israeli-Arab war of October 1973) the PLO adopted the notion of a two-stage struggle in which it was envisaged that a Palestinian state would exist next to an Israeli one, while the establishment of a full democratic state in historic Palestine was to be left to a later stage of the struggle. This 'transitional' co-existence of two states (one Palestinian, the other Israeli) was articulated further in November 1988 during the first Palestinian Intifada, when the PLO endorsed as a strategy the formula of 'two states for two peoples'. The borders of the Palestinian state were not specified. The implementation of Right of Return for Palestinian refugees (as specified by United Nations Resolution 194) remained an integral part of the two-state solution.

It was the Oslo Accords (signed in 1993 between Israel and the PLO) that defined clearly the occupied West Bank (including East Jerusalem)

3

and the Gaza Strip as the territory of the Palestinian state. It soon became clear, however, that Israel still viewed these territories as disputed areas, thereby giving itself the right to continue its colonial settlement activities, and to solidify its annexation and Judaization of East Jerusalem and the surrounding areas. The painful compromise that the PLO made by accepting a state on 22% of Palestine was rejected by Israel, and, as it turned out, also by the United States.

The explanation of the gradual acceptance by the main stream of the Palestinian national movement of a two-state solution to the Israeli-Palestinian conflict needs to recall the fast-changing situation of the PLO and the impact on it of regional and international shifts from the late 1960s to the late 1980s. The PLO's lack of a territorial base of its own led to frequent conflicts with the host governments of the countries in which it resided, as happened with Jordan, Lebanon, and Syria. It is also important to stress that the PLO bureaucracy grew rapidly during the 1970s, which limited its agility and created interests specific to this bureaucracy that made it resist change; at the same time it was able to use the relatively large 'rent' generated from Arab (mostly from oil-rich states) and international sources (mostly Soviet and socialist countries) to create a kind of a 'rentier' relationship with the Palestinian communities, particularly with the Palestinian camps. This took the form of providing employment, welfare, and services. But the PLO also provided empowerment to refugees through arming and organizing them (Sayigh 1979).

The special relationship with the oil-producing Arab states and the socialist camp ensured that the PLO listened to their political counselling; and this counselling tended towards the acceptance of a state on the West Bank and Gaza Strip. Attempts by the PLO to widen its relations with the Western countries were made conditional on its acknowledging the right of Israel to exist and its acceptance of Security Council resolutions 242 and 338. The loss to the PLO of its Lebanon base made it vulnerable to pressure and ultimately it settled for a state on 22% of Palestine.

The dispersal of the PLO forces as a result of the Israeli invasion of Lebanon in 1982 added political weight to the role of the occupied West Bank and Gaza Strip in the PLO's strategy. The immediate and most important aim for Palestinians in these areas was, and still is, freeing themselves from the Israeli occupation, which raised the question about the political future of the Palestinians. The obvious answer was to establish an independent Palestinian state. The first Intifada, which erupted in December 1987, made the two-state solution the logical solution, particularly following the announcement by Jordan in 1988 that it would cut all its administrative links with the West Bank. The collapse in the late 1980s of the PLO's main international ally (the Soviet Union and the socialist camp), and the political and financial siege imposed on the PLO by the rich Gulf states as a result of its stand on the Gulf War in the early 1990s, left the Palestinian movement exposed and vulnerable, and ready join the Madrid conference in 1991.

The Oslo Accords reflected the core PLO leadership reading of the balance of forces existing at the time. The Intifada gave that leadership the feeling that it could change the balance of forces once it returned to Palestine, to the extent of achieving an independent Palestinian state. Hence the PLO accepted the establishment of the Palestinian Authority (PA) as a government with limited powers on a part of the 1967-occupied Palestinian territories, and agreed to leave the issue of statehood to 'final status' negotiations (to come after a five-year transitional period of the self-governing entity). It thought, mistakenly, that Israel would try to deal with the 'final status' issues on the basis of international law, thereby to some degree redressing historic justice, and not on the basis of the balance of power, as in fact Israel did. The four main 'final status' issues left for negotiations were: the future of Jerusalem, the fate of the refugees, the question of Israeli settlements, and Israeli-Palestinian borders. When the final status negotiations were held at the Camp David summit in July 2000 between Arafat, Barak, and Clinton, it was the Palestinians who were asked to render concessions to Israel on all four issues.

One consequence of the Oslo Accords was the freezing of the PLO's national institutions and associations in favour of empowering the new PA. The result was the effective dismantling of the entire organizational superstructure that the PLO had constructed since the late 1960s, which provided a complex network of relations connecting Palestinians in their diverse and scattered communities and a forum for their political deliberations. The freezing of the PLO institutions and mass and professional organizations left Palestinians outside the 1967-occupied territories with a deep sense of abandonment and desertion (recorded by Nabulsi in Chapter 11).

5

The transformation of the Palestinian national movement

The second Intifada – which came soon after the collapse of the Camp David negotiations – deepened the polarization within the Palestinian political movement into two main political trends: one populist nationalist (represented by Fatah), the other populist Islamist (represented by the Islamic Resistance Movement or Hamas), with the left camp occupying a marginal space as it remained politically fragmented and organizationally sectarian. Since the late 1980s, the influence of political Islam had grown in line with the growth of Islamist influence in the region following the Iranian revolution in 1979 and following the failure of the Arab secular-nationalist states to deliver politically (in terms of democracy, human and civil rights, and Arab unity), and economically (in sustained economic development). The collapse of the Soviet Union and the socialist states in Eastern and Central Europe placed the Arab left in bewilderment, while the rapid growth of the financial capital available to the oil-producing Middle Eastern countries (particularly Saudi Arabia and other Gulf states) was used to bolster these countries' political and ideological influence. This expressed itself in their control of mass media, satellite television, the publishing of religious books, the growth in the building and use of mosques for political advocacy, and maintaining large charity networks. Apart from Iran since the Khomeini revolution, the oil-producing countries in the region were political clients of the United States.

The organizing of armed resistance against the Soviet occupation of Afghanistan (funded by oil-rich Gulf states and armed and supported by the US) provided the necessary networking and ideological indoctrination for political Islam in the Arab World. Hamas and Islamic Jihad owe their origins to the Muslim Brotherhood movement that was active in Egypt and Jordan long before the Iranian revolution and the Afghan war (see Chapter 8 by Abu-Amr and Chapter 9 by Knudsen and Ezbidi in this book). The Muslim Brotherhood was allowed to operate freely in Jordan as a challenge to the Arab secular pan-nationalist and the socialist left; and Israel, following its occupation of the West Bank and Gaza Strip, let the movement be and took no action against it till it began to engage openly in armed resistance against the occupation, upon the formation of Hamas early in 1988 – Islamic Jihad was formed a few years before that.

Hamas is clearly not al-Qa'ida; if anything it shares with Hizbullah its formation within the context of the Israeli occupation: the Israeli

6

occupation of the south of Lebanon between 1982 and 2000 in the case of Hizbullah, and the occupation of the Gaza Strip and West Bank since June 1967 in the case of Hamas.[4] There are important differences between the two, which will not be discussed here, arising mainly from the differences between the Lebanese and Palestinian situations in terms of state formation, social structure, confessional and religious composition and political geography. The fact that both were formed in a context of confrontation with the Israeli military occupation explains the nationalist-patriotic tenor of their discourse and policies, despite their different ideological origins.

The fact that Hamas owes its origins to the Muslim Brotherhood movement explains, in the context of Palestinian nationalism, its readiness to adopt pragmatic and conciliatory programmes. This can be witnessed from the politics of the movement's branches in Egypt and Jordan. Indeed, if given the chance, Hamas could follow the track taken by the ruling party in Turkey.[5] Islam, like other religions, provides ideological cover for all sorts of political and social formations.

In March 2005, Hamas joined its main secular rival, Fatah, and eleven other Palestinian organizations in endorsing what came to be known as the Cairo Declaration, whereby it agreed to halt attacks on Israel for the rest of the year, participate in the coming Palestinian parliamentary elections and commence discussions about joining the Palestine Liberation Organization (PLO).

In June 2006, all the Palestinian organizations, except Islamic Jihad, signed a document calling for a political settlement of the Israeli-Palestinian conflict based, effectively, on the creation of a Palestinian state beside the state of Israel. The document restricted the area of armed resistance to within the West Bank and Gaza Strip. It called for the formation of a government of national unity ready to open peace negotiations. The next day the Israeli army invaded areas of Gaza, under the pretext that an Israeli soldier had been taken prisoner. The Israeli incursion was accompanied by the bombing of power stations and PA buildings, arrests of PA ministers and legislators in the West Bank, and the continuation of a policy of destroying homes, targeted assassinations, and the use of civilians as human shields.[6]

The Legislative Council election in January 2006 pointed to a radical transformation in the Palestinian political movement. It announced the ascendancy of an agenda that called for the Islamicizing of state and society (in opposition to the secular political culture of the PLO),

7

and adopted a political programme that differed from that of the PLO. The January elections meant that Hamas was no longer another faction within the Palestinian political field; it had become a leading force ready to take over the role that Fatah had held for nearly four decades. What emerged in January 2006 was a Palestinian political system that was no longer dominated by one political party (Fatah), but by two competing political parties (Hamas and Fatah), with the clear possibility of Hamas replacing Fatah as the dominant party (Hilal 2006a, 2006b, 2006c).

This change in the Palestinian national political field had ramifications within the Palestinian movement and society, but it has also had an effect on Hamas itself. This is most obvious in the discourse of democracy, social development, and human rights that, in the months after the election, permeated the recent discourse of Hamas in a vein similar to that of other Palestinian political parties. This heralded a genuine change in Hamas's outlook and a shift towards the nationalist-populist paradigm of the national movement. This was not negated by the fact that the democracy-human rights discourse could have been initiated, on the part of Hamas, by the imperative of survival in a globalized world of capital and territorial nation states, and by the necessity for retaining the support of a large constituency. But more important, Hamas, like all Palestinian political formations, could not ignore the strength and vigour of Palestinian nationalism, nor could it ignore the Israeli occupation, and Israel's suppression and criminalization of the Palestinian national struggle. It is necessary, therefore, to situate the ascendancy of Hamas within the context of the political economy of the Israeli occupation and colonialism, as well as in the context of the long history of the Palestinian national struggle.

The fact that Hamas has been labelled by Israel and in the West as 'terrorist' did not diminish its popularity, despite the financial and political sanctions that were imposed on Hamas's government by Israel and the Quartet (US, Russia, EU, and UN) soon after its formation in March 2006. Such sanctions are seen to fit the long tradition of double standards in the Western world's dealings with the Palestine question. The sanctions have amounted to collective punishment of Palestinians in the West Bank and Gaza Strip, and rewarded Israel's ongoing military occupation and repression. Moreover, Israeli and Western reactions to Hamas's electoral win demonstrated clearly that their calls for the 'reform' and 'democratization' of the PA were merely a cover for a demand for changing its political agenda to suit that of Israel and the

8

USA. This is clear from the demands made by the Quartet on Hamas, which were: first, Hamas's acknowledgement of Israel's right to exist, without this being conditional on Israel's acknowledgement of the Palestinians' right to self-determination; second, Hamas's renouncing 'violence' (i.e. all forms of resistance), and dismantling its armed wing (and other armed wings of Palestinian factions) prior to Israel ending its occupation and dismantling its colonial settlements; third, Hamas's adherence to the agreements made between the PLO and Israel (including Oslo and the Road Map), although Israel has violated these agreements repeatedly.

The increase in the popularity of Hamas during the second Intifada needs to be explained by the collapse of the Camp David negotiations and the mounting Israeli repression since then. The resounding failure of the Oslo Accords in establishing an independent Palestinian state, and the ineptness of the PA (dominated by Fatah) and its humiliation by Israel are important factors that stand behind Hamas's popularity. Hamas's position against the Oslo Accords, and against the corrupt practices of the PA, its extensive welfare activities among the poor, and its continuing to raise the banner of resistance to the Israeli occupation are the main factors behind its electoral victory (see Chapter 8 by Abu-Amr in this book on the formation of Hamas and its ideology, and Chapter 9 by Knudsen and Ezbidi on the political impact and ramifications of its electoral win in January 2006).

Israel's failure to fashion a client Palestinian entity explains its unilateralism

It was Israel's failure to turn the PA into a subservient tool of its policies – particularly into a tool to suppress resistance to the occupation – that led Sharon, who opposed the Oslo agreement in any case, to use force against the PA and re-invade the West Bank in March and April 2002. Sharon exploited the events of September 11, and the sensibilities of the neo-conservative ideology of the Bush Administration, to label the PA as terrorist and Arafat as another Osama bin Laden. Sharon combined military, security, economic and political measures to weaken the PA and fragment Palestinian society in an attempt to implement unilaterally a system that has been described as creeping apartheid (Yiftachel 2005). This needed a policy declaring the non-existence of a Palestinian peace partner. This was how Sharon excluded Arafat, and – following the PLO leader's mysterious death – Mahmoud

9

Abbas after his election in January 2005. Abbas went out of his way to declare his commitment to ending the Infitada, and his unconditional acceptance of the Road Map, and worked successfully to persuade all the Palestinian factions to declare unilaterally a ceasefire (a *hudna*). However, the Israeli army continued its targeted assassinations, and the construction and fattening of settlements in the West Bank and the building of the Separation Wall acquired a faster pace. With the formation of the Hamas government in March 2006, Israeli unilateralism found its ultimate cover for an open war on the Palestinian movement, and for the burial of any viable and sovereign Palestinian state.

The burial of the Oslo Accords and of the Road Map was effective with the release of the text of Bush's letter of assurances to Sharon (published in April 2004). The letter, which has been compared to a new Balfour Declaration (Aruri 2005), absolves Israel from its obligation to withdraw to the 1967 borders (UNSC Resolution 242), from dismantling its settlements, from its annexation policy generally, and from its policy of the Judaization and annexation of Jerusalem. The letter absolves Israel from any responsibility towards the Palestinian refugees' Right of Return.

Bush's policy on the Palestine question has to be located within the existing global situation and the dominance in the United States of a neo-liberal and neo-conservative ideology. Bush's vision of a Palestinian state is a vision synchronized between the American neo-conservatives and the Zionist right wing (see Chapter 5 by Husam Mohamad in this book). It is a vision that sees a solution to the Israeli-Palestinian conflict within what US Secretary of State Condoleezza Rice, during the Israeli war on Lebanon in August 2006, called the 'new Middle East' – that is, a subservient and client Middle East to be fashioned by imperialist wars and military occupations, such as we have been witnessing in the area (Afghanistan, Iraq, Lebanon, and the West Bank and Gaza Strip).[7]

The Israeli war of July–August 2006, intended to destroy Hizbullah and Hamas following their capture of Israeli soldiers, shows how Israel understands its role in the Middle East in relation to US policy towards this oil-rich region. In destroying or weakening Hizbullah, whose resistance had forced Israel to withdraw from the south of Lebanon in 2000, and in destroying or weakening Hamas, Israel, as has been customary since its establishment, sought to demonstrate the heavy price it is determined to exact from those who challenge its military might and regional supremacy. But it was also a war that was intended to send a message to Iran and Syria about what they might face if they did not toe the US line.[8] This is the shape of the 'new Middle East' that the Bush Administration is trying to enforce by means of the recent Israeli wars against Hizbullah in Lebanon and Hamas and the Palestinian resistance in Palestine, with all the destruction and killing this entailed.[9] However, by many accounts, the 21st century Israeli-American wars in the region are initiating a substantially different Middle East from the one intended by the engineers of these wars.[10]

'Disengagement' and 'conversion' as apartheid

The policy imperatives of political Zionism have been oriented towards occupying land but with no, or the minimum of, Palestinians. This is a necessary requirement for establishing a Jewish state protected from the 'demographic peril' that the growing numbers of Palestinians pose for such a project (see Chapter 2 by Pappé and Chapter 3 by Ghanem). This imperative is behind much of the repressive Israeli policies towards the Palestinians; it is behind Israel's drive to build colonial settlements, bypass (or apartheid) roads, and the Separation Wall,[11] behind the annexation of Jerusalem and of large tracts of land, including the Jordan Valley (see Chapter 7 by Isaac and Powell).

In short, Israel's policy has amounted to a systematic negation of the basic conditions necessary for a viable and sovereign Palestinian state. During the 40 years of its occupation, Israel has succeeded in creating a totally dependent, unproductive and captive Palestinian economy, with total Israeli control of trade, natural resources (mostly land and water), urban planning, investment, movement of individuals and goods, and Palestinian borders (see Alissa, Chapter 6).

The colonial-settler ideology that dominates Israeli political thinking lacks the conceptual or moral tools to accept responsibility for the historic injustice inflicted on the Palestinians. It sees no problem in Palestinian refugees remaining dispersed (in *al-shatat)* or in exile (in *ghurba)*. In fact behind its envisioning a rump Palestinian state lies the possibility of turning Palestinian refugees into expatriates who carry Palestinian travel documents or passports, which will allow them to enter the territory of the Palestinian 'state', but not to exercise their Right of Return to their original homeland.

Sharon's 'disengagement',[12] and later Olmert's 'convergence' or 'alignment' plan,[13] need to be comprehended within the aim of maintaining a Jewish state. In an interview in the Israeli *Ha'aretz* newspaper,

11

published in November 2003, Olmert, well before he became Israel's prime minister in March 2006 and before Sharon's 'disengagement' from Gaza in August 2005 – explained the reasons behind this policy in the following words:[14]

> There is no doubt in my mind that very soon the government of Israel is going to have to address the demographic issue with the utmost seriousness and resolve. This issue above all others will dictate the solution that we must adopt. In the absence of a negotiated agreement – and I do not believe in the realistic prospect of an agreement – we need to implement a unilateral alternative.

He added:

> We don't have unlimited time. More and more Palestinians are uninterested in a negotiated, two-state solution, because they want to change the essence of the conflict from an Algerian paradigm to a South African one; from a struggle against 'occupation' in their par-lance, to a struggle for one-man-one-vote. That is, of course, a much cleaner struggle, a much more popular struggle – and ultimately a much more powerful one. For us, it would mean the end of the Jewish state. Of course I would prefer a negotiated agreement [for two states]. But I personally doubt that such an agreement can be reached within the time-frame available to us.

The policy can be summarized as follows: 'To maximize the number of Jews; to minimize the number of Palestinians; not to withdraw to the 1967 border and not to divide Jerusalem'. This means, as Olmert explained when he became prime minister, 'to divide the land, with the goal of ensuring a Jewish majority, is Zionism's lifeline'.[15]

The idea of 'unilateral separation' is not new. Some Israeli leaders seriously entertained the idea in the early 1990s. Before he was assassinated by the Israeli extreme right in 1995, Itzhak Rabin believed that he could achieve effective separation from the Palestinians by persuading their leaders to accept it by negotiation – something that Olmert or the next Israeli prime minister might be tempted to do. Rabin also believed that he would need to fall back on a Wall to enforce a separation between Israelis and Palestinians (Cook, May 2006).[16]

Israel's extreme right wing still adheres to Likud's policy, which stood throughout the 1990s against the idea of separation as giving away part of Israel. Likud stands for the intensification of colonial settlement, with some calling openly for the transfer of Palestinians by force or voluntarily through economic or other forms of pressure. The political outcome of the Israeli 2006 war in Lebanon and Palestine will induce both camps to rethink their options, but it remains doubtful if this would involve Israel accepting to live next door to a sovereign and viable Palestinian state on the whole of the 1967-occupied territories, and a just solution to the refugee problem. Whatever Israel concludes from its review of the latest war, its most profound significance lies in showing the limits of Israeli military power, however supreme it might have been thought to be, in exactly the same way that the occupation of Iraq has demonstrated similar limits of military power. Both wars establish yet again that the balance of power is not determined solely by military strength.

Barring Palestinian statehood, and banning bi-nationalism

The ramification of the war against Hizbullah seems to have persuaded the Israeli government to shelve the 'convergence' plan and to give priority to the war's repercussions.[17] But this shelving of the 'convergence plan' does not solve the Israeli predicament of how to reconcile its cherished colonialist spirit with its dread of a bi-national state. As one Israeli journalist put it (Levy, August 2007):

> The convergence/alignment option no longer has a chance – even the
> prime minister admits as much. And returning territory as part of
> an agreement is not acceptable to the right. Annexing the territories
> is not an option because even the right realizes that means the state
> becomes bi-national, which the right does not want. What remains?
> To wait. For what exactly? For the Palestinians to be a majority between the Mediterranean and the Jordan River? And then what? The
> Arab countries equip themselves with more advanced weaponry and
> ultimately with nuclear bombs? And then what?

Regardless of the fate of the convergence plan, the fact is that the Separation Wall is already there annexing the areas of large settlement blocs, the Jerusalem area and the Jordan valley. The Wall, once finished, is intended to ensure the following: first, that a Palestinian state will not be established on all the Palestinian territories occupied in 1967; second, that calling a collection of bantustans a 'state' does not make that state viable and sovereign, nor will it be acceptable to the overwhelming majority of Palestinians; third, the Separation Wall, together with the siege imposed on the Gaza Strip (with its 1.5

13

million inhabitants and 1.3% of the area of historic Palestine), and the totalitarian control regime imposed by Israel on the Palestinians, are sufficient, from the Israeli perspective, to prevent the emergence of a bi-national state on historic Palestine, which is something all Zionist political parties fear.

It was to halt the march towards bi-nationalism that Israeli leaders began to talk about a Palestinian state on parts of the West Bank and Gaza Strip. It was Sharon, who was vehemently against a Palestinian state west of the River Jordan, who told a Likud Party meeting in May 2003:

> The idea that it is possible to continue keeping 3.5 million Palestinians under occupation – yes, it is occupation, you might not like the word, but what is happening is occupation – is bad for Israel, and bad for the Palestinians, and bad for the Israeli economy. Controlling 3.5 million Palestinians cannot go on forever.[18]

The change came as Sharon realized that the 'demographic threat' facing Israel as a Jewish state was real. By 2010, Palestinians living in historic Palestine will form the majority of the population in the area. Disengagement and convergence are plans to intercept this reality.

The Road Map appeared in late 2002 (with Arafat under siege in his headquarters in Ramallah) and it envisaged a Palestinian state (in the year 2005) as the outcome of a negotiation process. Sharon accepted the plan but registered a number of reservations, and then announced that he had no Palestinian partner with whom to negotiate. It was soon afterwards that the disengagement plan was proposed as an enactment of a unilateral separation strategy. Sharon's aids were forthcoming in explaining that the aim of the disengagement plan was to outmanoeuvre the Road Map, and make sure that no Palestinian state worthy of the name came under consideration.[19]

The creation of Kadima came when Sharon failed to persuade the 'Greater Israel' old guard in his Likud Party to come to terms with the realization that the Palestinians would never give up their dream of independence and statehood. What Sharon proposed was a strategy of forced separation that would, so Kadima leaders believe, render Palestinians powerless to resist it.

Thus disengagement from the Gaza Strip cannot be seen outside a strategy to safeguard the 'Jewish character' of Israel, by isolating it physically from Palestinians without surrendering its overall control over the area. The 'convergence' or 'realignment' put forward by the new Israeli government that was formed following the Knesset elections in March 2006, is nothing more than the annexation of a sizeable area of the West Bank, leaving out the densely populated Palestinian centres. The result of this process would be a 'bantustanized' Palestinian population within well-guarded confines.

Any limited withdrawal (or redeployment) from the West Bank will, in all likelihood, be followed by Israel declaring the end of its occupation (as happened following the disengagement from Gaza), suggesting that the Palestinians are now free to construct their state on the territory from which the Israelis have withdrawn. That, in fact, leaves bits of the West Bank disconnected, impoverished, cut off from Gaza and from East Jerusalem, and deprived of its best agricultural land and sources of underground water.[20]

This is why the ongoing process of annexation, the Separation Wall, and unilateralism – or the refusal to negotiate with the legitimate representative of the Palestinian people – amount to the construction of an apartheid system that fosters conditions of ethnic cleansing. These conditions are present in high rates of unemployment, high rates of poverty, economic stagnation, and siege conditions restricting freedom of movement of people and goods. Such conditions drive those who can to emigrate.[21]

Imagining a future

European and United Nations conceptions had from early on favoured a two-state solution starting with the United Nations Partition Plan in 1947 and ending with the Road Map. But such proposals have always favoured the Zionist colonial project, both before 1948 and following Israel's establishment. From the 1920s to the early 1970s the Palestinian movement favoured one state on the whole of historic Palestine, and considered the two-state solution to be divisive of Palestine and an unjust solution to the Palestinian cause.

Israel's systematic undermining of a solution that facilitates the establishment of a sovereign and viable Palestinian state on part of historic Palestine can only lead to the perpetuation of the conflict. This puts enormous responsibilities on the Palestinian movement if it wants to avoid the extinction that the national movement faced in 1948. The Hamas-Fatah political polarization reflects a 'dual authority' situation institutionalized in the existing presidential-parliamentary

15

political system.[22] This polarization needs to find a peaceful resolution before it explodes into a civil war that would heap more tragedy on the Palestinians. The way out of this leadership crisis is a rejuvenated and democratized political movement, unified within renewed PLO institutions that are relevant to the present, equal to the tasks required to keep the unity of aims of the Palestinian people and the interaction between its diverse communities, and necessary for coordinating resistance activities to the Israeli occupation.

The withering Palestinian Authority

One of the urgent tasks facing the Palestinian movement is what to do with the PA, given the restrictions and obstructions that are imposed on it, particularly since the eruption of the second Intifada and more so since Hamas formed the government in March 2006. The pressures on the PA have been compounded by the United States and Europe joining Israel in putting it under siege. At the time of writing in September 2006, the PA was no longer able to pay regularly or in full the salaries of its 165,000 civil servants; it was unable to stop the military attacks that Israel unleashed on Gaza; nor was it able to prevent the arrest of several of Hamas's ministers (including the deputy prime minister) in the West Bank, or secure the release of any of nearly a third of the total PLC members (including its speaker) who in August 2006 were imprisoned in Israel. The capture of an Israeli soldier in June 2006, whose captors declared they wanted to exchange him for some of the many thousands of Palestinian prisoners held in Israeli detention centres, unleashed a military campaign (under the name of 'summer rains') against Gaza that brought death to hundreds of civilians.

The severe restrictions on movement of Palestinian ministers, officials, and parliamentarians, not to mention ordinary citizens and the fact that the Palestinian Authority cannot represent its people or promote their interests or provide them with vital services have raised questions about the usefulness of retaining such an entity. The absence of negotiations with Israel (since it refuses to negotiate with the PA), adds to the feeling among Palestinians that the PA has lost its relevance. The issue of its dissolution is no longer raised among intellectuals as a way to force Israel to be accountable for its policies as an occupying power under international law (Jarbawi 2005).

The idea of dissolving the PA and making Israel face its responsibilities toward the nearly 4 million Palestinians in the West Bank

16

and Gaza Strip began to acquire widespread circulation following the siege imposed on the PA in response to Hamas's success in form-ing the Palestinian government. Those who have examined the idea include Fatah leaders and a number of public figures.[23] In response to the intensification of Israel's repressive measures against the PA leadership and institutions, in August 2006, Palestinian Prime Min-ister Ismail Haniya found himself questioning the viability of the PA, since its key lawmakers and ministers were in Israeli jails. Through a video link between Ramallah and Gaza city, Haniya told the assembled members of the Legislative Council: 'All political elites, the presidency, the factions and the government are invited to discuss the future of the Palestinian Authority following this [Israeli] attack' (referring to Israel's arrest of Parliamentary Speaker Aziz Dweik of Hamas a week earlier). He asked: 'Can the Palestinian Authority function under the occupation, kidnappings and assassination?'[24]

If the PA continues to be unable to provide the minimum functions of self-government, and if it remains barred, because of repressive Israeli policies, from transforming itself into a viable sovereign state acceptable to a majority of Palestinians, it will wither away by virtue of losing its *raison d'etre*. The dissolution or otherwise of the PA is an issue that has to be thought out carefully and decided upon by the Palestinian movement as a whole. But whatever decision is taken on this issue it is absolutely vital not to leave the Palestinians, in the occupied territories and outside Palestine, leaderless. This would mean another Palestinian Nakba. Hence an urgent task of the Palestinian movement is the revival, restructuring and democratizing of the institutions of the PLO. This is necessary to enable the organization to reflect its new Palestinian constituency and to deal better with qualitative changes that have taken place in the local, regional and international situation since the late 1980s. But the fate of the PA should not be left to the Israelis, to the deliberations of the United States and Europe, or to interpretation by this or that Palestinian faction.

Where now for Palestine?

Palestinians face a critical moment in their confrontation with Israeli settler-colonialism. They cannot, by any means, accept a bantustan state – encircled by walls and electronic fences and watchtowers – on approximately 12% of their historic homeland, nor can they accept a denial of their Right of Return, or not having Jerusalem as their capital.

Israel could, to help market such a state, call it a state with provisional borders, leaving negotiations on the final status issues to a future date that could be postponed *ad infinitum*, given the special relationship Israel enjoys with the United States. The moment a 'provisional state' is accepted, the Palestinian issue will lose its colonial aspect and become another border dispute. This is why the idea of a Palestinian state with temporary borders on the Gaza Strip and parts of the West Bank should be rejected outright. The only realistic strategy open to the Palestinian movement here is to reject any Israeli attempt to cover up its apartheid project that is being forced on the Palestinians. If negotiations are to be resumed then they should deal with final status issues (i.e. refugees, Jerusalem, borders, Israeli colonial settlements, and compensating the Palestinians for dispossession, occupation and repression).

Negotiating the final status issues means seeking a solution based on the idea of 'two states for two peoples'. This has been the programme of the PLO since 1988; it is a programme that recognized the balance of power and accepted the erection of a sovereign Palestinian state on the whole area of the West Bank and Gaza Strip (that is on 22% of Palestine). It assumes a willingness on the part of Israel to dismantle all Jewish colonial settlements, to accept East Jerusalem as the capital of the Palestinian state, and to acknowledge the right of the Palestinian state to have full control over borders and natural resources, including water. It also assumes that this solution will in no way jeopardize the rights of Palestinian refugees as specified in United Nations resolutions (particularly resolution 194 of 1948). Such a solution still has the support of a majority of Palestinians, and could, if seriously adopted, gain the consent of Hamas (but probably not of Islamic Jihad).

Israel is not likely to accept a full sovereign Palestinian state as envisaged by the PLO as long as the balance of power (local, regional and international) remains unchanged. This should not be understood, as some have argued, to mean that Palestinians should lower even more the political ceiling of their demands, which are legitimate by any standard of relative justice, or principles of co-existence, or the exigencies of political compromise. But it does imply a need to work to change the existing balance of power, and to realize that the present balance of power is not permanent. The signs are already discernible that the tide seems to be beginning to turn against global American dominance, not only in Latin America, but also elsewhere, including the Middle East.

Because of the impasse of the present situation, the Palestinian movement should articulate a detailed proposal for a bi-national state, and begin to canvass for such an idea among Palestinians, and, more importantly, among Israelis. This should be done not as a scare tactic to get Israel to agree to a separate Palestinian state, but because the bi-national solution is better than all other solutions to the conflict, as more than one chapter in this book argues.

Palestinians can play a part in affecting a change in the balance of power by re-inventing their national movement, strengthening its mobilizing ability, adopting more participatory and creative modes of resistance, and articulating a discourse that debunks Israeli militarist and segregationist policy, strengthens and enlarges the anti-colonialist and anti-occupation camp in Israel, and campaigns for more active Arab and international support for the Palestinian cause.

Israel, the US and EU have be clear that the Palestinian question cannot be resolved by concocting a state out of what Israeli colonialism leaves behind for fear of the changing balance of demography. A client and dependent Palestinian state cannot provide Palestinians with the freedom, justice and emancipation they seek. The state they seek is one in which they can practise a tangible sense of justice and can restate their humanity. Europe, particularly, should cease acting as if the Palestinian question can be solved by being reduced to one of humanitarian aid.

Without a new balance of power that is reflected in the alignment of forces inside Israeli society itself, the ruling Zionist elite in Israel will continue to obstruct the emergence of a sovereign Palestinian state acceptable to a majority of Palestinians. It will also do all it can to prevent the solidification of conditions for a bi-national state (or a secular democratic state) through the cantonization of the Palestinian population, and calling the outcome a state, or, if this fails, it will attempt to move these population centres to Jordan and Egypt. The chance of such Israeli manoeuvres succeeding is almost nil, particularly in the presence of an active and alert Palestinian movement. The 'Jordan option', which was advocated during the 1970s and 1980s by Sharon, and envisaged the establishment of a Palestinian state in Jordan, is not revivable. It is an option that has been strongly rejected by both Palestinians and Jordanians, and the Israel-Jordan peace agreement abolished this as a serious option, despite statements now and then by Israelis about the transitory nature of the Hashemite regime (Lynch, June 2004).

The Palestine liberation movement needs to widen its options by revisiting the original vision that the Palestinian national movement had before 1948, and which was re-articulated by the PLO during the late 1960s: that is, the vision of the establishment of a secular democratic state (or a bi-national state) in Mandate Palestine for all the citizens of the country. The idea has gained increasing attention as the Oslo process collapsed and the two-state solution reached an impasse. In fact the main theme of this book is to show in some detail why and how this collapse has happened, and why some new solution has to be found. The most discussed alternative is the one-state or the bi-national state solution. The bi-national state model provides a sharing of power between Jews and Palestinians that could take various negotiable forms, but with the emphasis on collective rights. The other model is the secular democratic state with no distinctions between citizens according to religion, ethnicity or national origin, with emphasis on individual rights.

The one-state solution has been debated so far mainly by the left in Israel and in the West (Sussman 2004; Reuveny 2005; Benvenisti 2003; Gavron 2004; Judt 2003; Golan 2004). The factors that have contributed to the conclusion that the two-state solution is dead and buried have been discussed above, but many of those who argue for the adoption of a bi-national state solution agree with Tilley that there is no escaping 'the incontrovertible evidence that a stable two-state solution in Israel-Palestine is now on the trash heap of history'.[25]

As a matter of history the idea of a bi-national state was entertained by Zionist leaders and intellectuals before 1948, when the balance of demography was decidedly in favour of Palestinians and the idea of an independent Zionist state did not seem easily realizable.[26] At that time the Palestinian national movement was insisting on a one-state solution in historic Palestine promising Jews full and equal rights on a par with other religious communities (Muslims, Christians and others) within a modern Palestinian state.

Although not much public debate has taken place among Palestinians on the bi-national state solution, in mid-2004 public opinion polls showed that 26.5% of the adult population in the West Bank and Gaza Strip was in favour such a solution, in addition to just over 10% who preferred a Palestinian state in historic Palestine, and some 14% who saw no solution to the conflict. In fact only 44.5% said they preferred a two-state solution.[27] Intellectuals who argued publicly for the one-state solution tended to be Palestinians living in Israel (see Ghanem, Chapter 3) or Palestinians living in *al-Shatat* (see, for example, Said 1999; Karmi 2002; Bishara 1998). It was the Israeli devastation of Palestinian society and polity that revived the idea of a bi-national state, which was, up to the early 1970s, part of the Palestinian political discourse in the form of a secular democratic state.[28] The suggestion by Elmusa (Chapter 10) of a 'Greater Palestine' state to include Israeli Jews, Palestinians and Jordanians and to cover the whole area of Palestine and Jordan, is an innovative version of the bi-national state proposal. Indeed, as the viability of an independent Palestinian state recedes, the vision of the one state will gain more support among the Palestinians, and, eventually perhaps, among Israelis.

The attraction of the one-state solution (be it one state for two peoples or a secular democratic state with one person, one vote) is that it solves many problems: refugees, Jerusalem, the Wall, borders, democratic co-existence and equal rights; for it proposes a different paradigm to the two-state solution, which could risk power relations between the two states that are not in favour of the Palestinian state, unless this were seen as a transitional phase to the bi-national state. The main difficulty with the one-state solution resides in Zionism as a colonialist ideology and its insistence on a Jewish state conceptualizing Judaism as a nation, not a religion or an aspect of culture.

A warning and a hope

The elevation of the 'Jewishness' of the Israeli state above all other considerations, and its concretization in an apartheid system symbolized by the Separation Wall, means the isolation of Israel from its geography. Israel cannot remain the regional superpower that it sees itself to be. Such a role and attitude can only drag Israel into a ghetto culture and jingoism that prioritizes force as the determining factor in its relations with the other states and peoples of the region. This is explicit in the six major wars Israel has had with its neighbouring states since its establishment (in 1948, 1956, 1967, 1973, 1982, 2006), and explicit in the numerous military attacks and incursions on Arab lands. Such a self-representation and posture by Israel is a sign of moral bankruptcy, likely to lead to the erosion of its international political legitimacy and internal loss of values and direction that can only breed a culture of violence. Already there are Israeli voices that have been saying that Israel is only able to pursue its colonial and

21

apartheid policies because of its willingness to serve Western (mainly American) imperial interests, including acting as a galvanizing centre for global neo-conservative forces.[29]

Palestinians confront an extremely precarious and perilous moment. The Palestinian liberation movement is divided and leaderless at a time when it needs most a unified and unifying leadership. Both leaders of the two largest political movements (Hamas and Fatah) realize that open conflict between them is suicidal, but remain so far unable to set up the organizational structures necessary to resolve their conflicts and differences democratically and peacefully by recreating the PLO institutions. Neither Fatah nor Hamas has as yet put forward a strategy for national struggle that deals with the situation after the collapse of the Oslo process and the construction of the Separation Wall. Fatah needs to cease behaving as if it is still in power and stop deluding itself that the Oslo Accords and the Road Map can bring Palestinians the sovereign state they desire. Hamas has to cease behaving as if it is still in opposition and thinking that substituting slogans for thought-out strategies will confront creeping apartheid. Both have to realize that Israel after its war against Hizbullah is not what it was before that war. As one knowledgeable European journalist of the Arab-Israeli conflict noted:

It is not just Hizbullah's performance in itself that has changed the balance of power at Israel's expense; it is the example it sets for the whole region. In his way Hassan Nasrallah is now an even more inspiring Arab hero than Nasser was; Hizbullah's achievement has had an electrifying impact on the Arab and Muslim masses that largely transcends the otherwise growing, region-wide Sunni-Shia divide; it will contribute to their further radicalisation and, if that is not appeased by the Arab regimes, to upheavals in the whole existing order. (Hirst, August 2007)

Some Israelis, although still few and far between, are beginning to realize too that a new era is dawning for Israel:

Never before, even after the Yom Kippur War in 1973, did it become clear to what extent the era of relying on the army as the perfect fix to stabilizing national security must come to an end. Never before has such a short time elapsed between boasts about what we are going to do to the villains who are facing us and the appalling sight of the collapse of the promise. ... The real, profound reason is that the

IDF [Israel's Army] cannot win even in the cruel struggle against the Palestinian liberation movement. During the course of the effort in the north, beyond the headlines, the IDF killed nearly 200 Palestinians in Gaza, about half of them civilians, fired more than 10,000 shells, abducted government ministers, and starved the Gaza Strip. It did not prevent the Qassams [locally made rockets]. (Samet, August 2006)

The 20th century was the century of decolonization which freed millions of people in the non-Western world from extreme oppression. But the decolonization process remained incomplete, as the Palestinians were left fighting their war of liberation against a settler-colonialist and highly militarized state, which was aided and abetted by the world's strongest imperial power. One can only hope that the 21st century, long before it ends, will witness Palestinians freed from colonialism, apartheid, and military occupation, and the world freed from US hegemony and injustice.

Notes

1 Jews in Palestine before the Zionist colonization were considered part of the mosaic of indigenous populations, like the Christians and Muslims. In 1914 Jews in Palestine numbered about 60,000, half of whom were recent settlers. The Arab Palestinian population (Muslims and Christians, and others) numbered 683,000. Jews remained a minority in Palestine on the eve of the creation of Israel in May 1948 despite the backing that Zionist immigration into Palestine received from Britain.

2 Palestinian society in the 1930s and 1940s was undergoing rapid changes as a result of urbanization and the spread of education, but change remained curtailed by the repressive measures of British colonialism, and the exclusivist nature of the Zionist colonization.

3 The Israeli High Court of Justice decided on 14 May 2006 to uphold the 'Citizenship and Entry into Israel Law' which bars family reunification for Israeli citizens married to Palestinians from the Occupied Territories It specifically targets Israeli Palestinians who make up a fifth of Israel's population, and Palestinian Jerusalemites, for it is they who marry Palestinians from the West Bank and Gaza Strip.

4 Hizbullah is not a minor political force in Lebanon. As Alain Gresh observes; 'Hizbullah is Lebanon's largest political party, with 12 members of parliament. It is deeply rooted in the Shia community, the country's largest, and enjoys enormous prestige for having liberated the south of Lebanon in 2000. It is allied with major political forces, such as General Michel Aoun's Free Patriotic Movement, the Lebanese Communist Party, the Syrian Social Nationalist Party, and with influential figures including Sunnis Usama Saad and Omar Karami, and the Maronite Sleiman Frangié. To claim that Hizbullah is a pawn in the hands of Iran or Syria is absurd.' (Gresh, August 2006).

5 For a discussion of Hamas's political pragmatism, see Usher, August 2005.

6 On this and other Israeli violations of human rights, see reports by the Israeli Human Rights Organization, B'Tselem (www.btselem.org/English). One can ask with the Israeli journalist Gideon Levy (9 July 2006): 'What would have happened if the Palestinians had not fired Qassams? Would Israel have lifted the economic siege that it imposed on Gaza? Would it open the border to Palestinian labourers? Free prisoners? Meet with the elected leadership and conduct negotiations? Encourage investment in Gaza? Nonsense. If the Gazans were sitting quietly, as Israel expects them to do, their case would disappear from the agenda here and around the world. Nobody would have given any thought to the fate of the people of Gaza if they did not behave violently.'

7 A statement on Gaza by United Nations Humanitarian Agencies working in the occupied Palestinian territory (3 August 2006) stated the following: 'The United Nations humanitarian agencies working in the occupied Palestinian territory are deeply alarmed by the impact continuing violence is having on civilians and civilian infrastructure in Gaza, ... We estimate that since 28 June [until 2 August 2006], 175 Palestinians have been killed, including approximately 40 children and eight women, and over 620 injured in the Gaza Strip.

8 The US is wary of the emergence of Tehran as a powerful anti-western regional pole that would increase its influence in the Gulf with the fragmentation of Iraq, and possibly make it a worthwhile candidate for special relations with Russia and China.

9 Israeli commentators do not hide the link between the war against Hizbullah and curtailing the role of Iran and Syria in the region. One Israeli commentator put it as follows: 'Hezbollah is not the strategic threat posed to Israel at present. The real threat lies in Syria, which is arming itself with thousands of missiles and various and sundry warheads, and in Iran, which is only a heartbeat away from attaining nuclear weapons. The war in Lebanon, therefore, is not only a war against Hezbollah and its ability to continue to attack Israel. It is a war against Iran and Syria, which clearly have the ability to attack Israel' (Arlosoroff, August 2006).

10 On the Bush Administration's involvement in Israel's war against Hizbullah, see Hersh (14 August 2006).

11 The total planned length of the Separation Wall, when finished, is about 790 kilometres (see Ha'aretz, report by Amos Harel, 17 May 2006. The report based on Israeli army information, estimates the Wall to be completed in the spring of 2007).

12 'Disengagement' from Gaza in August 2005, as Israeli actions the following year have shown, has not been more than another term for redeployment of Israeli troops, with the difference of dismantling the Israeli settlements there (7,500 settlers, compared to something like 415,000 settlers in the West Bank).

13 'Convergence' or 'realignment', as an Israeli strategy for managing its occupation of Palestinian land, was put forward by Olmert's Kadima Party in the March 2006 Knesset election campaign. According to the plan, Israel would

move its soldiers and settlers from parts of the West Bank behind a unilaterally fixed 'eastern border' for the Israeli state. Olmert suggested, in August 2006, during Israel's war on Lebanon and Gaza, that one aim of the war was to facilitate the implementation of his 'convergence' plan. Some saw in Israel's war against Gaza and Lebanon an attempt to show that disengagement was not a mistake (Blecher, Summer 2006). However Olmert indicated that 'convergence' will not be a priority of his government following his war on Lebanon.

14 *Ha'aretz*, 15 November 2003, interviewed by David Landau.

15 See Jonathan Cook, 'Olmert old ruse', *Al-Ahram Weekly*, 11–17 May 2006. Issue No. 794.

16 According to Jonathan Cook (May 2006) who is a journalist and writer living in Nazareth, Israel, Rabin entrusted the wall project to a committee headed by his public security minister. The scheme was dropped by his two successors, Peres and Netanyahu, but returned with Barak, who advocated unilateral separation. In May 2000, he unilaterally withdrew troops from southern Lebanon. A fortnight before departing for talks at Camp David, he is reported as saying: 'Israel will insist upon a physical separation between itself and the independent Palestinian entity to be formed as a result of the settlement.' Cook also adds: 'In one typical commentary in June 2002, some 18 months before Sharon's own proposals for disengagement were revealed, Barak wrote: "The disengagement would be implemented gradually over several years. The fence should include the seven big settlement blocs that spread over 12 or 13 per cent of the area and contain 80 per cent of the settlers. Israel will also need a security zone along the Jordan River and some early warning sites ... In Jerusalem, there would have to be two physical fences. The first would delineate the political boundary and be placed around the Greater City, including the settlement blocs adjacent to Jerusalem. The second would be a security-dictated barrier, with controlled gates and passes, to separate most of the Palestinian neighbourhoods from the Jewish neighbourhoods and the Holy Basin, including the Old City."' (Cook, *Al-Ahram Weekly*, ibid; see also Cook's book; *Blood and Religion* 2006).

17 See statements by Olmert (*Ha'aretz*, 18 August 2006).

18 See Cook, May 2006.

19 Sharon's adviser, Dov Weissglas, told *Ha'aretz* in an interview published on 8 October 2004: '[The disengagement plan] supplies the amount of formaldehyde that's necessary so that there will not be a political process with the Palestinians.' He explained, 'The political process is the establishment of a Palestinian state with all the security risks that entails. The political process is the evacuation of settlements, it's the return of refugees, and it's the partition of Jerusalem. And all that has now been frozen.'

20 The West Bank aquifers provide Israel with half a billion cubic metres annually of the best quality water, a third of Israel's present supply. It is difficult to imagine that Israel will hand these aquifers over to Palestinians in the near future, or even after it has built all planned expensive desalination plants. Israel allocates 10 per cent of West Bank water to Palestinians, a fraction of what the Palestinian population needs.

21 Surveys, in the early part of 2006, indicate that a third of the adult

population in the West Bank and Gaza Strip (mostly young and educated) think of permanent emigration, given the very high rates of unemployment and poverty in the high-risk society that the Israeli occupation has fostered (detention without trial, home demolition, targeted assassination, military incursions, restricted movement ...).

22 The president of the PA controls the military and the presidential guards, and foreign relations, and represents the PLO; the Council of Ministers controls the police and civil defence, and some 20 ministries in the West Bank and Gaza Strip. In the presidential election of January 2005, Mahmoud Abbas (Abu Mazin) won the election gaining 62% of the votes. He became the leader of Fatah, and the chairman of the executive committee of the PLO upon the death of Arafat in November 2004. In the Legislative Council Elections of 2006, Hamas won the majority of the seats, and formed the Council of Ministers. Both movements have strong armed wings, and public opinion polls in August 2006 show the two movements as having equal support (about 30% each) among the adult population in the West Bank and Gaza Strip; see Near East Consulting, 'Palestinian Perceptions towards Politics, Peace and the Conflict in Lebanon', 7 August 2006 (http://www.neareastconsulting.com/).

23 A number of Fatah leaders counselled the PA president in March to dissolve the PA and make Israel and the international community face their responsibilities. Salam Fayyad, who is an independent PLC member and a former finance minister, declared: 'It is our right to question the benefits of the Palestinian Authority. The continuation of the Palestinian Authority will acquit Israel from its responsibilities as an occupying power' (ibid.).

24 See news agencies; also *Ha'aretz*, 9 August 2006.

25 See Tilley 2005a. See also Tilley 2005b in the *Arab World Geographer*. A critical examination by an Israeli writer, of the one-state solution as proposed by Tilley; see Peled 2006, and her reply, Tilley (2006). See also Anderson 2001, Mandron 2001, Piterberg 2001, Laor 2001. *The Arab World Geographer*, Vol. 8, No. 3 (2005) also tackled the issue of the one-state or two-state solution.

26 According to Sussman the idea of a bi-national state was propagated in mandatory Palestine by 'the likes of Henrietta Szold, Martin Buber, Judah Magnes and the Hashomer Hatzair movement.' He adds that 'prominent Zionist leaders like Chaim Weizmann and Chaim Arlosoroff supported the idea. David Ben Gurion, the first prime minister of Israel, toyed with bi-national ideas between 1924 and 1939, probably for tactical purposes. At a time when Jews were a minority (less than 20 percent) in the territory of mandatory Palestine, he surmised that the Zionists were too weak to take on both the British and the Arabs. Moreover, the demand for parity in political representation, implicit in the rally for bi-nationalism, clearly served the Zionist movement.' (Sussman 2004)

27 The question was phrased as follows: 'Some believe that a two-state formula is the favoured solution for the Arab-Israeli conflict, while others believe that historic Palestine cannot be divided and thus the favoured solution is a bi-national state on all of Palestine wherein Palestinians and Israelis enjoy equal representation. Which of these solutions do you prefer?' Only 44.5% said they prefer a two-state solution, of the remainder the highest per-

centage (26.5%) preferred a bi-national state solution, while 11.1% preferred a Palestinian state solution on all of Palestine, 13.6% said they do not see a solution to the conflict, and less than 2% said they preferred an Islamic state (Jerusalem Media and Communication Centre (JMCC), poll No. 51, June 2004 www.jmmcc.org).

28 Marwan Barghouti, a prominent Fatah leader in the West Bank, invited Israelis attending his trial (30 September 2003) for his role in the second Intifada to remember 'that the Palestinian people cannot be brought to yield with force. If an occupation does not end unilaterally or through negotiations then there is only one solution – one state for two peoples.' In December 2003, the prime minister at the time, Ahmad Qurei', responded to Sharon's announcement that he was going to move ahead with his unilateral disengagement plan at the annual Herzliya Conference by saying: 'This is an apartheid solution to put the Palestinians in cantons. Who can accept this? We will go for a one-state solution ... .' Yasser Arafat responded in similar tone in an interview published on 24 January 2004 by the *Guardian* (Sussman, ibid.).

29 See, for example, Halper (7 November 2005). This also can be glimpsed from Israeli comments (still marginal) following the summer 2006 war against Lebanon, such as the following: 'Instead of speaking with our enemies we speak with our friends, not to say our patrons, the Americans, as though we were lowly vassals. We have adopted English almost as a mother tongue and we relate to Arabic as almost an existential threat. Thus far, the subordination of our lives, our values and our future to the Americans has not proved itself. We have never been as insecure as we are today. As part of our despair we are surrounding ourselves with a wall and turning the symbol of national rebirth into a fortified Jewish ghetto closed on all sides' (Simon, August 2006).

References

Anderson. P (2001), 'Scurrying towards Bethlehem', *New Left Review*, 10, July–August.

Arlosoroff, M. (8 August, 2006) 'The cold arithmetic of blood'. Tel Aviv, *Ha'aretz*.

Aruri, N. (2005). 'U.S. Policy and the single state in Palestine/Israel', *The Arab World Geographer*, Vol. 8, No. 3.

Benvenisti, M. (2003) 'Cry, the beloved two-state solution', interview by A. Shavit, *Ha'aretz*. 6 August.

Bishara, A. (1998) 'Reflections on the realities of the Oslo process', in G. Giacaman and D. J. Lønning (eds), *After Oslo: New Realities, Old Problems*, London and Chicago: Pluto Press.

— (Winter 2006) 'The pitfalls of a U.S.–Israel vision of a palestine state', *Journal of Palestine Studies*, Vol. XXXV, No. 2.

Blecher, R. (July 2006) 'Converging upon war', *Middle East Report Online*.

Cook, J. (2006). *Blood and Religion: The Unmasking of the Jewish and Democratic State*, London: Pluto Press.

— (11–17 May 2006) 'Olmert's old rose' in *Al'Ahram Weekly*, No. 794.

Gavron, D. (2004). 'One state awakening', interview by Peter Hirschberg, *Ha'aretz*, 6 February.

Golan, A. (2004) 'Enough of this demographic panic', *Ha'aretz*, 10 August.

Gresh, A. (August 2006) 'After Hizbullah and Hamas: Middle East – what will emerge from the ruins', *Paris: Le Monde diplomatique*.

Halper, J. (7 November 2005). 'Israel as an extension of American Empire', *Counterpunch*.

Hersh, S. M. (14 August, 2006) 'Watching Lebanon', *The New Yorker*, (http://www.truthout.org/docs_2006/061306y.shtml).

Hilal, J. (2002) *The Formation of the Palestinian Elite* (in Arabic), Ramallah and Amman: and Al-Urdun Al-Jadid Research Centre.

— (2006a) *The Palestinian Political System After Oslo* (in Arabic), Beirut: Institute for Palestine Studies, and Ramallah: Muwatin – The Palestinian Institute for the Study of Democracy.

— (2006b) 'Hamas's rise as charted in the polls, 1994–2005', *Journal of Palestine Studies*, Vol. XXXV, No. 3.

— (2006c) *Palestinian Political Organizations and Parties* (in Arabic), Ramallah: Muwatin-The Palestinian Institute for the Study of Democracy.

International Crisis Group (13 June 2006) 'Palestinians, Israel, and the Quartet: pulling back from the brink', *Middle East Report*, No. 54.

Jarbawi, A. (2005) 'The remaining Palestinian options', *The Arab World Geographer*, Vol. 8, No. 3.

Hirst, D. (17 August 2006) 'Hizbullah has achieved what Arab states only dreamed of', *The Guardian*, (http://www.guardian.co.uk/israel/comment/0.. 1851814.co.html).

Judt, T. (2003) 'Israel: the alternative', *New York Review Of Books*, 23 October www.nybooks.com/articles/16671.

Karmi, G. (2002). 'A secular democratic state in historic Palestine: an idea whose time has come?', *CAABU Information and Press Library*. www.caaabu.org/press/articles/secular-state.html.

Khalidi, R. (1997). *Palestinian Identity; The Construction of Modern National Consciousness*, New York: Columbia University Press.

Kimmerling, B. and J. S. Migdal (2003). *The Palestinian People; A History*, London and Cambridge, MA: Cambridge University Press.

Laor, Y. (2001) *'Tears of Zion'*, *New Left Review*, 10, July–August.

Levy G. (9 July 2006) 'Who started it?', Tel Aviv, *Ha'aretz*.

— (21 August 2006) 'What the right has to offer', Tel Aviv, *Ha'aretz*.

Lynch, M. (June 2004), 'No Jordan option', *Middle East Report Online*.

Mandron, G. (2001) *'Redividing Palestine?'*, *New Left Review*, 10, July–August.

Masalha, N. (1992). *Expulsion of Palestinians: The Concept of Transfer in Zionist Thinking, Planning and Action.* Beirut: Institute for Palestine Studies (in Arabic).

Morris, B. (1987) *The Birth of the Palestinian Refugee Problem 1947–1949*, Cambridge: Cambridge University Press.

Mushtaq, H. with G. Giacaman and I. Amundsen (eds) (2004) *State Formation in Palestine; Viability and Governance During Social Transformation*, London and New York: RoutledgeCurzon.

Pappe, I. (1994) *The Making of the Arab-Israeli Conflict, 1947–1951*, London: I.B. Tauris.

Peled, Y. (2006) 'Zionist realities', *New Left Review*, 38, March–April.

Piterberg, G. (2001) *'Erasures'*, *New Left Review*, 10, July–August.

Porath, Y. (1974) *The Emergence of The Palestinian Arab Movement, 1919–1929*, London: Frank Cass.

Reuveny, R. (2005). 'The binational state and the colonial perspective: Israeli-Palestinian conflict in historical perspective', *The Arab World Geographer*, Vol. 8, No. 3.

Said, E. (1999) 'An interview with Edward W. Said by D. Barsamian', *The Progressive*, 63.

Samet, G. (17 August 2006). 'It's a new era, if you haven't noticed', Tel Aviv, *Ha'aretz*.

Sayigh, R. (1979) *Palestinians from Peasants to Revolutionaries*, London: Zed Books.

Simon D. B. (18 August, 2006). 'Talking only to ourselves', Tel Aviv ; *Ha'aretz*.

Sussman, G. (Summer, 2004), 'The challenge of the two-state solution', *Middle East Report Online*.

Tilley, V. (2005a). *The One-State Solution: A Breakthrough for Peace in the Israeli-Palestinian Deadlock*, Ann Arbor and Manchester.

— (2005b) 'From "Jewish State and Arab State" to "Israel and Palestine"? international norms, ethnocracy and the two-state solution', *The Arab World Geographer*, Vol. 8, No. 3.

— (2006) 'The secular solution; debating Israel-Palestine', in *New Left Review*, 38, March–April.

Usher, G. (August 2005) 'The new Hamas; between resistance and participation', *Middle East Report Online*.

Rouhana, N. N. (Winter 2006) ' "Jewish and Democratic"? the price of a national self-deception', *Journal of Palestine Studies*, Vol. XXXV, No. 2.

Yiftachel, O. (2005), 'Neither two states nor one: the disengagement and 'creeping apartheid' in Israel/Palestine', *The Arab World Geographer*, Vol. 8, No 3.

2 | Zionism and the two-state solution

ILAN PAPPÉ

A clear sense of 'Palestine' as a coherent geo-political unit dates back, according to both the Palestinian and Zionist narratives, to 3000 BCE. From that time onward, for 1500 years, it was the land of the Canaan-ites. In around 1500 BCE the land of Canaan fell under Egyptian rule, not for the last time in history, and then successively under Philistine (1200–975), Israelite (1000–923), Phoenician (923–700), Assyrian (700–612), Babylonian (586–539), Persian (539–332), Macedonian (332–63), Roman (63BC–636CE), Arab (636–1200), Crusade (1099–1291), Ayubi (1187–1253), Mamluk (1253–1516) and Ottoman rules (1517–1917). Each rule divided the land in an administrative way that reflected its political culture and time. But apart from the early Roman period and the early Arab period when vast populations were moved out and in, the society remained – ethnically, culturally and religiously – the same. Within what we recognize today as Mandatory Palestine this society developed its own identity and distinctive features.

In modern times, some of the above periods were manipulated and co-opted into a national, or colonialist, narrative to justify the take-over and conquest of the country. This historical chronology was used, or abused, by the Crusaders and later European colonialists and the Zionist movement. The Zionists were different from the others as they deemed – as did the powers that be when the Zionists emerged in 1882 – the historical reference to be crucial for justifying their colonization of Palestine. They did it as part of what they termed 'the Return' to or 'Redemption' of the land, which was once ruled by Israelites; as the historical checklist above indicates, this is a reference to a mere century in a history of five millennia.

Away from the national narrative, we should say that Palestine as a geo-political entity was a fluid concept since the rulers of the country quite often were the representatives of an empire, which disabled any local sovereignty from developing. The question of sovereignty began to be an issue – one that would inform the land's history and conflict until today – once the empires disappeared. The natural progress from such disintegration, almost everywhere in the world, was that the indigenous population took over. Ever since the emergence of the concept of nationalism, the identity of this historical revolution is clear and common. Where the vestiges of imperialism or colonialism refused to let go – such as in the case of white settlers' communities in north and South Africa – the national wars of liberation lingered on. In places where the indigenous population was annihilated by the settlers' communities, the latter became the new nation (as happened in the Americas and Australasia).

The takeover from the disintegrating empires followed a longer process, so many of the theoreticians of nationalism believe, of social and cultural cohesiveness. The liberated lands varied in structure and composition: some, with a heterogeneous ethnic, religious and cultural society, found it difficult to become a nation state; others were fortunate due to their relative homogeneity – although they had their share of economic polarity, social differentiation and constant struggle between modernity and tradition. A liberated Palestine would have belonged to the latter model, which developed in Egypt and Tunisia – and been less similar to the more troubled cases of Iraq and Lebanon.

At the turn of the 21st century, the political map of the world was consolidated in such a way that in only a very few areas does the building of the nation state still continue or the issue of sovereignty remain open. A rare case, which distresses the world at large and destabilizes it, is Palestine. Why this Arab land did not become another Arab nation state – as did all the other states in the Middle East (including the smallest of the emirates in the Persian Gulf) – is a well-known story. What is quite often neglected is the fact that the present geo-political reality, while it has been depicted in the world as normal, is in fact *sui generis* and runs contrary to the land's history and the wishes of its native population, who still constitute a vast majority of the people (the Palestinian refugee community and those living inside Palestine are double that of the Jews inside the land). The gap between the external depiction of the reality and the reality itself as perceived by the Palestinians is the major source of the conflict, and only attempts to tally the former with the latter have a chance of bringing reconciliation and peace to the torn country of Palestine.

The purpose of this chapter is to stress the pattern of continuity in

31

Palestine's modern history (beginning with the late Ottoman period) as a geo-political entity, with its own cultural cohesiveness and distinctiveness, and contrast it with the dominant mainstream Zionist perception of Palestine as formed of two units: one Jewish and one not Jewish (Jordanian or Palestinian as the circumstances would have it).

Even a cursory journey into the past reveals that Palestine was most of the time ruled as a unitary political unit; namely, the political structure fitted the ethnic, social, cultural and religious realities on the ground. Such a long span of time, lying on deeper layers of ancient existence, explains the emergence of unique features such as dialects, customs and local patriotism in what we recognize today as Palestine.

The rise of ideologies such as nationalism, the intervention of European colonialism and the decline of Ottomanism contributed to a clearer conceptualization of what Palestine meant and stood for, both to its inhabitants and those coveting it from the outside.

Palestine in the late Ottoman rule

The above heading is the title of a book published by my own university in 1986. More than 25 historians, most of them Israeli Jews, reconstructed life in Palestine: a geo-political unit that was predominantly Arab in ethnicity (more than 95% of half a million population). In fact the old Jewish community also considered itself to be Arab, and only a few thousand Jewish settlers, who arrived for the first time in 1882, regarded their ethnicity, and not only religion, as Jewish.

Palestinian historians would have no problem with defining the land in 1882–1917 as Palestine in the late Ottoman period. However, they would find it bizarre to learn from the book's introduction that in that period there were two communities, Jewish and Arab 'which began aspiring toward national liberation' and, therefore, both groups were anti-Ottoman. It was 'only natural that much of their protest and grievances be directed against their Ottoman masters'. Historical fabrication at its best, one should say. The naive reader would think Palestine in the late Ottoman period, and centuries, if not millennia, before, was the land of Jews and Arabs, equal in number, presence and claim, who disliked each other, and the Ottomans. In this typical Zionist narrative from the mid-1980s, Palestine is already partly Israel. Partition was already in the air.

We need Palestinian scholarship to remind us that even in 1917 the vast majority of people in Palestine were Palestinians – 600,000

– with a few thousand foreign settlers hoping to colonize the land on behalf of European Jewish nationalism or Christian millenniarism. A year later Palestine was clearly defined as such with the name Palestine given to it officially for the first time as a political unit, and through dramatic dispossession, colonization and aggressive British imperialism became a historical case study lying somewhere between the annihilated indigenous populations and the liberated colonies of the European empires. It is still there today.

As long as the demographic, social and cultural realities on the ground fitted the political structure of the land, conflicts were sparse and very localized. For most of the Ottoman period, Palestine was only divided administratively, but, as mentioned, maintained a cohesion distinguished by dialect, customs and the people itself.[1] The country was composed of three principal Ottoman subdistricts, Acre, Nablus and Jerusalem, which were connected by history and tradition. These similarities had all along been recognized by the people themselves, which is why the people of Jabal Nablus had made every possible effort to remain connected to Jerusalem. When Nablus was officially annexed in 1858 to the vilayet of Beirut, a protest movement arose, so massive that it turned into a bloodbath in which, according to the British consul in Jerusalem, 3,000 people were killed. The consul was, however, known to have exaggerated in the past, so the number could well have been much lower.[2]

In the very last years of their rule, the Ottomans allowed the Arab elite to take a more intensive part in the politics of the land – turning its cities such as Jerusalem, Jaffa, Haifa and Nablus – into epicenters of social, and later even national, unity.[3] Like all the Arab lands around Palestine, under the spell of nationalism, Palestine progressed into becoming a *wataniyya* – a geo-political locality – within a *qawmiyya* – the pan-Arabist sphere of belonging. The new ruler of Palestine, the British Empire, did not stop this process, nor did it create a political structure that collided with the cohesiveness of the society and its uniqueness. But it did lay the foundations, through the various political solutions it offered, for the construction of a new Palestine – which deprived the Palestinians of their land – and making it into Israel.

One Palestine complete

Here we have, yet again, a title by a Zionist historian, this time Tom Segev. Here too Palestinian historiography would not object to the title,

33

but Segev's English title is misleading. The book was originally written in Hebrew and entitled 'Eretz Israel in the Mandatory Period', a typical Zionist parlance. 'The One Palestine', is thus an aberration, almost a foreign occupation by a very civilized culture, according to Segev, which enabled the native population, which here too includes the Zionist settlers and colonialists, to live in relative peace and prosperity.

Palestine became more complete – in this Segev is right – because the British continued where the Ottoman reformers, before they collapsed, had left the work of unison. The British combined the three Ottoman sub-districts into one geo-political unit (a smooth operation that was carried out with great local satisfaction compared to the uneasiness that accompanied similar unifications in Iraq, where Kurds, Shiites and Sunnis were to become the Iraqi nation state under British rule). The making of a unitary mandatory state was a calm historical process that corresponded to the harmonious ethnic and religious fabric on the ground. It lasted until 1923, and the final stages were devoted to negotiating over the land's final border, creating a better defined space for the national movement to identify with, but also for colonialism and Zionism to fight for.

This was Palestine's tragedy: that in the same period when it crystallized as a typical Arab nation state, it enabled the Zionist movement to define clearly what it meant geographically by the concept of Eretz Israel, or the land of Israel; with Zionism came also the idea of partitioning Palestine.

The political elite of the native Palestinians conceived its homeland as a unitary state. In fact, in the very early years of British occupation and nascent Zionist presence it imagined the future more in pan-Arabist than Palestinian terms. But the balance of forces on the ground undermined the dream of a pan-Arabist entity stretching from Morocco to Iran and subverted even less ambitious plans such as creating a Greater Syria out of the eastern Mediterranean countries. By 1922, the majority of the Palestinian leaders, and, one guesses, the population at large, conceptualized Palestine as the national homeland of the Palestinians lying between the River Jordan and the Mediterranean. When this was the trend, and given the vast majority they enjoyed in the country, the Palestinians, through their elected leaders, became aware of their need to make a claim to a land that was theirs, until a foreign movement challenged them. Their entry into the game of diplomacy in the post-1918 global arena was hesitant and ineffective,

34

compared to the European-based Zionist movement with its growing power base in America.

On the face it, being such a vast majority, they should have succeeded, despite their leaders' lack of experience. The new system of nation states in the Middle East was promised independence, under the guidance of the League of Nations, based on principles of democracy and self-determination. Had Palestine been treated according to these measures, it would today have been in a similar position to any other Arab nation state.

But, unlike with any other Arab state, the international verdict on Palestine's future, in the form of the mandatory charter, included clauses that defeated the right of the Palestinians to their homeland. The Balfour Declaration, and with it the ambiguous British promise to make Palestine a homeland for the Jews, was incorporated in the charter. A few violent outbursts and more reflective British strategic thought led London to rethink its previous concepts. This is probably why, until 1937, the British were still visualizing the future within a one-state paradigm. In 1928, these fresh insights turned into the first significant peace initiative. In a country that by then had a majority of Palestinians (85% of the population), the British must have felt triumphant when they succeeded in persuading the Executive Committee of the Palestine National Congress – the de facto government of the Palestinians – to share the land with the Jewish settlers. The idea was to build a state on the basis of parity – in the executive, legislative and judiciary system. It was a concept of a unitary state that was accepted by a Palestinian leadership – in a rare moment of unity in a polity that hitherto and after was divided by clannish cleavages of prestige and ancestry.[4]

It was also an opportune moment for allowing the two communities to try and coexist within an acceptable political structure. But the Zionist leadership refused to partake in such a solution. Interestingly, as long as its leaders had been aware of a total rejection of the idea on the Palestinian part, the official Zionist position was that this kind of a solution was acceptable. Once the intelligence unit of the Jewish Agency reported a change of wind on the Palestinian side, the Jewish leadership reversed its policy and rejected the idea of parity.[5]

The Zionist leaders preferred the idea of partition, with the hope of annexing more of Palestine when favorable conditions for such expansion would develop.When the future of Palestine was discussed once

35

more in the wake of the British decision to leave Palestine in February 1947, the Zionist leadership, although representing the minority group of settlers, determined the peace agenda. A very inexperienced inquiry commission was appointed by the UN – the international body took responsibility for Palestine after the British withdrawal. The new commission acted within a vacuum which was easily filled by Zionist ideas. In May 1947 the Jewish Agency provided the inquiry commission, UNSCOP, with a map that included the creation of a Jewish state over 80% of Palestine – more or less Israel of today without the occupied territories. In November 1947 the commission reduced the Jewish state to 55% of Palestine and formulated the plan as UN General Assembly resolution 181. Despite the Palestinians' rejection of the plan, which did not surprise anyone as they had been opposed to partition ever since 1918 – and to the Zionist endorsement of it – and which was foretold since partition was after all a Zionist solution to the problem, it was in the eyes of the international policeman a solid enough basis for peace in the Holy Land. Imposing the will of one side on the other was hardly a productive move towards reconciliation and indeed, rather than bringing peace and quiet to the torn land, the resolution triggered violence on an unprecedented scale in the history of modern Palestine.[6]

The partitioning of Palestine, 1947–67

The Jewish leadership returned to its May 1947 map; if the Palestinians rejected the Zionist idea of partition, it was time for unilateral action. The map showed clearly which parts of Palestine were coveted as the future Jewish state. The problem was that within the desired 80% the Jews were a minority of 40% (660,000 Jews and one million Palestinians). But this was also a passable hurdle. The leaders of the Yishuv[7] had been prepared ever since the beginning of the Zionist project in Palestine for such an eventuality. They advocated in such a case the enforced transfer of the indigenous population so that a pure Jewish state could be established. Therefore, on 10 March 1948, the Zionist leadership adopted the by now infamous Plan Dalet, which ordered the Jewish forces to ethnically cleanse the areas regarded as the future Jewish state in Palestine.

The international community realized that the partition plan was more an incentive for bloodshed than a peace programme, and, five days after the 1948 war erupted, once more attempted a reconciliation effort. The mission was entrusted to the hands of the first UN mediator in the history of the post-mandatory conflict, Count Folke Bernadotte. Bernadotte offered two proposals to end the conflict by partitioning the land into two states. The difference between them was that in the second proposal he suggested the annexation of Arab Palestine to Transjordan. But in both proposals he stipulated the unconditional repatriation of Palestinian refugees as a precondition for peace. He was ambivalent about Jerusalem, wishing it to be the Arab capital in the first proposal but preferring it to be international in the second. In any case, he seemed to place the refugees and Jerusalem at the centre of the conflict and perceive these two dilemmas as indivisible problems, for which only a comprehensive and just solution would do.[8]

Even after Bernadotte's assassination by Jewish extremists in 1948, the Palestine Conciliation Commission appointed to replace him pursued the same policy. The three members of this commission wished to build the future solution on three tiers: the partition of the land into two states – not, however, according to the map of the partition resolution, but corresponding to the demographic distribution of Jews and Palestinians – the internationalization of Jerusalem and the unconditional return of the refugees to their homes. The new mediators offered the three principles as a basis for negotiations, and while the Arab confrontational countries and the Palestinian leadership accepted this offer, during the UN peace conference in Lausanne, Switzerland in May 1949, as the UN General Assembly had done before them in resolution 194 of December 1948, the offer was nevertheless buried by the intransigent David Ben Gurion and his government in the summer of that year. At first, the US administration rebuked Israel for its policy and exerted economic pressure on it, but later on the Jewish lobby succeeded in reorientating US policy onto pro-Israeli tracks, where it has remained until today.[9]

Palestine was not divided; it was destroyed and most of its people expelled. The expulsion and the destruction has kindled the conflict ever since. The PLO emerged in the late 1950s/1960s as an embodiment of the Palestinian struggle for return, reconstruction and restitution. But it was not a particularly successful struggle. The refugees were totally ignored by the international community and the regional Arab powers. Only Gamal Abd al-Nasser seemed to adopt their cause, forcing the Arab League at least to show concern for their case. As the ill-fated Arab manoeuvres of June 1967 showed, this was neither enough nor efficient.

In those days, when the PLO phoenix hatched (1948–67), a more systematic conceptualization of the idea of one state emerged. In the paper *Filastinuna* several writers envisaged a secular democratic state as the only viable solution for the Palestine problem. But a thorough reading shows that the concern was an unidentified 'Palestinian entity' that would trigger the rebirth of the movement, rather than focusing on actual political models or structures.[10] The debate was mainly with a pan-Arabist point of view, wishing to oppose what they called separatism from the *qawmi* (the pan-Arabist version of nationalism) future in the name of a Palestinian *wataniyya* (nation-state territorialism).

Neither was the nature of a future Palestinian entity seriously discussed in the regional or international arenas. There was a lull in the peace efforts in the 1950s and 1960s, although up-in-the-air schemes such the Anglo-American Alpha programme and the Johnston Plan were mooted.[11]

These and more esoteric initiatives, almost all of them American, wished to adopt a businesslike approach to the conflict. This meant a great belief in partition with regard to the security interests of Israel and its Arab neighbours, while totally sidelining the Palestinians as partners for peace. The Palestinians were cancelled as a political partner in this approach; they existed only as refugees whose fate was treated within the economic framework of the American Cold War against the Soviet Union. Their problem was to be solved within a new Marshall Plan for the Middle East. This plan promised American aid to the area in order to improve the standard of living as the best means of containing Soviet encroachment. For that, the refugees had to be resettled in Arab lands and serve as cheap labour for their development (thus also distancing them from Israel's borders and consciousness). Although the PLO showed enough resistance to encourage Arab regimes to leave the refugees in their transitional camps, despite the perception of them as a destabilizing factor, the association of the PLO with the Soviet Union pushed the Palestinians, wherever they were located, further from any prospective Pax Americana.

The two-state formula and its demise, 1967–2000

In June 1967, the whole of Palestine became Israel – a new geopolitical reality that necessitated a renewed peace process. At first, it was the UN that took the initiative, but soon it was replaced by American peacemakers. The early architects of Pax Americana had some original ideas of their own, which were flatly rejected by the Israelis and hence remained on paper. Then the mechanism of American brokering became a proxy for Israeli peace plans. At the centre of the Israeli perception of a solution stood three presumptions: the first was that Israel should be absolved from the 1948 ethnic cleansings, with that issue no longer being mentioned as part of a prospective peace agenda; secondly and consequently, negotiations for peace would only concern the future of the areas Israel had occupied in 1967, namely the West Bank and the Gaza Strip; and, thirdly, the fate of the Palestinian minority in Israel was not to be part of a comprehensive settlement for the conflict. This meant that 80% of Palestine and more than 50% of the Palestinians were excluded from the peacemaking efforts in the land of Palestine. This formula was accepted unconditionally by the USA and sold as the best offer in town to the rest of the world.

At the heart of this formula stood an equation of territories for peace, produced by the Israeli peace camp and marketed by the Americans. It is a strange formula, if you stop and think about it: at one end of the equation you have a quantitative and measurable variable; at the other, an abstract term, not easily conceptualized or even illustrated. It was less bizarre as a working basis for bilateral peace between Israel and its Arab neighbours where indeed it operated quite well for a while in the case of Egypt and Jordan. And yet we should remember it produced 'cold peace' in the case of these two countries, as it did not offer a comprehensive solution to the Palestine question. And indeed what had this equation to offer to the ultimate victims of the 1948 war, whose demand for 'justice' is the kindling for the conflict's fire?

The architects of the Oslo Accords thought they had something to offer. They resold the merchandise of 'peace for territories'. Hollow concepts such as Israeli recognition of the PLO and 'autonomy' for the Palestinians was meant to strengthen the businesslike approach for a solution. The reality on the ground was one state, 20% of which was under indirect Israeli military occupation, while it was represented as the making of a two-state solution with the display of a dramatic discourse of peace.[12]

I am not underestimating the progress made in Oslo, but one should never forget the circumstances of the Accords' birth – they tell you why it was such a colossal failure. Dramatic changes in the global and regional balance of power, and an Israeli readiness to replace the Hashemites of Jordan with the PLO as a partner for peace, opened the way to an even more complicated formula of 'territories for peace'. Oslo was a celebration of the idea of partition: territories and everything else which was visible and quantifiable could be divided between the two sides. Thus the only non-Jewish parts of post-1948 Palestine – 22% of the land – could be re-divided between Israel and a future Palestinian autonomous entity. Within this 22% of Palestine, the illegal Jewish settlements could be divided into 80% under Israeli control and 20% under the Palestinian authority. And so on: most of the water resources to Israel, most of Jerusalem in Israeli hands. Peace, the quid pro quo, meant a stateless Palestinian state robbed of any say in its defence, foreign or economic policies. As for the Palestinian Right of Return, according to the Israeli interpretation of Oslo, which is the one that counts, it should be forgotten and erased. This Israeli conceptualization of a solution was presented to the world at large in the summer of 2000 in Camp David.

For Palestinians the summit in Camp David was meant to produce the final stages in the Israeli withdrawal from the West Bank and the Gaza Strip (according to resolutions 242 and 338 of the UN Security Council) and prepare the ground for new negotiations over a final settlement on the basis of UN resolution 194: the return of the refugees, the internationalization of Jerusalem and a full sovereign Palestinian state. Even the US voted in favour of this resolution at the time and has done ever since.

The Israeli left, in power since 1999, regarded the Camp David summit as a stage for dictating to the Palestinians its concept of a solution: maximizing the divisibility of the visible (evacuating 90% of the occupied areas, 20% of the settlements, 50% of Jerusalem) while demanding the end of Palestinian reference to the invisible layers of the conflict: no Right of Return, no full sovereign Palestinian state and no solution for the Palestinian minority in Israel. After Camp David an acceptable solution for the Israelis meant that, as long as the Palestinians refused to succumb to the Israeli dictates, the occupation, exile and discrimination would continue. With or without Ariel Sharon's violation of the sacredness of the Haram al-Sharif in September 2000, the second uprising broke out in the territories in late September, and in Israel a month later, in October 2000, and it is still going on in one form or another while this chapter is being written.

In the first four years of the second Intifada, 'territories for peace' was absent from the peace table. The uprising spilled over into Israel itself, leading the Palestinian minority there to call for the de-Zionization of the Jewish state, allowing West Bankers to demand the Palestinianization of Muslim and Christian Jerusalem, and the inhabitants of Gaza to raise arms against the continuing occupation, as well as uniting Palestinian refugees around the world in their call for the implementation of their Right of Return. What this last Intifada made abundantly clear was that, in the eyes of the Palestinians, the end of occupation was a precondition for peace and could not be peace itself. The Israeli peace camp, so we are told by its 'gurus', was insulted in October 2000. The narrative provided by the Israeli prime minister at the time of the Camp David summit, Ehud Barak, was widely accepted by the peace camp. According to this version the Israeli leadership maximized the equation of 'territories for peace' by offering most of the territories Israel occupied in 1967, and the Palestinians stupidly rejected this 'generous' offer.

This version was endorsed by the United States, although several European governments and personalities doubted its validity. The narrative delineated very clearly what was the final settlement in the eyes of the political camp led at the time by the Israeli Labour Party and its leader Ehud Barak. Such a 'comprehensive' solution was in essence an Israeli demand of the Palestinians to recognize the Zionist narrative of the 1948 war as exclusively right and valid: Israel had no responsibility for the making of the refugee problem, and the Palestinian minority in Israel – 20% of the population – was not part of the solution to the conflict. The solution also included an Israeli demand of the Palestinians to acquiesce in the new reality Israel had created in Greater Jerusalem and the West Bank. A final peace settlement was therefore one in which the world recognizes as eternally Jewish the settlement belt encircling Jerusalem and planted at the heart of Palestinian cities such as Nablus and Khalil (Hebron).

This dictate returned as a peace process in 2004 under the auspices of a new body, the Quartet – a committee composed of the most senior UN, American, European and Russian diplomats. They presented a 'Road Map', which was an international endorsement of the Israeli ideas of how best to divide the occupied territories between the Jewish state and a future Palestinian entity, that could be called, even according to Israeli Prime Minister Ariel Sharon (who won the elections of 2001 and 2003) a 'state'. When the two sides failed to move ahead toward the Road Map, for the same reasons that they had failed to reach an agreement in the previous 36 years of Israeli occupation, Sharon offered his own

Zionism and the two-state solution

41

version of the Map. He suggested a unilateral Israeli withdrawal from the Gaza Strip and four settlements in the north of the West Bank. The Quartet wished this disengagement to be part of the Map; Sharon did not care one way or another. He was motivated by an Israeli consensus that regards half of the West Bank (the big settlement blocs and Greater Jerusalem) as an integral part of future Israel in a solution that has no Right of Return for the refugees. In a way, Sharon, backed by the political centre in Israel, was moving towards the implementation of a one-state solution that includes a Palestinian bantustan (in fact two Bantustans: one in the Gaza Strip and one in the shrunken West Bank), and which the world has already hailed as a two-state solution.

The Israeli elections of 2006 brought this Sharonite conception to full fruition. The idea begot a party – Kadima – and even without Sharon it won a vote of confidence from the Jewish electorate. One state with two bantustans is the ideal Zionist solution according to these elections. It is a political vision accepted not only by Kadima, but also by Labour, and all the smaller centrist parties. It is still marketed as a two-state solution and a peace programme, although the reality on the ground attests to a scheme that perpetuates the occupation of the whole of mandatory Palestine by direct or indirect means. The two-state solution, once a major theme in Zionist strategy and Israeli ideology, has been replaced by 'ingathering' (*Hitkansut*), taking over 88% of historical Palestine, and the isolation and imprisonment of the remaining 12%.

Emptying Palestinian statehood of meaning

The historical perspective on the peace efforts offered hitherto indicates that the attempt to focus on the fate of the territories Israel occupied in the June 1967 war – territories which constitute 22% of Palestine – has been a total failure. Even Israeli offers to withdraw from most of the territories (at Oslo, through Camp David 2000, the Ayalon-Nusseibeh initiative, the Road Map and the Geneva Accords) could not elicit a meaningful Palestinian consent to end the conflict. These offers had one thing in common: they emptied the concept of statehood of its conventional and accepted notion in the second half of the 20th century. These peace offers, without exception, limited the future independence of the Palestinians in that 22%, accrediting Israel an exclusive say in security, foreign and economic matters in the future mini-state of the West Bank and Gaza Strip.

42

The mini-state structure failed to offer a solution to the refugee question; nor did it relate to the internationally recognized Right of Return. It is also a political structure that has no relevance to the fate of the 1.4 million Palestinians who live inside Israel, subjected to formal and informal apartheid policies. And finally, as the annexation of most of east Jerusalem has been tolerated by the international community for such a long time, it seems that a two-state solution retains much of Jerusalem in Jewish hands and disables the Palestinians from having a proper capital there.

What unites these four unsolved problems is the extension of the peace effort both geographically and chronologically. Geographically, we are looking for a political structure that is different from the contemporary one in the whole area of mandatory Palestine. Chronologically, we are looking for recognition of the significance of the 1948 Nakba (literally 'catastrophe') in determining the future chances of reconciliation.

The two are interconnected in a required recognition, globally and locally, of the disparity built into this conflict. More precisely, it means that the whole process of reconciliation cannot be activated unless Israel acknowledges the ethnic cleansing it committed in 1948 and is willing to be accountable for it.

I have written elsewhere on the various possible mechanisms for such a process;[13] here I would like to associate the end of conflict and the question of the desirable political structure that should 'accompany' such a process and eventually a solution. I use the term accompany, as I believe the process of mediation and reconciliation between Israel and its Palestinian victims is a first preconditional stage that should commence even before the final construction of an appropriate political structure.

Both the outstanding problems and the mechanism of reconciliation have a better chance of being dealt with once the idea of two states is abandoned, and with it the paradigm of parity is substituted with recognition of the imbalance between colonizer and colonized, expeller and expelled and occupier and occupied.

Buds of new thought: contemporary support for the one state

Reaching such noble objectives may rightly seem now sheer utopia. Such a way forward is vehemently rejected by most of the Jews in Israel and objected to by a considerable number of West Bankers. In the long run it may be, for good or for ill, the only game in town as recognized even by those who are still ardent supporters of the idea of two states, such as Mustafa Barghouti.[14]

In Israel two long-time comrades of Barghouti's struggle for two states, Haim Hanegbi and Meron Benvenisti (see also next chapter) decided at the end of the summer of 2003 that the time had come to forsake the two-state solution.[15]

The former sees a one-state solution as just; the latter laments it as unfortunately the only feasible one, given the range of Jewish settlements in the occupied territories, the unwillingness of any Israeli government massively to withdraw settlers and the growing demography of Palestinians inside Israel. However, both advocate the bi-national model, a kind of a federation between two national entities which share the executive, legislative and constitutional authorities between them on a parity and consensual basis.

The more veteran advocates of such a solution tend to prefer the idea of a secular democratic state for all its citizens. But some of them also regard the bi-national structure as a more feasible one to begin with. As Tony Judt put it recently in a *New York Review of Books* article on the subject,[16] it will be easier to win over those disappointed with the chance of a two-state solution to the notion of a bi-national state. A similar argument was made in 2004 by two Israeli academics, a Palestinian and a Jew.[17]

The powers that be – whether in politics, the economy or the media – are still putting all their energies into consolidating in Palestine a two-state solution; each according to its own understanding. The political elite in Israel wishes for a structure that would shrink Palestine into oblivion; the Quartet asserts that it could convince Israel to allow a mini-state over 15% of what used to be Palestine and this bantustan seems to satisfy some of the Arab regimes that are within the American sphere of influence.

Given such local, regional and global balances of power, can there be a return to political structures that would reflect more fairly and usefully the history, geography, culture and demography of Palestine?

The time has not yet arrived for detailing the nature of the political structure that would replace the two-state solution, and the two models of the secular state and the bi-national state that would compete in the theoretical discussions on the subject.

Surely, one way forward is to continue the extrapolation of the concept of one state as the only sensible solution that can prevent a civil war in Israel, grant equal rights to the Palestinian minority in Israel, and provide equitable solutions to the Right of Return and the status of Jerusalem. Much work is still to be done in this theoretical sphere beyond the stage of slogans and rhetoric. Moreover, there is a need to draw into the discussion other groups, such as feminists and ecologists, to widen the scope of the debate on how to structure the requisite political entity.

This can begin with joint historiographical effort that seeks non-ethnocentric, polyphonic reconstruction of the past that in its turn can produce more reflective and humanistic attitudes towards the suffering of those victimized by structures of evil in the land. The historiographical endeavour is not merely academic, as it looks for a de-nationalized, as well as de-genderized and de-colonized history. This means that salvaging the deprived voices of the past requires giving them a voice today and a vista of a different future.

However, it is an almost impossible task to move from historical deconstruction to future reconstruction. The comparative historical lessons, one has to admit, are not very encouraging in this respect. And thus, with all due respect to an important and significant debate that continues today between the proponents of the various ideal types of one-state solution in Palestine, one has to assess the chances of arriving at the moment when these theoretical broodings will become real models on the ground – albeit inevitably reduced.

More urgent, therefore, is the deconstruction of the present political power controlling the life of newcomers, indigenous and future inhabitants of Palestine – a power that suckles from an international system governed by ideals and motivations that seem to seek perpetuation of the present reality rather than its change.

Four processes have to be looked at closely, if the chances for a new reality to emerge in Palestine are to be assessed. These processes are intertwined in a dialectical relationship that, as a whole, is likely to impact on the reality on the ground in contemporary Palestine.

The first is Israeli policy – with the backing of global powers such as the American military-industrial complex, Christian Zionists and the pro-Zionist Jewish lobbies around the world. This policy, if unabated and unhindered, will continue to destroy Palestine, in the name of a two-state solution.

The second is the growing resentment with this reality in the Third,

Muslim and Arab worlds. So far, this anger is only reflected in extremist fanaticism, which feeds and benefits the first trend, but it can grow into a far more lethal, effective, and even acceptable force countering Israel and its policies.

The third is a fundamental change in Western public opinion and in what can be called, for lack of a better term, civil society. In July 2005, a survey showed that only 14% of Europeans and 42% of Americans showed sympathy and understanding of the Israeli position; and the trend is towards reducing these percentages even further. Against these statistics, one can appreciate the mushrooming of the boycott, divestment and sanctions campaign against Israel, reminiscent of the way the anti-Apartheid movement grew in the 1960s.

The fourth is a cautious emanation of desegregated spaces of coexistence, on a parity basis, inside areas in Israel where Palestinians and Jews live in proximity, such as the Galilee. It is reflected mainly in the opening of joint kindergartens and schools, but it is also beginning to pervade the business, judicial and municipal fields. It is early days to assess the significance of the phenomenon, a drop in a sea of segregation from above. But if the three processes mentioned above have their impact, this may develop both as a refuge for people who wish to live differently from the reality around them, or even as a model for a future Palestine.

Notes

1 See Jamil Hilal (2002) *The Making of the Palestinian Elite from the Emergence of the Palestinian National Movement until the Aftermath of the Palestinian Authority*, Ramallah: Muwatin (Arabic); Beshara Doumani (1995) *Rediscovering Palestine: Merchants and Peasants in Jabal Nablus, 1700–1900*, Berkeley and New York: University of California Press; and Rashid Khalidi (1997) *Palestinian Identity: The Construction of Modern National Consciousness*, New York: Columbia University Press.

2 See more details in Ilan Pappé (2004) *A History of Modern Palestine: One Land, Two peoples*, Cambridge: Cambridge University Press, pp. 14–26.

3 Butrus Abu Manneh, 'The rise of the Sanjak of Jerusalem in the late nineteenth century', in I. Pappé (ed.) (1999) *The Israel/Palestine Question*, London and New York: Routledge, pp. 41–52.

4 Eliakim Rubenstein (1995) 'The treatment of the Arab question in Palestine in the immediate period after the 1929 events and the establishment of the political bureau – Political aspect' in Ilan Pappé (ed.), *Jewish–Arab Relations in Mandatory Palestine: A New Approach in the Historical Research*, Givat Haviva: Institute of Peace Research, pp. 65–102 (Hebrew).

5 Ibid.

6 This is detailed in Ilan Pappé, *The Making of the Arab-Israeli Conflict,* *1947–51*, New York and London: I. B. Tauris, pp. 16–46.

7 The Yishuv is literally the 'settlement' and this refers to the Jewish community in Mandatory Palestine.

8 Ilan Amitzur (1989) *Bernadotte in Palestine 1948: A Study in Contemporary Humanitarian Knight-errantry*, London: Macmillan.

9 See Pappé, *The Making*, pp. 203–43.

10 Helena Cobban (1984) *The PLO*, Cambridge: Cambridge University Press, pp. 28–9.

11 Avi Shlaim, *The Iron Wall: Israel and the Arab World*, New York and London: W. W. Norton and Company, pp. 109–10.

12 See Ilan Pappé (1999) 'Breaking the mirror – Oslo and after' in Haim Gordon (ed.), *Looking Back at the June 1967 War*, Westport, CT and London: Prager, pp. 95–112.

13 Ilan Pappé (2001) 'Fear, victimhood, self and other', *The MIT Electronic Journal of Middle East Studies*, May 2001.

14 Mustafa Barghouti (2004) 'Sharon's nightmare', *Al-Ahram Weekly*, 690, 13–19 May 2004.

15 *Ha'aretz*, 8 August 2003.

16 23 October 2003.

17 See for instance, As'ad Ghanem and Sarah Ozacky-Lazar, 'The status of the Palestinians in Israel in an era of peace: part of the problem but not part of the solution', *Israel Affairs*, 9/1–2 (Autumn/Winter 2003), pp. 263–89.

3 | Israel and the 'danger of demography'

AS'AD GHANEM

Despite the fact that many analysts are addressing the Oslo Accords as the cornerstone for any peace process or historical agreement between the Israelis and Palestinians, it is clear that in recent years the political situation that prevailed at the time of signing these agreements has fundamentally changed. Responding to internal politics and impeded hopes for establishing an independent Palestinian state beside Israel, in 2006 the Palestinians elected a new government and a legislative council led by Hamas; they have practically closed the Oslo chapter and declared the beginning of a new stage. The Palestinians were following in the footsteps of Israel, who took the lead in ending Oslo and its bilateral agreements once then prime minister Ehud Barak had deliberately thwarted the reaching of an interim agreement with Yasser Arafat at the Camp David summit of 2000. Barak was succeeded as prime minister by Ariel Sharon, who boasted of his bloody record in dealing with the Palestinians and of the fact that he did not 'shake hands with Arafat' even when he was a minister during the Netanyahu government and a member of the Israeli negotiating team in 1996–99. Sharon launched the new Israeli project (see below) while avoiding any official negotiations with the Palestinians, even after the death of Arafat and what the Israelis claimed to be the 'positive' transfer of power to Mahmoud Abbas (Abu Mazen). Sharon succeeded in establishing a new political game based on shifting from a policy of seeking a solution to the conflict to a policy of 'conflict management' in tackling the future of the Palestinian territories occupied in 1967.

The discourse on the future of Israel is based, according to most of Israel's leaders, elite, and average public, on what is known in Israel as the 'demographic danger'. Related to the 'demographic danger' is the fear that Israel, within its extended borders, including the West Bank and Gaza, or within the limits of the borders before the June 1967 war, would, sooner or later, turn into a 'bi-national' state. This chapter is an attempt to analyse the Israeli official and public stance on this issue and to give background to this discussion with emphasis on the post-Oslo era and precisely after Israel ended the Oslo process.

The politics of fear: the 'demographic danger' vs. the 'bi-national' reality

The demographic factor constitutes a basic component in drafting executive planning for present-day communities. This is especially true of the divided communities that were established following the Jewish immigration. Demography constituted an important component for the Zionist movement in dealing with the Palestinians before and after the establishment of Israel. During the Mandate period, Zionist decision-makers prepared strategies of ethnic cleansing that were carried out in 1948. Referring to the Palestinians, Theodor Herzl (1860–1904), the father of modern Zionism, intended to 'spirit the penniless (indigenous) population across the border' to create the Jewish state (Masalha 1992).

After the establishment of the state, Israel continued to consider the demographic factor as paramount in relation to the Palestinians, whether citizens of Israel or not. Since the 1950s, Israeli policy and Jewish housing plans have focused on 'improving' the demographic ratio generally, and locally by settling Jews in the Arab areas. The Galilee judaization project was the first step in this regard, aimed at enforcing control over the land through spreading Jewish settlements and communities on large areas of land in order to create a Jewish majority in the Galilee (Lefshetz and Leon 1993). As part of the implementation of this project, Arab lands were confiscated and tens of new Jewish settlements and towns were built around Arab villages.

The Galilee judaization project was followed by another judaization project for the Negev desert. The aim of this programme has been to gather all of the Arab residents into seven bounded, government-planned communities. These programmes are inherently repugnant to the native Arab Bedouin population, whose traditionally distinct clans and nomadic life styles were previously unrestricted. While the Bedouin have been subjected to restricted herding for allegedly inhabiting too much land, dozens of cooperative villages and communities continue to be established for Jews in the Negev area, where government planning aims at absorbing thousands of future Jewish settlers. These general judaization policies have been coupled with ending the majority status of Arab communities throughout the country, and included the estab-

49

lishment of Nitseret Elit city with a view to checking demographically the Arab population of Nazareth, and developing Beer Sheva city to become the central city in the Negev area.

Demography has become an essence of the conflict in recent years, and many conferences have been held and articles written to deal with its effect on the character of the Jewish state and the possible future solution with the Palestinians. It is the catalyst for the discussion in support of or opposing withdrawal from the 1967-occupied territories. The demographic discussion has also broadened to include a link between withdrawal from the West Bank and Gaza Strip, to the possibility of relinquishing predominantly Arab areas along the Green Line to a future Palestinian state, as well as the solution to the Palestinian refugee problem. The goal of this demographic discussion is, of course, to research ways to preserve and ensure the steady growth of the Jewish majority.

Israeli sociologists have used statistics to encourage withdrawal from or annexation of the 1967-occupied land (Arieli, Shfarts and Tegari 2006). In a demographic study, the Jewish demographer Sergio de la Pergula concluded that Jews make up 78% of Israel's population and predicted a decline on that percentage to range between 65% and 69% in 2050. Pergula also established that Jews make up 53% of the population in historic Palestine and that this will dwindle to 26%–35% by 2050 (*Ha'aretz* 13/2/2002). This prompted Pergula to call for a speedy disengagement between the two peoples.

The demographic reality is also causing concern among Jewish politicians and academics anxious about the character and identity of the state. This has led many of them to seek new ways to guarantee a Jewish majority in light of a now declining Jewish immigration, an immigration that helped to maintain a Jewish majority over the last five decades. Different suggestions were proposed during the debate, including the surrender of Arab areas within the Green Line, as part of the final solution with the Palestinians.

One of those most prominent in bringing this discussion to light was Professor Arnon Soffer. Professor Soffer presented a paper to Prime Minister Ariel Sharon detailing his vision for solving the 'demographic crisis'. This paper was discussed by the Knesset's Foreign and Security Committee and the Herzliya Conference for Security and National Defence. Soffer proposed giving the Triangle (Muthallath) area and East Jerusalem to the PA, thereby reducing the Arab population of Israel by

400,000 (210,000 in East Jerusalem and 190,000 in the Triangle area. These 400,000 Arabs are expected to increase to 800,000 by 2020). With this reduction, in 2020, Israel would expect to have 1,350,000 Arabs in its population alongside 6 million Jews (Soffer 2002).

Soffer's demographic concern and justification for disengagement, including that from East Jerusalem, were explicit in his paper. He wrote to Sharon: 'the absence of disengagement means the establishment of an Arab majority, and consequently the end of the Jewish state of Israel.' He added 'it's important to remember that when the Israeli army makes efforts and succeeds in assassinating a militant here or there, at the same time 400 children are born in the western land of Israel; some of them will become new militants – everyday 400 children! Do you understand that?' (*Ha'aretz* 28/6/2002). After reading the paper, the director of planning at the US State Department, Richard Harris, asked Soffer how much of his project was based on security and how much on demography. Soffer responded it was 100% based on demography (*Ha'aretz* 28/6/2002).

The obsession with annexation, disengagement and demography is not the monopoly of a specific few. For example, work groups have been established to draft border demarcations based on the demographic factor rather than on security. In 2006, a number of demography and geography researchers continued to meet with some settlers at the Van Lair Institute. This group drafted different scenarios for demarcating the most suitable borders to ensure that 80% of Israeli citizens are Jews and 20% are Arabs. Every dunum drafted for annexation to Israel must have a population ratio of 8:2 to ensure a Jewish majority. This ratio explains the objection raised by this group to the disengagement plan that annexes some Arab villages in the northern Triangle area.

The Van Lair Institute is not the only place in Israel to discuss demography and annexation. These issues were also discussed at universities and research institutes, the Israeli National Security Council and even the US State Department and the CIA (*Ha'aretz* 28/6/2002). The Herzliya Center, one of Israel's elitist security and academic research establishments, also held several meetings to discuss the demographic issue in Israel.

Shimon Peres was one of the most ardent believers in the importance of demography in the post-Oslo era. He based his vision for 'peace' and withdrawal on making the demographic factor convincing enough to enlist support for his plans in and after the Oslo agreements. This was especially the case during the right-wing surge in Israel that caused his concerns over the annexation and settling of Palestinian land. Uncharacteristic of his own history, Sharon followed in the footsteps of Peres upon his assuming the prime minister's office. Both found common ground in the Kadima party, and promoted the 'necessity' to withdraw in order to keep a 'demographic balance'.

Sharon was the most vocal Israeli leader to express his ideas, political views and the policy that he thought Israel should follow to achieve its goals. On assuming office, Sharon faced a basic dilemma that Israel had failed to resolve since it occupied the West Bank and Gaza Strip in 1967. This chronic dilemma resulted from the contradiction between the Zionist nature of expansion and the need to preserve the Jewish character of Israel. The annexation of the occupied Palestinian land practically abolishes the Jewish character of Israel and makes it a binational state with a majority and growing Arab Palestinian population. Withdrawal, on the other hand, contradicted Sharon's basic belief concerning the 'Greater Land of Israel'. Because of this demographic dilemma, Sharon sought to establish unilaterally a separation system while rejecting withdrawal to the June 1967 borders. Sharon's vision is to withdraw from the Gaza Strip and 42% of the occupied Palestinian West Bank in return for annexing those Palestinian areas where Jewish settlements are established and other West Bank areas with coveted resources (mainly water and land).

After its establishment by Sharon, the Israeli party 'Kadima', which won a sizeable victory in the March 2006 Knesset elections, continued stressing the need to withdraw unilaterally from parts of the West Bank. In an Israeli TV interview aired on 7 February 2006, Ehud Olmert, as leader designate of Kadima, said: 'We shall keep the Jordan valley, we can't abandon control over Israel's eastern borders ... Our intention is clear, we are heading for disengagement with the Palestinians [in the West Bank] and for establishing final borders for the state of Israel ... We shall disengage from most of the Palestinian residents in Judea and Samaria [West Bank].' Olmert added 'this would force us to abandon territories presently held by Israel.' The Kadima platform included keeping 'the state of Israel as the safe national homeland for the Jewish people in the land of Israel', and introducing 'a national component to the character of the state of Israel besides providing full equality in rights for the minorities living in Israel so as to ensure ... a balanced Jewish democratic state.' In this context, Kadima envisioned using the negotiation process with the Palestinians as a means of demarcating and developing the permanent borders of Israel. The leaders of Kadima hoped this strategy would achieve calm and realize the national and security interests of Israel. So, 'the interest in keeping Israel as a Jewish national state requires accepting the principle of two nationalist states, on demographic bases, that live side by side in peace and security.' (Madar website: www.madarcenter.org)

Israel's strategy on the 'demographic danger' and the 'bi-national' reality

Sharon depended on large public support to pursue a long-term interim solution. He believed the time had not yet come for achieving a comprehensive peace on the basis of the US-EU understanding, and that, in the light of what happened at Camp David 2000, 'fast solutions' usually fail. He realized that retaining Israel's control over the Palestinians of the West Bank and Gaza would add an economic burden to Israel. He saw it would make it difficult for Israel to respond to the many international and Israeli-Palestinian peace initiatives, such as the joint Geneva initiative by Yossi Beilin and Yassir Abed Rabbo, and the Nusseibeh-Ayalon initiative, both of which gained wide Israeli public support but ignored the Right of Return.

Sharon, as was the case with his preceding prime ministers, faced a basic dilemma which Israel has so far failed to deal with following its occupation of the Palestinian territories in 1967. The dilemma is caused by the contradiction between the Zionist nature of annexation and expansion, and preserving the character of Israel as a Jewish state (for more details see: Ghanem 2005a; Kabha 2005; Muhareb 2005; Mansour 2006; Nawfal and Shalhat 2006).

Despite attempts to revive them, the Oslo Accords, which involved a mutual recognition between Israel and the PLO and were the basis for establishing the Palestinian National Authority (PNA), ceased to be the basis for the negotiation process once Sharon assumed office.

The fact is that Sharon developed a new Israeli vision for dealing with the issue of occupation and the future of Palestine. This vision was patterned in Israel's shift from pursuing a solution to the conflict with the Palestinians according to the Oslo Accords and related US-sponsored agreements, to a vision based on 'conflict management'. This management was intent on ensuring Jewish demographic superiority within the Israeli borders, while positively responding to the

Israeli public demand for achieving a period of calm. The calm would, however, be fragile, as the Sharon vision was not ready to pay the price required by the international resolutions, or indeed by the majority of those Israelis who support the establishment of a Palestinian state with limited sovereignty and independence – these Israelis consider themselves as part of the peace camp, even though their stand falls far short of the minimum Palestinian aspirations and the requirements of international resolutions.

Sharon gave his vision a political context by putting forward the unilateral withdrawal project as the only Israeli project for dealing with the Palestinian issue in the short run. The labelling used does not hide the fact that it was based on Sharon's old vision of annexing large areas of the West Bank along the Green Line and the Jordan valley, whilst concentrating the Palestinians in segregated enclaves, or at best connected by roads, tunnels and bridges to narrow land strips. Gaza was the first enclave to be established. The substantive change in Sharon's stand was not in accepting the need for dividing the 'land of Israel', but rather in agreeing to call the Palestinian enclaves a 'state'.

In October 2004, Israeli lawyer, Dov Weissglass, Sharon's adviser and architect of the disengagement plan and of the Israeli-US understandings on the plan, revealed, in a lengthy interview with *Ha'aretz*, the motives and goals behind it. He openly stated that the goals of the plan were to neutralize and freeze the proposed alternative political plans (particularly the Road Map) and to project 'terrorism' as the main problem. He also exposed the marketing interest in strengthening the Israeli allegation that 'there was no Palestinian partner', in order to stop any Israeli concessions and to make the Road Map peace plan irrelevant through diverting attention to an alternative plan (*Ha'aretz* 15/10/2004).

Ariel Sharon decided to make public his ideas and new policy through the Herzliya Conference held in December 2003. The main points of his speech outlining the new Israeli policy were as follows:

1. Israel continues to commit itself to the Road Map peace plan.
2. Israel makes implementation of each part of the Road Map conditional on the cessation of 'terrorism', the eradication of 'terrorist organizations' and reforming the PA.
3. Israel warns the Palestinians that if they do not eradicate the 'terrorist infrastructure' and adopt comprehensive reforms within a few

54

months, Israel would take unilateral measures for disengagement, which Sharon described as based on pure non-politically motivated security measures.

4. The intended Israeli disengagement would include a new redeployment of the Israeli army along a 'security line' within the Palestinian territories, and would include evacuating some settlements. The settlements to be relocated would be those settlements not to be included within Israel 'in any possible future solution'. In return for this, Israel would strengthen its hold over certain parts of the occupied Palestinian territories which would become indivisible parts of the state of Israel in any possible future solution.

5. Israel would accelerate the building of the separation wall.

6. Israel would coordinate its unilateral measures with the United States of America.

7. Israel would remove the random illegal settlement outposts and commit itself to freezing settlements according to understandings with the USA.

8. The plan aimed at providing the highest standard of security to the Israelis and the least degree of friction with the Palestinians.

After assuming office following Sharon's illness, Ehud Olmert adopted the same vision: the unilateral dismantlement of a number of West Bank settlements and the implementation of similar withdrawals in the West Bank over the coming years. On the last day of the Herzliya Conference on Israeli security, 21–24 January 2006, Olmert stressed that the first dramatic and important mission for Israel was to 'demarcate permanent Israeli borders so as to ensure a Jewish majority in the state'. In his statement Olmert echoed Ze'ev Jabotinsky on the significance of having a Jewish majority:

The term 'Jewish nation' is absolutely clear: it means a Jewish majority. With this, Zionism began, and it is the basis of its existence, it will continue to work towards its fulfillment or it will be lost.

The existence of a Jewish majority in the State of Israel cannot be maintained with the continued control over the Palestinian population in Judea, Samaria [the West Bank] and the Gaza Strip. We firmly stand by the historic right of the people of Israel to the enitre Land of Israel. Every hill in Samaria and every valley in Judea is part of our historic homeland. We do not forget this, not even for one moment. However, the choice between the desire to allow every Jew to live anywhere in the

Land of Israel to the existence of the State of Israel as a Jewish country – obligates relinquishing parts of the Land of Israel. This is not a relinquishing of the Zionist idea, rather the essential realization of the Zionist goal – ensuring the existence of a Jewish and democratic state in the Land of Israel.

In order to ensure the existence of a Jewish national homeland, we will not be able to continue ruling over the territories in which the majority of the Palestinian population lives. We must create a clear boundary as soon as possible, one which will reflect the demographic reality on the ground. Israel will maintain control over the security zones, the Jewish settlement blocs, and those places which have supreme national importance to the Jewish people, first and foremost a united Israel under Israeli sovereignty. There can be no Jewish state without the capital of Jerusalem at its center.

Basic components of the Israeli 'post-Oslo' posture

The main goal of Israel's post-Oslo policy is based on the following considerations: to demarcate the permanent borders of Israel unilaterally (that is, not through bilateral agreements); to retain a numerical Jewish majority within the borders of this state; and to establish an accommodating authority on the Palestinian side to provide security and deliver basic economic functions and services. This would enable Israel to annex all of the land along the Green Line and the Jordan valley, in addition to annexing large areas to establish contiguity between the Jordan valley and the Dead Sea.

Furthermore, Israel would fatten settlements that will not be evacuated, by stepping up construction and encouraging Jews to settle there. This vision implies ceding control over densely populated Palestinian areas to a PA and entails the removal of Israeli settlements from these areas. Consequently, eight to nine segregated Palestinian enclaves would be established. Each of these enclaves would be surrounded by Israeli settlements and military structures. As such, Israel would not object if these enclaves were called a 'Palestinian state'. Practically, this post-Oslo policy necessitates the following measures:

1. *Unilateral withdrawal* The unilateral withdrawal plan was formulated in light of Ehud Barak's experience at Camp David. It was actually Sharon who drafted and presented this plan as a new approach to dealing with conflict in general and the occupation in particular. Sharon

formulated his vision and drafted his plan before presenting it during the Herzliya Conference on 18 December 2003, when it was referred to as the 'unilateral disengagement plan'. Sharon rejected withdrawal to the 4 June 1967 borders and at the same time warned of what Zionism calls the 'demographic danger'. Sharon sought to establish a segregation system in historical Palestine by agreeing to withdraw from the Gaza Strip and 42% of the occupied Palestinian West Bank, in return for annexing the Palestinian areas where the Jewish settlements are established and other strategic Palestinian West Bank areas (for more details see Ghanem 2005b, Amara 2005, Kabha 2005, Muhareb 2005, Mansour 2006, Nawfal and Shalhat 2006).

A number of factors contributed to Sharon's success in freezing the Road Map peace plan and making his plan 'the only game in town'. The main factors included Israel's strong and special relationship with the USA in a uni-polar world, a weak Arab world with its regional conflicts and competing attempts to woo the American administration, the lack of Israeli opposition (apart from the Israeli extremist right wing and the Likud Party), and the unequivocal support of the Israeli left wing for Sharon's plan.

The disengagement document appeared in the form of a letter sent by Israeli Prime Minister Ariel Sharon to US President George Bush on 14 April 2004. In the preface to the letter, Sharon insisted that 'Israel is committed to the peace process and aspires to a negotiated settlement, on the basis of two states for two peoples: the state of Israel for the Jewish people and a Palestinian state for the Palestinian people'. Sharon justified the unilateral disengagement on the grounds that 'Israel has arrived at the conclusion that today there is no Palestinian partner to proceed with in a reciprocal peace process'. Sharon stressed that the unilateral disengagement plan was not contingent upon Palestinian cooperation and that it would take Israel to a 'better security situation'. Sharon further elaborated that Israel would withdraw from the Gaza Strip and parts of the northern West Bank, and that 'in any future settlement there would be no Israeli settlements in the Gaza Strip. It is clear that there would be areas, in Judea and Samaria, considered as part of the state of Israel, including civil settlements and security zones, in addition to other areas where Israel has interests'. The Israeli leader added that the disengagement plan 'would counter allegations concerning Israel's responsibility for the Palestinians in the Gaza Strip'. He ended his letter alleging that the disengagement

Ghanem | 3

plan would not violate the signed agreements between Israel and the Palestinians and that 'when there are indications on the Palestinian side of their readiness and ability as well as practical action to combat terrorism and conduct reforms according to the Road Map, then Israel can return to the track of dialogue and negotiation'. Sharon explained that Israel would withdraw from the Gaza Strip, including the existing settlements, except for the border between the Gaza Strip and Egypt, and added that after accomplishing the Gaza Strip withdrawal 'there would be no basis for allegations that the Gaza Strip is an occupied area'. As for the redeployment in the occupied Palestinian West Bank, Sharon stated that 'Israel would evacuate an area in the northern West Bank (settlements of Ganim, Kadim, Humish and Sanour) besides all permanent military structures in that area'.

In mid-September 2005, Sharon visited the UN where he addressed the annual meeting of the General Assembly to explain the unilateral step taken by the Israeli government. In his address he said: 'Early this week, the last Israeli soldier left the Gaza Strip and the military rule of this area has ended. As such, Israel has proved its willingness to undertake painful concessions so as to find a solution to the conflict with the Palestinians.' He added; 'now it's time for the Palestinians to prove their wish for peace because ending Israeli rule in this area and ending Israel's responsibility over the Gaza Strip would allow the Palestinians to develop their economy and build a society that seeks peace.' (Quotations translated from Arabic: Nawfal and Shalhat 2006).

During the preparations for the 17th Knesset elections, held on 28 March 2006, Kadima's candidate for prime minister, Ehud Olmert, declared his party's intention to go ahead with the unilateral disengagement and unilateral demarcation of Israel's permanent borders. This declaration was made without seriously considering negotiating with the Palestinian partner ('The Israeli View', Madar, edition 128, 7/3/2006), supporting the view that Israel has moved to a new stage in managing the conflict with the Palestinians. The Gaza disengagement plan was the first stage of the project to deal with the issue of occupation in light of what is seen as Israel's demographic danger, but without any real readiness to pay the price demanded by the Palestinians or related international resolutions.

2. *Allowing the Palestinians to have partial self-determination.* One of the most important components of the post-Oslo Israeli posture is the

58

evasion of responsibility for the daily needs of the occupied Palestinians and the shifting of that burden on to the PA.

From the start of the Oslo negotiations, it was obvious that Israel was facilitating the establishment of a Palestinian Authority. Israel made clear its demands on the form, content and tools of this authority, including the introduction of legislative and institutional changes that suited Israeli interests (Ghanem 2001).

During the second (Al-Aqsa) Intifada, Israel took several measures to hold back the PA. In 2002, it waged a full-scale military offensive against the territory ruled by the PA. The Israeli army systematically destroyed the Palestinian infrastructure, crushed their security forces, and ended communication between the presidency in Ramallah and the rest of the territories under PA rule, obstructing social services and seriously restricting Palestinian diplomatic relations, especially with Europe and North America.

However, Israel stopped short of total destruction of the PA. The official existence of the authority was intentionally spared so as to claim that there was a Palestinian body responsible for providing basic needs and services to its people, and to exonerate Israel from these responsibilities under international law. It gave Israel a convenient scapegoat for the conflict, and a tangible enemy to be held accountable for actions against Israel, and for Palestinian domestic problems.

After the death of Arafat, Israel continued the same policy. It stopped negotiations and obstructed President Abbas's negotiation efforts, but backed down on steps that could have ended the PA. When Abbas called for legislative elections in January 2006, Sharon announced that he would prevent their holding elections in PA territory if Hamas and the Popular Front, 'murderers of Minister Zeevi' (a firm supporter of Israel's assassination strategy), participated. Furthermore, he said that he would not allow Palestinian residents of Jerusalem to participate in these elections on the basis of arrangements made for the 1996 Palestinian elections. He added, Jerusalem is 'the capital of Israel where there is no place for the Palestinian Authority and its organizations', suggesting that Palestinians who wanted to vote should do so outside Jerusalem and in Ramallah. Sharon advised Abbas to focus more on eradicating terrorism, work on collecting the weapons of Hamas and the other militant groups before thinking about legislative elections.

On the eve of the Palestinian legislative elections, Sharon's government backed down on the issue of Palestinians in Jerusalem

59

participating in the elections ostensibly in response to a call by the US president. The Israelis and Palestinians held meetings to discuss arrangements and methods of campaigning for the elections, and ensuring for calm and order on election day (25 January 2006). The Israeli side promised to abstain from military incursions, arrests and assassinations and to ease restrictions on travel on election day. Late in 2005 the Israeli leaders had publicly declared their intention to boycott any Hamas-led government. Nevertheless it was clear that Israeli threats would not go as far as ending the PA, but that the Authority would be kept only in so far as it was convenient for Israel to do so, even if this meant having to acknowledge the Palestinian entity as a state.

3. *Continued settlement.* Sharon's government followed in the footsteps of previous Israeli governments in dealing with the peace process with the Palestinians. It declared that its policy was to refrain from building any new settlements in the occupied territories – a policy appearing in the government's basic platform and also mentioned in several official statements (Muhareb 2005, Nawfal and Shalhat 2006). However, Israeli government statements have always included the caveat that the 'natural growth of settlers' would be taken into consideration. The 'natural growth of settlers' has always been used as a pretext for annexing more land, enlarging settlements and constructing settlement roads. The size of the land and number of housing units added to the settlements substantially exceeds any natural growth of settlers. In some settlements thousands of housing units were built, while there were dozens of flats remaining vacant.

It is worth mentioning that Israel (and particularly former Prime Minister Ariel Sharon) has repeatedly announced that it was committed to the Road Map peace plan as proposed by US President George Bush. The American Road Map specifies complete cessation of settlement expansion in return for Palestinian cessation of all forms of violence and military operations against Israeli targets.

Although international law considers all forms of settlement in the occupied territories illegal, Israel only considers settlement 'outposts' illegal. These 'outposts' are new colonies that can in no way be considered as proximate to already existing settlements. Ironically, Sharon was a big supporter of establishing settlement outposts from the 1980s, and especially in the 1990s, when he himself was on the opposition benches, and later when he assumed the Likud government's ministerial portfolios. In the mid 1990s, Sharon encouraged settlers to occupy the West Bank hills to establish facts on the ground before reaching any agreement with the Palestinian leadership.

Recently, an official Israeli report, the Sasson Report, has supported the conclusion that all Israeli departments and ministries are engaged in funding illegal settlements or outposts. The 300-page report reveals a steady official channelling of services and maintenance funds to these outposts even in the absence of government construction approval. Accomplices in establishing these outposts include the ministry of defence, the Israeli army, the so called 'civil administration', occupation police, ministries of infrastructure, education, industry and trade, finance and others. The report reveals that all officials in these ministries and departments, including the ministers and lower position holders, ignored the violation of law when settlers took over land owned by Palestinians or land designated 'state-owned land' by the occupation authority. Until the end of 2005 the settlers established 120 illegal settlement outposts with the aim of making them new independent settlements or new settlement neighbourhoods within nearby settlements.

4. *Building the separation wall.* In mid-March 2006, two weeks before the Israeli general elections, the Likud candidate Ehud Olmert declared his intention to make the separation wall a permanent borderline for Israel. The idea of building the separation wall was not devised by the present or former Israeli government, but was suggested by the leaders of the Labour party (mainly Itzhak Rabin and Chaim Ramon, after the Beit Lydd operation in 1994). They first proposed the idea of total separation between the two peoples as a solution that included sealed borders demarcated almost along the Green Line (with some amendments based on Israeli security considerations). The Likud government substantially developed Ramon's idea for 'security amendments' in many ways. These developments made the idea of establishing a Palestinian state with geographical contiguity almost impossible to realize. The proposed path for the separation wall (including already built and planned parts) annexes large areas of the remaining Palestinian land and allows the settlement blocks and infrastructure to segregate and encapsulate the territories where the Palestinian state would be established according to the proposed Road Map peace plan.

When the Palestinians approached the International Court of Justice

61

(ICJ) in the Hague, the Israeli media launched a campaign to foil their campaign and at the very least mobilize international support for Israel's stand, so as to minimize the effects of any possible ruling by the ICJ. When the court issued a ruling supporting Palestinian rights, the Israeli media embarked on a process of refuting the ruling and justifying the pretexts of the Israeli government (Ghanem 2005b, Amara 2005, Kabha 2005, Muhareb 2005, Mansour 2006, Nawfal and Shalhat 2006). The ICJ ruling required Israel to stop building the wall instantly, dismantle those parts of the wall already constructed, and compensate the Palestinians. The ruling included the following: 'The Court considers that the construction of the wall and its associated regime create a "fait accompli" on the ground that could well become permanent, in which case, and notwithstanding the formal characterization of the wall by Israel, it would be tantamount to de facto annexation.' The ICJ acknowledged that the Israeli building of the separation wall was not justified by security reasons. It considered that 'the construction of the wall and its associated regime cannot be justified by military exigencies or by the requirements of national security or public order'. (Breach by Israel of various of its obligations under the applicable provisions of international humanitarian law and human rights instruments. Quotations translated from Arabic: Nawfal and Shalhat 2006).

It is important here to point out that any delay in constructing the separation wall is not due to budget constraints, nor to pressure exerted by the international community, and certainly not to the ICJ's ruling. The slow pace of construction is due rather to the pressure exerted by some extremist right-wing groups and Likud extremists who are worried about the separation wall becoming the de facto border. In their minds, this would undermine and negate the acquisition of the whole land of Israel, in all the territory of historic Palestine.

5. *Practical annexation of the Jordan valley.* Israel adopted a policy of tight restrictions on the movement of the Palestinians in the eastern part of the West Bank. As concluded by B'Tselem, the Israeli Information Center for Human Rights in the Occupied Territories, this policy has practically annexed this area to Israel. Generally, the Israeli army prohibits the entry of Palestinians to the Jordan valley, and confines access only to those officially registered as residents of that area. B'Tselem warned that isolating the Jordan valley from the rest of the West Bank is a dangerous violation of the human rights of many

Palestinian residents. This isolation of the Jordan valley is happening without any formal government decision and without informing the public (Nawfal and Shalhat 2006).

Following the occupation of the West Bank, all Israeli governments have considered the Jordan valley as the eastern border of Israel and have worked on annexing it to Israel. In order to consolidate its presence, Israel established 26 settlements in the Jordan valley where around 7,500 settlers have lived since the early 1970s. Since then, Israel has gradually claimed most of the land in the Jordan valley as state-owned land, which was annexed to the jurisdiction of the Israeli regional councils Arfout Hirian and Mgilot. The Oslo agreements classified most of this area, except for an enclave that includes Jericho and its environs, as area 'C', or area under *full Israeli control*. The acting Israeli Prime Minister Ehud Olmert said on many occasions during the 2006 election campaign that the Jordan valley would remain under Israeli control in any future settlement.

Israel erected seven permanent roadblocks along the area from the western Jordan valley to the northern part of the Dead Sea. Four of these roadblocks besiege the Jericho enclave, and have been used, since 2002, by the Israeli army to place significant restrictions on the movement of Palestinians. A spokesman for the Israeli army responded to the B'Tselem report (Nawfal and Shalhat 2006: 63) of January 2006, saying that access through these roadblocks was restricted only to the residents of the Jordan valley on the basis of the address indicated on their identity cards; their address had to be in one of the villages in the Jordan valley. Other West Bank residents would be required to have a special permit issued by the Civil Administration, without which only humanitarian cases would be allowed. These restrictions do not apply to West Bank residents passing to Jericho, but those travelling from Jericho north towards the other parts of the Jordan valley, including residents of Jericho without special permits. 'Palestinians caught in the Jordan valley without permits will be handed over to the police', said the army spokesman.

Israel's actual policy in the Jordan Valley, and the statements of high-ranking officers, indicate that the motive behind Israel's policy is not a security-military one but rather political. What is taking place is an annexation of this area to Israel, as is the case of other large Palestinian areas that fall on the western side of the separation wall, in flagrant violation of the Palestinian right to self determination. The control of the Jordan valley is also important for the control by Israel of the movement of Palestinians and goods between Jordan and the West Bank.

6. Improving relations with neighbouring Arab countries. Israeli changes of policy towards the PA in late 2004 and early 2005, especially following the death of Yassir Arafat and the election of President Mahmoud Abbas, have affected Israeli-Arab relations, particularly Israeli relations with Egypt and Jordan. After President Abbas assumed office and Sharon resumed implementing the Road Map, relations improved and an activation of political and mutual security efforts was noted. As the implementations of the 'disengagement' plan neared, communications intensified between Israel and Egypt while the US Administration stepped up communications between the three parties. US Secretary of State Condoleezza Rice succeeded in mobilizing Egypt's support for the evacuation of the Israeli settlers and army from the Gaza Strip.

Egypt contributed to reaching an understanding about the houses of settlers, in which Israel committed itself to demolishing the houses and moving the rubble to the Egyptian desert. It is worth mentioning here that economic relations between Israel and Egypt continued with the two sides exchanging goods and cooperating on tourism.

In 2005, relations between Jordan and Israel resumed as normal, especially after the return of the Jordanian ambassador to Tel Aviv. In fact they continued and even strengthed in trade, economy and tourism because Jordan served as a springboard for Israeli goods to the East, the Gulf countries and Iraq (shipping military supplies to the American forces). Security cooperation between the two sides was maintained on the basis of signed agreements and a shared interest in combating extremism and terrorism. Both sides continued their security cooperation on international terrorism, especially after hotels in Amman were targeted by Zarqawi (one of the leaders of al-Qa'ida) suicide bombers.

Proposing 'bi-nationality' in Israel

There is no doubt that the Israeli public and government stand against the bi-national state solution. The overwhelming majority of the Israeli public agrees with their political leaders, and with most writers, journalists and academics, in rejecting every solution other than that of Israel remaining a Jewish state, and as the embodiment of the 'Jewish right to self determination'. It is clear that a sort of consensus emerged during the 17th Knesset elections, held on 28 March 2006, that the majority of Israeli leaders and the public prefer Israel to be an ethnic-Jewish state, even at the cost of withdrawing from parts of the West Bank and Gaza Strip. Very few contemplate having a future 'bi-national state' with the Palestinians.

This is not to deny that some Israeli politicians and scholars remain ready to consider and even support the possibility of establishing a bi-national state. Their beliefs are based on various grounds, and may carry different conceptions of the proposed 'bi-national state'; nevertheless, they do consider the bi-national option. Besides the small number of Jewish activists, Palestinians in Israel are, in general, in favour of the bi-national state, as well as supporting the two-state solution, Israel and Palestine.

Support for the bi-national solution among the Jewish left

Since British Mandate times, there have been Jews calling for sharing Palestine, its power and resources, between the two peoples. Some called for this to be done on proportional bases, in addition to sharing government and other portfolios. The Jewish movement 'Brit Shalom' publicly called for this (Ghanem 2002; 2005c). The Kedma Mizraha movement came out of the Brit Shalom movement and also advocated close cooperation with the Arabs (Kardahji 2005). The Ihud movement that was established as a continuation to the 'Bat Shalom' project of 1942, continued calling for the 'Equality' solution (Hiller 2006). Hashomer Hatzair and Poale Zion were leftist Zionist movements that attempted to advocate bi-nationalism and equality. Also, importantly, the League for Jewish-Arab Rapprochement and Cooperation was formed in the late 1930s as an umbrella organization to combine all the efforts of the different factions supporting bi-nationalism in historic Palestine (Kardahji 2005).

Some researchers believe that these people called for a bi-national state simply on moralistic grounds (Herman 2005). However, I believe that the Jewish supporters of the joint state drafted their political platform based on a balanced analysis of the facts, and the interests of the Jews at the time. Whether or not moralistic motives played a part, these proposals were a real and substantial political project, based on thorough political analysis.

65

After the establishment of Israel, secondary parties continued calling for a bi-national state. But these calls faded away with the success of the Ben Gurion project, which was based on compiling power and using force against the Palestinians and Arab states, and manifested itself in the dispersal of the Palestinians and the establishment of a Jewish state.

Since the 1980s, some Jewish scholars have revisited the one-state solution. One of these is the prominent scholar, journalist and historian Meron Benvenisti, a long-time leftist Zionist activist and a member of the West Jerusalem Municipal Council under its renowned Mayor Teddy Hollek. Benvenisti projected his ideas as part of his analysis of the Israeli occupation of the West Bank, and on the basis of what he called 'cutting edge annexation' as a result of Israeli settlement in the West Bank and Gaza Strip (Benvenisti, 1983, 1988; *Ha'aretz* 21/8/1987). After Oslo and the establishment of the PA, Benvenisti continued tackling the conflict in the light of persistent Israeli settlement in the occupied Palestinian territories, particularly in East Jerusalem. He considered the Al-Aqsa Intifada another indication supporting beliefs he had held in the 1980s. In an interview with *Ha'aretz*, the most prominent liberal Israeli newspaper, Benvenisti reiterated what he had called for in the past:

In the 1980s I believed it wasn't possible to share this country; settlement construction and control of territories is an irreversible reality ... We have realities that don't allow us to change the situation. Neither Oslo nor the talk about a Palestinian state can change this situation. Our life situation is that of bi-nationality. It's a fixed reality that can't be ignored ... All that we can do is to adapt our thinking to this reality. We need to find a model that fits this reality. We need to ask the right questions even if they awaken anti-Semitic feelings and even if they awaken feelings that accuse us of abandoning the dream of a Jewish state (Shavit 2003).

Other Israeli political activists and scholars expressed support for establishing a joint bi-national state based on their belief that the Oslo agreements had failed. Consequently they voted for Benvenisti's choice, but as a conclusion they had arrived at in recent years. Haim Hanegbi, a prominent leftist activist, previously supported the Oslo process and believed, like many other Israelis, that the time was ripe for establishing a Palestinian state beside Israel. In the same newspaper

66

that published Benvenisti's views, Hanegbi published an interview in which he stated:

> Right after the 'second' intifada, I ... changed my idea and thought of suggesting, again, the joint-state solution ... Early last summer, I wrote an article against the occupation, at the end of which I included my idea of having a state for the two peoples, a joint bi-national state ... In recent years I had discovered my mistake, and, like the Palestinians, I, too, was allured to the lie; I took the Israeli allegations seriously and didn't notice their actions ... When I realized that the settlements were doubling themselves I realized that Israel had wasted the chance it had been given ... that's how I realized that Israel can't abandon its expansionist character; it is shackled, by arms and legs, to its institutionalized ideology, structure, actions and theft. (Shavit 2003)

Many other Israeli scholars followed in Hanegbi's steps, keeping the issue of a bi-national state on the Israeli agenda (see Green 2005, Kalir 2002, Hiller 2004, Herman 2005, Sussman 2005). The leftist professor Oren Yiftachel of Ben Gurion University in the Negev also proposed that a bi-national state be established after the establishment of a Palestinian state beside Israel.

Besides the aforementioned scholars, a prominent historian, Ilan Pappé, is considered one of the most prominent Israelis calling for adopting the bi-national state as a way out of the complicated post-Oslo political situation. Commenting on Benvenisti's and Hanegbi's political statements, Pappé stated:

> Calls for the 'bi-national state' are getting louder, like the calls made by Meron Benvenisti and Haim Hanegbi, who are central figures in the Israeli peace camp. After calling for years for the establishment of two states, they now ... say it's not possible to realize a just peace through the two-state solution. There are people who have always called for the bi-national state without apology, like my late friend Edward Said. What is important here is that the ideas on a 'bi-national state' are arrived at through realistic politics and proposing new solutions. That's why the solutions proposed by academics might lead to new solutions, as they aren't politicians – politicians are usually preoccupied with ideas and solutions of the past. These old solutions frequently fail, and unfortunately, the two peoples pay for that failure' (*Al-Mashhad Al-Israeli* newspaper, Madar, 26/3/2004).

Thus a new vision developed in Israel based on the belief that the two-state solution had become unrealistic and impossible. The supporters of this idea believed that Israel was to blame for this situation and that Israel's settlement policy ended the possibility of achieving a historical reconciliation through a two-state solution, and consequently paved the way for discussion of a joint state for Israelis and Palestinians. This proposed solution is slowly surfacing in public discourse through the media, political, and academic symposiums at universities and research centres, as well as the political platforms of those supporting or objecting to the idea. Those opposing are influential and greater in number, but a legitimate discussion of the bi-national state idea is unprecedented in Israel, even as far back as the Mandate time, when there were organized Jewish parties that supported it.

The Palestinians in Israel and the 'bi-nationality' demand

Palestinians in Israel are the only group of Palestinians calling clearly for bi-nationality. Their brethren in exile, in the Arab world and other countries, seek to return to their country and property, but without much interest in the character of the Israeli state. This group of Palestinians also differs from large sectors of Palestinians in the West Bank and Gaza Strip who demand the establishment a Palestinian state beside Israel with little regard for the future nature and character of the state of Israel. The Palestinians in Israel remain a distinct group with a special vision based on the fact that they are in Israel and will stay there in the event of a two-state solution. A sweeping consensus has emerged among the Palestinians in Israel since the mid-1980s concerning the demand for a Palestinian state in the West Bank and Gaza Strip, with Jerusalem as its capital. Opinion polls conducted in the recent years again reveal sweeping support for this demand. (Ghanem 2005a; Smooha 2005).

Establishing a Palestinian state is considered a demand for most of the Palestinians in Israel, not only because such a state would solve the problem of the other Palestinians by giving them a national homeland, but also because the state would contribute to improving the life of Palestinians in Israel (Ghanem 2001b). This belief is based on the assumption that the continuation of the conflict keeps Israel and the world busy looking for a solution and consequently distracts attention from internal neglect of the Palestinians in Israel. In addition, external conflict results in internal stress and increased suspicion of

TABLE 2.1. Degree of equality between Jews and Palestinians in Israel demanded by Palestinians (February 2006) (%)

Sphere	Full equality	Almost full equality	Partial equality	No need for equality
1 Resource allocation	75.5	10.9	10.1	3.5
2 Define the state character	72.1	13.0	10.0	4.9
3 Define the goals of the state	75.3	11.1	8.4	5

the Palestinians in Israel. This suspicion regarding their 'intentions' towards Israel leads to policies that marginalize and alienate them.

Another area of interest for Israeli Palestinians is improving their individual and collective equality. Palestinians in Israel have made strong demands for equality with the Jewish majority. Statistical figures on different areas show that the majority of Palestinians in Israel seek total equality between themselves and the Jewish citizens of Israel. In other words, the Palestinians in Israel strongly support bi-nationality in Israel as an expression of their Palestinian identity, in the same way that the Jewish majority has and is able to express its own group identity.

Table 2.1 presents some data supporting the argument that the Palestinians in Israel want a bi-national state based on group and individual equality for the two national groups inside the Green Line: Jews and Palestinians. The table is based on a public opinion poll conducted by the polls centre Mihshov at the request of the Department of Government and Political Thought at Haifa University. The sample included 500 participants with an error margin of (+/−4.5%). The participants represented different sectors of Palestinians in Israel.

The poll results support previous polls (Ghanem 2001a, 2005a), which have indicated that most Palestinians in Israel were generally dissatisfied with their living conditions, especially those related to them as a group. The question asked was 'what kind of equality do the Palestinians want? What collective changes and achievements do the Palestinians in Israel seek?'

It is well known that the Palestinians in Israel want complete equality with the Jewish majority. In answer to the question 'How important is the realization of full equality for the Palestinians in Israel for

69

improving the collective situation of the Palestinians?', 93.8% of the participants responded by rating it as 'very important' (Ghanem 2001a). The need for equality was emphasized in a poll where questions were asked about a number of spheres with gaps between the Jews and Palestinians in Israel, such as resource allocation, and equality in defining the goals and character of the state (see Table 2.1).

Palestinians in Israel expressed dissatisfaction with their living conditions as a national group and demanded that the state cater for their needs in the same way as it caters for the needs of Israeli Jews. This means stopping discriminating against them in resource allocation, public services and employment opportunities in the public sector, and allowing their political parties the opportunity to participate in government coalitions on the same footing as other political parties. They also demand from the Israeli state a role in defining the goals and character of the state such that it become a state for all its citizens.

The Jewish-Zionist character of the state is clearly manifested in the preference for Jews in almost all areas related to the state and to Israeli society. Palestinians surveyed were fully aware that Israel serves primarily its Jewish citizens instead of all its citizens, and most of those interviewed (75%) agreed that Israel is a Zionist-Jewish state, which means, in practice, that it prefers Jews to Arabs. In addition, some 17.5% of those interviewed responded to this issue saying that 'yes, somehow' Israel prefers Jews to Arabs, while some 7% rejected the view that there is preference.

Palestinians in Israel believe that equality must be realized between themselves and Jewish Israelis, but that realizing this is almost impossible in Israel as long as it is a Zionist-Jewish state. Palestinians believe that the state should not intervene in order to preserve a Jewish majority in the country, so it has no right to encourage only Jews to immigrate into the country. This consequently implies abolishing the law of 'right of return' for the Jews, and halting all state efforts and activities in the country and abroad to encourage Jews to immigrate to the country. Second, it implies that no attempts should be allowed to obstruct or prevent the growth of the Palestinians in Israel into a majority. In other words, they believe that the state should not prefer one ethnic group over another, since members of both ethnic groups are citizens of Israel (Ghanem 2001a).

Palestinians in Israel seek to develop a democratic model in Israel that is based on components of bi-nationality. The change that they seek has two dimensions. First, they seek integration within the state organizations with full equality with Israeli Jews (including in the area of the allocation of resources, jobs and ability to influence and change the decision-making process and policies of the state). Second, they seek institutional autonomy in order to achieve that equality. When discussing this issue, Palestinians stress the significance of 'Israeli recognition of their group as a national minority' (84% support that) and emphasize the areas in which to realize autonomy within the state, such as educational autonomy manifested in establishing an Arab university and an autonomous Arab administration in the education department and the cultural life within the Palestinian community (including structures, curriculum and staff in educational programmes and others).

Additionally, Palestinians seek the establishment of a full network of institutions for themselves in Israel in order to achieve organizational autonomy. These include: Arab labourers' syndicate, Arab health insurance fund, delegation of the administration of the Islamic trust to an Arab administration, delegation of more powers to the Arab local authorities, and the Israeli government recognition of the Arab Higher Follow-up Committee as a representative of the Palestinians in Israel. The participants in the poll stressed the significance of their 'direct election' to this committee (85% supported this).

Survey data reveals that Palestinians in Israel are dissatisfied with their collective situation and aspire to achieve integration within state organizations, and institutional autonomy within the framework of the Israeli state, as well as their commitment to equality with the Jewish majority. As a matter of fact, such a form of autonomy within the state constitutes a model for a bi-national system and would function to protect the national identities of the two distinct national groups, Jews and Palestinians.

Conclusion

In 1993, prior to the political coup that followed the Knesset elections of 1992, Israel recognized the PLO as the sole legitimate representative of the Palestinian people and signed the Oslo agreement as a first step in a process aimed to achieve an Israeli-Palestinian peace. The Israel that signed that agreement was not ready to meet the requirement of that peace or to implement the relevant international resolutions.

Three years after signing the Oslo Accords, Israeli Prime Minister Itzhak Rabin was assassinated by a Jewish extremist who was seeking

71

(successfully it turned out) any way to stop the peace process. Following that, the right-wing candidate Benjamin Netanyahu was elected prime minister in the 1996 elections, and declared the beginning of a new era in relations with the Palestinians.

As Israel came under the leadership of Sharon, its policy shifted from seeking to solve the conflict with the Palestinians to adopting a new strategy for 'conflict management' according to narrow Israeli interests, and so Israel proposed a policy of 'unilateral disengagement'.

Olmert will follow the same policy as Sharon towards the Palestinians. Declaring that the elected Hamas government is a 'terrorist' government, Israel will act without any serious attempt to negotiate with the Palestinians. Israel will seek to establish a 'separation system' without any historic settlement. As a result, an entity will be created which is 'more than autonomy and less than a state'. This situation will result in a crisis for the Palestinians and force them to seek an alternative option to that of an independent Palestinian state. This has led some Israeli and international parties to try to bring the bi-national state project to the discussion table.

Israel and a majority of its citizens are not ready to give up the Jewish nature of the Israeli state. Also it is quite clear that the majority of Israelis and policy makers are not ready to pay the full price of a satisfactory resolution of the Palestinian-Israeli conflict, including the return to 1967 borders, the evacuation of all Jewish settlements, the division of Jerusalem, and the return of refugees.

The commitment to the Jewish nature of the Israeli state and Israel's refusal to reach a compromise with the Palestinians have resulted in the dominance of the politics of fear of the 'demographic threat'. This has meant adopting policies to guarantee a Jewish majority unnaturally in as wide a border as can be demarcated. This Jewish majority and character of the state consequently is expressed favourably to Jews in almost all spheres of activity of the Israeli state. The aim of Israeli policies has been centred on avoiding the possibility of establishing a bi-national system.

The future solution to the conflict cannot be foreseen now, as we are almost as far from the two-state solution as we were before the Oslo Accords. However, as we distance ourselves from the two-state solution, the possibility of a solution based on the idea of a joint or bi-national entity should not be ruled out.

Bibliography

Alpher, Joseph and Shai Feldman (1989) *The West Bank and Gaza: Israel's Options of Peace*, Tel Aviv: Jaffee Center for Strategic Studies, Tel Aviv University.

Amara, Mohammad (2005) 'The political situation' in As'ad Ghanem (ed.), *Madar Strategic Report: Israel 2004*, Ramallah: Madar – The Palestinian Center for Israeli Studies, pp. 73–113 (Arabic).

Arieli, Shaul, Doubi Schwartz and Hadas Tagari (2006) *Injustice and Folly: On the Proposal to Cede Arab Locations from Israel to Palestine*, Jerusalem: Floersheimer Institute (Hebrew).

Benvenisti, Meron (1983) 'The day of the collapse of the illusion: The second republic', *Davar* 26 December. (Hebrew)

— (1988) *The Sling and the Club*, Jerusalem: Keter (Hebrew).

— (2003) 'Which bi-nationalism: that is the question', *Ha'artez*, 20 November (Hebrew).

Ghanem, As'ad (2001a) *The Palestinian Regime: A Partial Democracy*, London: Sussex Academic Press.

— (2001a) 'The Palestinians in Israel: Political orientation and aspirations', *International Journal of Inter-Cultural Relations*, Vol. 26, pp. 135–52.

— (2002) 'The Bi-national idea in Palestine and Israel: Historical roots and contemporary debate', *The Holy Land Studies Journal*, 1/1, pp. 61–84.

— (2005a) *Marginalized Groups in Israel: A Challenge to Ashkenazi Dominance*, Ramallah: Madar (Arabic).

— (ed.) (2005a) *Madar Strategic Report*: Israel 2004, Ramallah: Madar (Arabic).

— (2005b) 'The bi-national solution for the Israeli-Palestinian crisis: Conceptual background and contemporary debate', in Mahdi Abdul-Hadi (ed.), *Palestinian-Israeli Impasse: Exploring Alternative Solutions to the Palestine-Israeli Conflict*, Jerusalem: PASSIA (Palestinian Academic Society for the Study of International Affairs) pp. 19–44.

Green, Dror (2005) *The Vision of Dual Nationality*, Safad: Sfareem (Hebrew).

Herman, Tamar (2005) 'The bi-national idea in Israel/ Palestine: Past and present' *Nation & Nationalism*, Vol. 11 (3): 381–401.

Hiller, Joseph (2004) *From Briet Shalom to Ihud*, Jerusalem: Magnes.

Kabha, Mustafa (2005) 'The strategic situation', in As'ad Ghanem (ed.), *Madar Strategic Report: Israel 2004*, Ramallah: Madar, pp. 115–45 (Arabic).

Kalir, Eli (2002) *Breaking Point*, Jerusalem: Carmel.

Kardahji, Nick (2005) 'Dreaming of co-existence: A brief history of the bi-national idea', in Mahdi Abdul-Hadi (ed.), *Palestinian-Israeli Impasse: Exploring Alternative Solutions to the Palestine-Israeli Conflict*, Jerusalem: PASSIA, pp. 1–18.

Lefshetz, Gabriel and Yobert Leon (1993) 'The new settlement in the Galilee: Aims and characteristics', *Research in the Geography of Iretz Yisrael*, Vol. 13.

Mansour, Jonny (ed.) (2006) *Madar Strategic Report: Israel 2005*, Ramallah: Madar (Arabic).

Israel and the 'danger of demography'

73

Masalha, Nur (1992) *Expulsion of the Palestinians*, Washington, DC: Institute for Palestine Studies.

Muhareb, Mahmoud (2005) 'Israel: The Palestinian question and international relations', in As'ad Ghanem (ed.), *Madar Strategic Report: Israel 2004*, Ramallah: Madar, pp. 37–70 (Arabic).

Nawfal, Mamdouh and Antoine Shalhat (2006) 'Israel, the peace process and international relations', in Jonny Mansour (ed.), *Madar Strategic Report: Israel 2005*, Ramallah: Madar (Arabic).

Pappé, Ilan (1999) 'Bi-national reality against national mythology: The death of the two state solution', *Nativ*, 2: 57–64 (Hebrew).

Shavit, Ari (2003) 'Forget about Zionism', *Ha'aretz*, 8 August (weekend supplement), pp. 10–14.

Smooha, Sammy (2005) *Index of Arab-Jewish Relations in Israel – 2004*, Haifa: Jewish-Arab Center, University of Haifa.

Soffer, Arnon (2003) *Israel's Demography 2003–2020: Risks and Opportunities*, Haifa: Haifa University, The National Security Study Centre.

Sussman, Gary (2005) 'The viability of the two-state solution and Israeli unilateral intentions', in Mahdi Abdul-Hadi (ed.), *Palestinian-Israeli Impasse: Exploring Alternative Solutions to the Palestine-Israeli Conflict*, Jerusalem: PASSIA, pp. 45–66.

4 | The paradox of Palestinian self-determination

NILS BUTENSCHØN

The main argument in this chapter is that contemporary diplomatic initiatives – which have all failed to produce a solid foundation for peace in the Middle East – have been based on political premises that deviate fundamentally from well-established legal interpretations of the principle of self-determination. The diplomacy, reflecting the huge imbalance of power between Israel and the Palestinians, pursues contradictory interpretations of the principle of self-determination. Furthermore, this inconsistency or 'dual commitment' to self-determination is applied specifically in the case of Palestine with reference to an historical pattern introduced by the Great Powers as a core element of the political reorganization of the Near East after World War I.

The policy implications implied in the pattern indicated is that any solution to the question of Palestine would have to be based on the recognition of a Jewish national right in the country and that the rights of the non-Jewish population (i.e., the Palestinians), while respected as far as possible, would have to be subordinated to that policy. This is the core meaning of the Balfour Declaration, issued by the British Government in 1917 without consulting the existing people of Palestine. The latest telling example of this approach is the non-recognition by the West of the result of the democratically organized elections for the Palestinian Legislative Council (PLC) in January 2006, on the ground that the new Hamas government was elected on a programme that *inter alia* rejects the legitimacy of the state of Israel. The paradox is that recognition of Palestinian national rights has been conditioned on Palestinian renunciation of their right to the same, leaving any Palestinian leadership with a catch 22 situation, i.e., the impossible choice of either struggling for the fundamental right of its own people to self-determination and risk being excluded and punished and losing ground to the enemy, or accepting the demands by powerful external powers and thus yielding to the logic of a political order imposed from the outside with no guarantees for the future aspirations of the Palestinian people.

The ongoing relevance of the question of Palestinian self-determination

It has often been pointed out that the Israeli-Palestinian conflict began as an inter-group or inter-ethnic conflict in the country around World War I between Jewish Zionist settlers and indigenous Palestinian Arabs; that it primarily became an inter-state conflict as the result of events in 1947–1949 (Palestinian defeat and flight, the establishment of the state of Israel and the first broader Arab-Israeli war) culminating in the 1967 Arab-Israeli war when Israel occupied large stretches of Arab territories, including the remaining area of Palestine (named after 1948 as the West Bank and Gaza Strip); and that the original inter-ethnic core of the conflict since that time gradually has re-emerged as the Palestinians have fought their way back onto the centre stage of the conflict.[1]

The state territory of Palestine as defined under the League of Nations regulations by the British mandatory power in 1922 is today effectively under the control of the state of Israel as an integrated 'control system', either as part of its sovereign territory recognized by the United Nations (within the ceasefire lines of 1949, known as the Green Line and comprising 'Israel proper') or under its de jure or de facto occupation since 1967 (the West Bank, Gaza Strip and East Jerusalem).[2] The latter part of the territory is today also known as the Occupied Palestinian Territory (OPT). Following the establishment of the Palestine Liberation Organization (PLO) in 1964, the entire state territory of Palestine came to be contested in the conflict between it and Israel. Gradually the PLO as the weaker party moderated its position in order to establish a platform for negotiations with Israel on the partition of Palestine and a two-state solution to the conflict. In 1988 the Palestine National Council (PNC, the highest PLO authority) passed resolutions that de facto recognized the state of Israel by accepting the United Nations General Assembly (UNGA) Partition Resolution of 1947 (which preceded the establishment of the state of Israel in 1948) and the United Nations Security Council (UNSC) Resolutions 242 (1967) and 338 (1973) that introduced the principle of 'land for peace', i.e., that the Arab states should recognize Israel within secure borders in return for Israeli withdrawal from 'territories occupied in the recent war'.[3] In addition, the PNC declared the establishment of the state of Palestine, implicitly confined to the Occupied Palestinian Territory and thereby limited their territorial claims on behalf of the Palestinian people.[4] The PLO made its recognition of Israel Proper de jure in 1993 as part of an exchange of letters of mutual recognition between Israel and the PLO in connection with the signing of the Oslo agreement in September of that year. The Israeli letter which recognizes the PLO as 'the representative of the Palestinian people' did however not explicitly commit Israel to recognizing an independent Palestinian state or define a specific territory within which a Palestinian national entity of some kind could be established.

By signing the Oslo Accords with the PLO Israel accepted officially the existence of a Palestinian people (though not necessarily Palestinian nationhood), a historic step in itself; but it did not relinquish its own claim to sovereignty in the OPT of 1967 (and consequently its position that this territory should not be considered as 'occupied').[5]

In effect therefore, the Oslo agreement (and later agreements between the parties), while narrowing the gap between the two parties, did not end the deep-seated conflict over the title to the country of Palestine as defined in 1922. Since the end of World War I, this conflict has been expressed as a conflict over the right to national self-determination, with the World Zionist Organisation (and the state of Israel since 1948) claiming this right on behalf of world Jewry, and thus challenging the same right as claimed by representatives of the Palestinians (that is the PLO since 1964) based on their status as the indigenous population of the country. The conflict has over the years involved a large number of additional actors both regionally and internationally in wars, as well as in diplomacy, and conditions on the ground have changed considerably. But the contentious issues of national self-determination, known in the diplomatic parlance as 'the final status issues' remain to this day unresolved.[6] The *question* of Palestinian self-determination has thus re-emerged, but the *right* to self-determination has by no means been secured.

The principle of self-determination and the issue of 'dual commitment' in Palestine

What makes the Israeli-Palestinian conflict unique and particularly complicated from a legal (and consequently political) point of view can be derived from the way in which the principle of self-determination has

77

been interpreted and applied in this case. The 'international community' (or more precisely dominant powers in the international system) has contributed directly to creating the conditions of intractability of the conflict that has been a pronounced feature since World War I, by accepting a dual commitment to the two parties. The incompatibility of the conflicting claims was from the very start inherent in declarations, treaties and agreements related to the political future of Palestine. Six observations come to mind and can be summarized as follows:

First, the Zionist claim to Palestine on behalf of world Jewry as an extra-territorial population was unique and not supported (as admitted at the time[7]) by established interpretations of the principle of national self-determination, expressed in the Covenant of the League of Nations (and later versions), and as applied to other territories with the same status as Palestine ('A' mandate).

Second, at the same time, the Zionist claim was supported, somewhat conditionally, by Great Britain as mandatory power. The British government issued the Balfour Declaration in 1917, in spite of British promises to support Arab independence in the area (the exact definition of which has been contested) as negotiated during the world war and explained in the Hussein-McMahon Correspondence 1915–16. The principal allied powers, at the San Remo conference in 1920, recognized the pro-Zionist Balfour Declaration and so did, at the time, the League of Nations itself in the provisions of the Mandate for Palestine, tentatively approved by the League Council on 22 July 1922.[8]

Third, also at the same time, neither the League of Nations nor any of the individual allied powers explicitly invalidated the right of self-determination of the indigenous people of Palestine. Taken together, international bodies had given a contradictory dual commitment as regards the title to Palestine; one that was consistent with the principle of self-determination (as a right that belongs to the indigenous population of a country) and another based on a 'historical connection' with Palestine of an external non-territorial population, with a clear political priority to the latter (i.e., to the Zionist claim).

The contradictions of the 'dual commitment' are clearly contained in the Preamble of the Mandate: First, it starts with a general reference to Article 22 of the Covenant and thus to the principle of national self-determination. Second, it incorporates the 1917 Balfour Declaration in favour of 'the establishment in Palestine of a national home for the Jewish people, it being clearly understood that nothing should be done which might prejudice the civil and religious rights of the existing non-Jewish communities in Palestine … ' Third, it recognizes 'the historical connection of the Jewish people with Palestine' and 'the grounds for reconstituting their national home in that country', however – and significantly – without defining who 'the Jewish people' are.[9]

The point here is that, taken together, the mandate gave representatives of both the indigenous people and the immigrant-settlers reasons to claim an internationally recognized title to self-determination in Palestine and to demand implementation of this right with reference to specific resolutions of the League of Nations.

Fourth, the dual commitment in the League of Nations Mandate for Palestine was confirmed and taken over by the United Nations when it took responsibility for Palestine in 1947, as expressed in the plan for the partition of Palestine adopted by the UN General Assembly in November of that year.[10] Paradoxically again, the new world organization, based even more firmly on the principle of the right to national self-determination than its predecessor, made its decision about the political future of Palestine against the aspirations of the majority of the people of that country. Other considerations, i.e., the hope of finding a lasting political solution to the historical 'Jewish problem' in the aftermath of the World War II genocide against the Jews and the failure of the mandatory government of Palestine to find a solution within a unitary state were given as reasons by the majority of UN members to ignore the principle of self-determination for the Palestinians. The Palestinian right to a separate state was recognized, but only in less than 50% of the country. At the time the Jews constituted some 30% of the population and owned about 6% of the land. This two-state solution represents still today, after almost 60 more years of conflict and diplomatic manoeuvres, the model thinking that can be extracted from the large number of UN resolutions relevant to the question of Palestine.

Although Palestine and the Palestinians almost disappeared from the international vocabulary of the Middle East conflict between the late 1940s and the late 1960s – as a result of the Arab defeat in the 1948–1949 war, the mass expulsions of the Palestinians and the political collapse of their leadership over the last four decades or so – the Palestinian claim to national self-determination has regained universal recognition.[11] The UN Security Council for the first time in its history explicitly expressed its support for a two-state solution in March 2002

79

(UNSCR 1397). The resolution foresees 'a region where two states, Israel and Palestine, live side by side within secure and recognized borders'. The follow-up 'Road Map to peace' represents an effort to define the practical steps that must be taken to implement the two-state solution based on the double commitment, and is officially the only game in town as far as diplomacy is concerned. In this sense we are today back to the idea of the UN plan of 1947 for a partition of Palestine and the creation of two states in the country, an Arab and a Jewish state. The presumption then as now is that Palestinian self-determination can be accommodated in a separate territory in Palestine *alongside* the Jewish state – and thus enable the parties to get around the problem of incompatibility of the national claims. But this in itself presumes that we are faced with two clearly identifiable societies within clearly identifiable territories. That was not the case in the 1940s and is still not the case, as illustrated in the following two points.

Fifth, the picture is particularly complicated by the fact that partition or some other method of power-sharing should accommodate not only those who actually live in the country today, but also millions of Palestinian refugees (according to established Palestinian positions) and the millions of Jews world-wide (according to established Zionist positions), both of which represent part of the respective national collectivities with mutually exclusive inalienable rights to settle in the country, as seen by the PLO and Israel, respectively. The implication is that there is no agreement between the parties as to who should be included in the demographic composition of the future political order of the country.

Finally, the unresolved question of state *territory* should also be mentioned. This is not only a question of borders between Israel and Palestine in case of partition, the Kingdom of Jordan is also in the picture and included in many designs for a future political settlement of the Palestine conflict. (Trans)Jordan was considered part of Palestine prior to 1922 and its character as a 'residual territory' without any independent political history has brought it into the territorial equation in discussions of how to establish a workable political order in the area.[12]

A contemporary legal perspective: the International Court of Justice

The extraordinary circumstances under which elections in the OPT have taken place since the establishment of the Palestinian Authority

(PA) in 1994 have many aspects. To understand these circumstances and the controversies that surround them, the legal framework is arguably one of the most important.

We are not dealing with elections for political institutions of an internationally recognized state. The elections may on the face of it resemble elections for a transitional national government in a post-conflict situation, but the Palestinians' conflict with Israel has not been settled, neither on paper nor on the ground. Furthermore, the elections, both in 1996 and later, have been held for an 'authority', not even fully recognized as a *national* authority, with limited powers and with a yet-to-be defined status. The most exceptional aspect of the situation is not only that elections are being organized under occupation, but that the *occupying* power is a contender for sovereignty in (parts of) the occupied territory, as is evident in the documents defining the legal framework of the elections (i.e., the Oslo Accords). In addition, related to the fact that there is still a situation of occupation and conflict, the elections have had to be organized under widespread constraints on civil and political rights, including freedom of movement and freedom of association and assembly. These and other violations of contemporary international standards of humanitarian and human rights law (like house demolitions, excessive use of force, etc) are executed by the occupying power with reference to legal provisions enacted by and inherited from previous rulers and adopted to varying degrees and amended by Israeli military orders.[13]

New legislation has been enacted by the PLC elected in the first general Palestinian elections in January 1996 with a view to initiating democratic reforms and establishing a unified legal system based on modern standards of the rule of law. Most importantly, this includes a Basic Law adopted in 2002 and amended later. The reforms have strengthened the Palestinian political system, but their effects have until now been limited due to the breakdown of the negotiations, patrimonialism and authoritarianism in the exercise of power by Arafat and the Executive, and the collapse of the self-governing Palestinian institutions, particularly since the outbreak of the second (Al-Aqsa) Intifada in the autumn of 2000.

These complex and for the Palestinian population extremely difficult circumstances reflect the still unresolved underlying contentious issues related to the status of the Occupied Palestinian Territory (the West Bank and Gaza Strip) under international law. It is not the purpose of the present study to analyse conflicting legal arguments on that question as presented by the parties involved.[14] What follows is a short discussion of the position as stated by the most authoritative international legal body that has dealt with the question, namely the International Court of Justice (ICJ) in its Advisory Opinion from 2004.[15] The ICJ as a United Nations court was responding to a question from the General Assembly in its resolution ES-10/14 of 8 December 2003 that requested an advisory opinion on 'the legal consequences arising from the construction of the wall being built by Israel, the occupying Power, in the Occupied Palestinian Territories'.[16] In order to answer the question the court had to clarify its position on the legal status of the OPT. Any serious discussion on political system formation in the OPT, including elections as a core element in such system formation, must relate to this opinion.

The most striking aspect of the advisory opinion is the overwhelming agreement among the fifteen sitting judges on the basic issue of the status of the OPT and the legal consequences that follow. This consensus includes Thomas Buergenthal, the American judge (and renowned human rights expert) even though he voted against the conclusions in the advisory opinion relevant to the construction of the wall. The reason he gave for voting against was that in his opinion the Court had been presented with insufficient facts on Israel's security concerns and should consequently have declined to render the requested advisory opinion.[17] In a separate declaration, however, he stated: 'I share the Court's conclusion that international humanitarian law, including the Fourth Geneva Convention, and international human rights law are applicable to the Occupied Palestinian Territory and must be faithfully complied with by Israel.'[18]

There is no disagreement, therefore, within the ICJ as the authoritative legal body of the international society that international law relevant to occupied territories applies to the OPT and that indeed these territories are 'occupied'. The Court discusses in some length the Israeli position that the Fourth Geneva Convention does not apply de jure to the OPT because of 'the lack of recognition of the territory as sovereign prior to its annexation by Jordan and Egypt'. The Court does not accept this argument and concludes that the 'Convention is applicable in the Palestinian territories which, before the conflict [in 1967], lay to the east of the Green Line[19] and which, during the conflict, were occupied by Israel, *there being no need for any enquiry into the precise prior status of those territories.'*[20] This conclusion is based, *inter alia*, on a brief discussion of relevant legal documents relevant to the question of Palestine since the country was established as a class 'A' Mandate under the League of Nations in 1922, establishing the boundaries of Palestine as a state territory.

The fact that what is today identified as the Occupied Palestinian Territory was annexed or administrated by external powers for a certain period of time before 1967 does not impinge on the status of the OPT as a Palestinian state territory.[21] Summing up the discussion, paragraph 78 of the ICJ advisory opinion states:

> The court would observe that, under customary international law as reflected in Article 42 of the Regulations Respecting the Laws and Customs of War on Land annexed to the Fourth Hague Convention of 18 October 1907 ..., territory is considered occupied when it is actually placed under the authority of the hostile army, and the occupation extends only to the territory where such authority has been established and can be exercised.
>
> The territories situated between the Green Line and the former eastern boundary of Palestine under the Mandate were occupied by Israel in 1967 ... Under customary international law, these were therefore occupied territories in which Israel had the status of occupying Power. *Subsequent events in these territories ... have done nothing to alter this situation.* All these territories (including East Jerusalem) remain occupied territories and Israel has continued to have the status of occupying Power.[22]

The Court furthermore discusses doubts that have been expressed by Israel as to the applicability in the OPT 'of certain rules of international humanitarian law and human rights instruments.'[23] First, the advisory opinion observes that it is a basic rule that 'No territorial acquisition resulting from the threat or use of force shall be recognized as legal.'[24] Secondly, as regards the principle of self-determination, the Court observes that the existence of a 'Palestinian people' is no longer in issue.'[25] Reference is made in this context to the exchange of letters of 9 September 1993 between Yassir Arafat, at the time chairman of the Executive Committee of the PLO, and the prime minister of Israel, Itzhak Rabin. In reply to the PLO's explicit recognition of 'the right of the State of Israel to exist in peace and security' and other commitments, Rabin states that, in light of those commitments, 'the

Government of Israel has decided to recognize the PLO as the representative of the Palestinian people'. A reference is also made to an earlier ruling by the Court whereby it emphasizes that current developments in 'international law in regard to non self-governing territories, as enshrined in the Charter of the United Nations, made the principle of self-determination applicable to all [such territories].[26] Thirdly, the Court discusses the Israeli contention that in addition to the de jure inapplicability of the Fourth Geneva Convention, a basic instrument of international humanitarian law, international human rights law does not apply to the OPT because it applies only in times of peace. Israel has ratified the International Covenant on Civil and Political Rights, the International Covenant on Economic, Social and Cultural Rights, as well as the United Nations Convention on the Right of the Child. In conclusion, the Court finds beyond doubt that all the said human rights instruments apply to the OPT.[27]

Two observations are of particular interest: 'The Court would observe that, while the jurisdiction of States is primarily territorial, it may sometimes be executed outside the national territory. Considering the object and purpose of the International Covenant on Civil and Political Rights, it would seem natural that, even when such is the case, States parties to the Covenant should be bound to comply with its provisions.'[28] Moreover, 'It would also observe that the territories occupied by Israel have for 37 years been subject to its territorial jurisdiction as the occupying Power. In the exercise of the powers available to it on this basis, Israel is bound by the provisions of the International Covenant on Economic, Social and Cultural Rights. Furthermore, it is under obligation not to raise any obstacle to the exercise of such rights in those fields where competence has been transferred to Palestinian authorities.'[29] Finally, referring to a number of Security Council resolutions, the Court 'concludes that the Israeli settlements in the Occupied Palestinian Territory (including East Jerusalem) have been established in breach of international law.' It refers, *inter alia*, to resolution 465 (1980) where the Council describes 'Israel's policy and practices of settling parts of its population and new immigrants in [the occupied] territories' as a 'flagrant violation' of the Fourth Geneva Convention, which is the main legal source in this context.[30]

On the basis of the ICJ advisory opinion we can safely conclude that the status of the Occupied Palestinian Territory under international law is not particularly ambiguous or disputed among the most authoritative international experts on international law. The territory, including East Jerusalem, is occupied, the Palestinian people has the right to national self-determination, all relevant rules and instruments of international humanitarian law and international human rights law apply, and all Israeli settlements in the OPT, including in and around East Jerusalem, are illegal. Diplomatic developments resulting in a number of Israeli-Palestinian agreements and the establishment of Palestinian proto-state institutions, as well as the unilateral Israeli withdrawal from and decolonization of the Gaza Strip do not fundamentally alter this legal situation.

The historic implications of the Oslo Accords

Whether or not one considers the Oslo Accords dead or alive, relevant or irrelevant in today's political setting, one cannot deny that they 'have irreversibly altered the legal and political landscape in the Middle East. Even if the peace process remains stalled for the next decade, the Accords will continue to furnish the basis for Israeli-Palestinian relations, to serve as a sort of "Basic Law" or constitution for an unhappy polity.'[31] The 'Oslo Accords' refers to the Declaration of Principles on Interim Self-Government Arrangements, Israel–Palestine Liberation Organization (DOP or Oslo I), signed 13 September 1993 and subsequent implementing agreements, notably the Israeli-Palestinian Interim Agreement on the West Bank and the Gaza Strip, Israel–PLO ('Oslo II'), signed 28 September 1995.

The Oslo Accords do not constitute a peace settlement between the State of Israel and the PLO, but agreements on a method and timetables for reaching a lasting solution and interim institutional and security arrangements. The Oslo I and Oslo II Agreements are not treaties in the legal sense, since the PLO is not a state. The Accords could, however, be seen as legally binding as agreements between subjects of international law.[32] The most contentious issues related to questions of sovereignty, borders, Jewish settlements in OPT, the future status of Jerusalem, and the rights of Palestinian refugees to return to their country were to be negotiated in 'permanent status negotiations' to be concluded by the end of a five-year interim transitional period (that expired in May 1999). The parties agreed that nothing should be done in the interim period that could change the status of the OPT or prejudice future negotiations over the permanent status issues. Article xxxi of the Oslo II Agreement, paragraphs 6 and 7, states:

6 Nothing in this Agreement shall prejudice or pre-empt the outcome of the negotiations on the permanent status to be conducted pursuant to the DOP. Neither Party shall be deemed, by virtue of having entered into this Agreement, to have renounced or waived any of its existing rights, claims or positions.

7 Neither side shall initiate or take any step that will change the status of the West Bank and the Gaza Strip pending the outcome of the permanent status negotiations.

A critical question that arises from these core paragraphs is what 'status' paragraph 7 refers to, considering the fact that the parties to the Accords fundamentally disagree on that question and that their conflicting positions and claims have not been forsaken or changed by entering into the agreements, as stated in paragraph 6. Paragraph 7 therefore does not refer to a status that the parties agree upon or to the status of the OPT under international law as expressed in all relevant UN General Assembly and Security Council resolutions, confirmed by the ICJ in its advisory opinion as discussed above. On the contrary, the cited paragraphs leave the question of the legal status of the OPT open to conflicting interpretations, giving Israel a reference for its claim that the status of the territories is 'disputed'.[33]

The 'agreement not to agree' as regards the legal status of the territories explains on the one hand how it was possible for the parties to enter into the Accords in the first place, but also why they had such opposing approaches to the implementation of the agreements. In contrast to their stated commitments in the Oslo Accords, the parties did almost everything that they considered politically possible to pre-empt the outcome of future negotiations on the permanent status. The opportunities to do this were, however, unevenly distributed, to say the least. Israel was in control of all relevant power resources and enjoyed a de facto impunity with regard to violations of international law within certain limits acceptable to the USA. On the other hand, the establishment of the PA created a universal expectation that a Palestinian state worthy of the name was in the making. Within its limited space of independent action, the Palestinians could exploit this at least for symbolic purposes, presenting the PA as a *national* authority with Jerusalem as its future capital. A dynamic was thus set in motion, with the continuing expansion of Israeli settlements as a particularly harmful development, which undermined a cooperative strategy for implementing agreements. This was to be expected for a number of reasons. First, there was no mechanism for third party monitoring of the implementation of the Accords and consequently no provisions for sanctions to be imposed in cases of any party breaching their commitments. Second, each party knew that it was almost impossible for the opponent to officially call off the historic peace process given the way it was initiated and the international support it had attracted. Third, hardliners on both sides[34] were critical or totally against the Accords, putting considerable pressure on the respective political leaderships to demonstrate national 'steadfastness' in the OPT.

Since the signing of the DOP in 1993 the Israeli-Palestinian conflict has focused on the question of the future status of the OPT. Whereas the PLO has based its claims on the position that all Palestinian territories occupied by Israel in 1967 should be handed over to a Palestinian authority as the territorial foundation for a future independent and sovereign state, the Israelis have challenged this position and never renounced their self-proclaimed rights to expand the Israeli-Jewish society into parts of or the entire OPT. This has been possible with the tacit support (or non-opposition) of the USA. Thus it has *not* been possible for the Security Council to impose sanctions or other mandatory measures to force Israel to comply with UN resolutions. On the other hand, in terms of prevailing international law, Israel has not been able to change the status of the OPT as 'occupied', as clearly demonstrated in the advisory opinion by the ICJ. It is worth noting that the Oslo Accords (and agreements pursuant to those Accords, including the 2003 Road Map) – which could be taken to advocate the view that the OPT is not 'occupied' but 'disputed' – have not in any way impacted on the legal status of the OPT. Thus, international humanitarian and human rights law relevant to occupied territories is fully applicable to the West Bank, including East Jerusalem, and the Gaza Strip.

Can self-government be transformed into substantive state sovereignty?

The challenges and dilemmas that faced Yassir Arafat when he set out to build a Palestinian state on the basis of the Oslo Accords were numerous.

First, he had in effect accepted that building a Palestinian state was, from now on, subordinated to Israeli security concerns. The Israeli veto power over Palestinian developments was not easily accepted by the

Palestinians (or by Arafat himself), and was a major source of wide-spread Palestinian opposition to the Oslo Accords. At the same time, the Israeli supremacy over the PLO in the peace process reflected the realities of power relations between the parties.[35] The purpose of the PLO was to 'liberate Palestine', as formulated in the Palestine National Charter from 1968. But what should the 'liberation of Palestine' from Israel mean now when it would have to be achieved on the basis of Israel's goodwill? The Palestinian liberation doctrine had been limited by the Palestine National Council (PNC) in 1988 to include only the West Bank (including East Jerusalem) and the Gaza Strip, constituting some 22% of the original state territory of Palestine.[36] But since Israel as the occupying power – in clear breach of international law, but with impunity – had expanded its state-building endeavour into the OPT (the districts of Judea, Samaria and Gaza in Israeli terminology), even this residual 22% and the prospect for establishing meaningful national sovereignty in any part of historic Palestine was in question. The first Palestinian Intifada that started in December 1987 can be seen as a popular response to this development. The DOP, in Article VIII, authorized the PA to establish a 'strong police force', but Arafat could not use his constantly growing number of security forces to liberate the OPT. That would be a material breach of the Oslo Accords, it would be condemned internationally, and the PA would have no chance of surviving an all-out war with the overwhelmingly stronger Israeli army. Israel, for its part, had no such restrictions and could make full use of its military strength to quell Palestinian resistance if it so decided. The tasks of the Palestinian security forces were limited therefore to defending the new PA regime from internal threats and preventing Palestinian violence and armed resistance against Israel, Israeli occupation forces and settlers.

Second, Arafat had to meet the expectations of his own people for progress and liberation which for most people meant the withdrawal of Israeli occupation forces, economic development and the establishment of an independent state. He was himself a symbol of national liberation. He was greeted as a hero in July 1994 when he returned from his exile in Gaza and Jericho with thousands of PLO followers, fighters and officials that were to constitute the core of his future PA regime.

On the face of it, Arafat's return from exile represented a new historical beginning for the Palestinian people in their own land. But the circumstances, conditions and restrictions under which Arafat's new regime was established were in fact not so different from the previous PLO administrations that he had been heading, particularly the Palestinian state-within-the-state in Lebanon between 1972 and 1982.[37] Again, as had been the case when he first started to re-build the PLO as an independent liberation organization in Jordan in the late 1960s, he had to set up an administration that lacked sovereign control over a distinct territory and population, and which existed at the mercy of a host government (in this case Israel). Again he would have to base his survival on informal alliances according to his understanding of the balance of power locally, regionally and internationally. This strengthened patterns of secrecy, power manipulation and patrimonialism so typical of Arafat's ruling techniques in exile.[38] Arafat therefore was not the guerrilla leader who became the statesman and leader of a liberated nation state (like Fidel Castro, Nelson Mandela, etc) as he had so strongly hoped for. And again Arafat sought international recognition and support with 'almost obsessive determination' to compensate for the lack of sovereignty and territorial control.[39]

Before the Oslo Accords, a majority of states recognized the PLO as the sole legitimate representative of the Palestinian people. It enjoyed full membership in the League of Arab States, Non-Aligned Movement and other multilateral groupings of Third World states, as well as an observer status in the United Nations. The phantom state declared by the Palestine National Council in the OPT in 1988 was recognized by more than 100 states. This was a remarkable achievement by a liberation organization without a stable territorial base. The Oslo agreement brought the PLO universal recognition, even by Israel, as the representative of the Palestinian people. Arafat tried to capitalize on this new international status in his efforts to build a viable state in the OPT, with a particular view to keeping as good relations as possible with the US government. The other side of this coin was, as Nathan J. Brown convincingly argues, that the 'logic of the peace process' augmented the tendencies towards authoritarian and patrimonial rule.[40] Israel and the United States, the dominating actors in the peace process, 'focused on security rather than governance'. Brown continues: 'Such priorities suggested establishment of a strong presidency and effective security services. Thus the PA presidency and its security apparatus were built two years before the first democratic elections and the convening of the Palestinian Legislative Council.'[41] Israel and the US wanted an Arafat who was weak and dependent in relation to them, but strong and authoritarian in relation to his own people. He should deliver the peace that Israel could accept, and be given enough power to control and, if necessary, destroy and disarm opponents of this peace.[42] It should be added that Arafat accepted, however reluctantly and not without severe internal infighting, the development of a relatively independent civil society and democratic practices not seen elsewhere in the Arab world.

But in the final analysis, the self-governing Palestinian Authority retained many of the characteristics of an authoritarian state-in-exile, dependent as it continued to be on the personal style of its charismatic leader. In that sense, it did not develop very differently from its old patterns in terms of leadership and decision-making, either because the conditions for running an independent national authority had not changed fundamentally or because the PLO elite found the old ways to be the most convenient or efficient in order to maintain control and leadership. This in turn contributed to the structural problems that came to characterize the PA and its relationship to the population in the OPT and the different political and social factions and forces that had been in operation during the first Intifada that was ended by Arafat's signing of the DOP in 1993.

This conclusion should not be taken to indicate that the establishment of the PA was an insignificant event in the history of the PLO and the Palestinian people. The point has been to suggest that – in spite of the new historical opening for the Palestinians to concentrate all their efforts on building a state in their own country – there were important structural continuities in the way the PLO operated and which pointed towards weaknesses and vulnerabilities in the Palestinian state-building strategy. The peace process with its priority on Israeli security concerns and a political economy in the hands of international donors did not produce much incentive for political reform. This priority, and the dependence of the PA on Israel and external donors, has made it possible for Israel to define unilaterally at any time if it has a 'partner for peace' or not. This has significantly humiliated and weakened the PA leadership, not least under Mahmoud Abbas, who has undeniably done everything within his power to comply with outside demands, but is still rejected by the Israelis.

Conclusion

The combined effects of the extreme hardship experienced under continued Israeli occupation, the lack of progress on the diplomatic front, and the paralysis, mismanagement and corruption of the PA created conditions for yet another Palestinian uprising. The popular anger and frustration was however channelled into electoral processes and led to what really became an Intifada of the ballot: Hamas, a political movement that emerged outside the PLO and PA and condemned by Israel and the West as a terrorist organization, won sweeping victories in the elections for local councils and the Palestinian Legislative Council. This is remarkable, not least considering that Israel in the preceding years had extra-judicially assassinated a number of the movement's senior leaders and arrested many scores of its activists. Western countries also interfered in the electoral process by trying to discourage Palestinians from voting Hamas and threatening with sanctions should Hamas be voted into a position of power. The result of these elections is the latest expression in the long history of the Palestinian quest for self-determination, a quest that is firmly supported by international law.

Up to this moment, the dominating international actors have treated the question of Palestine as an exceptional case whereby universally accepted standards of democracy, human rights and humanitarian law do not fully apply. The hope has been that the Palestinians would 'accept the inevitable', i.e., that their position in Palestine would have to be subordinated to the principle of a secure Jewish national state in the country. But the Palestinians have countered time and again that they refuse this fait accompli as long as their own basic rights remain unsecured. The question is if the West (often taken as the meaning of 'the international community') will ever learn that conflicts cannot be solved by manipulating justice, as has consistently been the case with Palestine over the last 90 years, and if it will take notice of the latest message from the Palestinian people.

Postscript

As I finish writing this in May 2006, two notable developments have taken place. One was the plan presented by the Israeli Prime Minister Ehud Olmert unilaterally to establish Israel's borders on the West Bank (the 'convergence plan'). The other was PA President Mahmoud Abbas's plan to let the Palestinians in the occupied territories vote in a referendum (replaced by a 'dialogue') on a platform for 'national conciliation'. The platform has been worked out by leading Palestinian activists currently held in Israeli prisons, representing both secular organizations affiliated with the PLO, and Islamic movements, including Hamas – and

91

even Islamic Jihad (with reservation).[43] In a nutshell these two plans represent the fundamental contradiction on the question of Palestinian national self-determination and illustrate that little or nothing has been achieved on this front since the start of the peace process in Madrid in October 1991. If we take these two plans to represent basic positions, the parties stand as far from each other as ever. The Israeli convergence plan implies that Israel's eastern border will roughly follow the track of the illegal Wall currently under construction on the West Bank (which was broadly suspected to be the case, but typically denied by Israel, when the work was initiated). The plan is a follow-up on former Prime Minister Ariel Sharon's master plan, which was to annex large tracts of the West Bank to Israel in order to secure Israel's permanent supremacy in the state territory of Palestine and prevent the emergence of a viable independent and sovereign Palestinian state. During his first official visit to Washington (in May 2006) as prime minister, Olmert obtained American support for the plan with reference to a letter sent by Bush to Sharon in April 2004.[44]

The national conciliation platform is a firm declaration of the right to Palestinian national self-determination in all the Palestinian territories occupied by Israel in 1967. It restates the right of Palestinians to armed resistance to liberate occupied territories and the right of the refugees to return to their country. In this sense the platform restates PLO positions on a two-state solution prior to the diplomatic process and, notably, goes against positions that President Abbas himself has taken in recent years.[45] If the Prisoners' Letter – widely believed to have been drafted by Marwan Barghouti, the popular number one on the Fatah list for the 2006 PLC elections – turns out to be adopted as a new unified Palestinian position, an entirely new political situation on the Palestinian side may result.

The fundamental challenge seems not so much to be differences over the two-state solution as such (and consequently recognition, at least de facto, of the state of Israel),[46] but rather *how* a unified position should come about. Who is in a position to define the rules of the game? This is not only a technical question of procedure, but a question of who represents the popular will and who will emerge as the leading Palestinian political force. As leader of the PLO and PA president, Abbas is constitutionally in a position to engage in negotiations with Israel, a position recognized by the Hamas government. But the Letter also contains recognition of the PLO as the sole legitimate representative of the Palestinian people. That is more difficult for the Hamas government to accept. By embracing the Letter and setting a deadline for the government to accept it or face a referendum, Abbas and the PLO Executive Committee may hope to regain the political initiative, building on the undisputed legitimacy that the prisoners enjoy among the Palestinians. The ball is thus in the court of the Hamas government who, as far as legitimacy is concerned, also feels entitled to speak on behalf of the Palestinians in the West bank and Gaza Strip. It is, on the one hand, not easy for the already hard-pressed government to reject a clearly popular platform of national reconciliation. On the other hand, it is unacceptable for the government, having won a sweeping victory in the recent elections, to accept a fait accompli from Abbas that would imply a subordination of the Hamas movement to the PLO as the sole legitimate representative of the Palestinian people.

The present internal political crisis on the Palestinian side will be difficult to solve, therefore, until a way is found whereby the two different trends in current Palestinian politics merge, either within the existing PLO or within a reconstituted PLO. The current crisis is not only a conflict over national authority. Such conflicts frequently occur in other cases where the president and prime minister represent different parties as a result of separate elections for president and parliament. The Palestinian crisis goes deeper as long as there has not been established an overriding national institutional structure, reflecting a unified *state idea*, with reference to which the conflict of authority can be negotiated and solved.

Nobody can deny the Palestinian resolve to struggle for their right to national self-determination as demonstrated in uprisings and elections alike. The current internal political crisis, the outcome of which may be known when this book is published, can determine to what extent this resolve will be transformed into a unified and effective strategy of state-building. A successful outcome would present the outside world with a position, not worked out in secrecy with the Israelis, but emerging from the day-to-day struggle for basic rights and dignity for the entire Palestinian people, as seen by most Palestinians. Such a position would have an undeniable legitimacy based in expressions of Palestinian popular will. And it would challenge more acutely than before the Western interpretation of its 'double commitment' to self-determination in Palestine that traditionally has tilted so clearly in favour of Zionist and Israeli positions.

93

Notes

1 For a recent study, see H. Ben-Yehuda and S. Sandler (2002) *The Arab-Israeli Conflict Transformed: Fifty Years of Interstate and Ethnic Crisis*, New York: State University of New York Press.

2 B. Kimmerling, 'Boundaries and frontiers of the Israeli control system – analytical conclusions' in B. Kimmerling (ed.). *The Israeli State and Society: Boundaries and Frontiers*, New York: State University of New York Press (1989). Cf. J. Halper, 'The 94 percent solution – a matrix of control', *Middle East Report*, 216 (Fall 2000), <http://www.merip.org/mer/mer.html>.

3 This famous (or infamous) formulation has been taken by Israel to imply that it is not obliged to withdraw from *all* territories occupied in the 1967 war, an interpretation that is *not* supported by any international legal opinion.

4 R. Khalidi (1990) 'The Resolutions of the 19th Palestine National Council', *Journal of Palestine Studies* 19, 29–42.

5 For a legal discussion of the Oslo agreement and the status of OPT see, for example, G. Watson, *The Oslo Accords. International Law and the Israeli-Palestinian Peace Agreements* (Oxford University Press, Oxford, 2000).

6 Article V(1) of the Oslo agreement defines these issues as: 'Jerusalem, refugees, settlements, security arrangements, borders, relations and cooperation with other neighbors, and other issues of common interest.' Cf. *supra* note 5. The parties in fact came close to an agreement on the final status issues in negotiations at Camp David in 2000 (and at Taba in January 2001) with President Bill Clinton as mediator. After the breakdown of these talks, negotiations were continued *non-officially* for two years by Israeli and Palestinian negotiators and prominent personalities. The talks were supported by several governments and produced the so-called Geneva Accords (for full text, see http://www.mideastweb.org/peaceplans.htm). The Geneva Accords represent the most elaborate compromise to date within the 'Oslo paradigm' between established political and military elites on both sides.

7 Arthur Balfour, the British Foreign Minister, stated in 1919: The Four Great Powers are committed to Zionism. And Zionism, be it right or wrong, good or bad, is rooted in age-long traditions, in present needs, in future hopes, of far profounder import than the desires and prejudices of the 700,000 Arabs who inhabit that ancient land'. Cited in W. Khalidi (ed.) 1971, *From Haven to Conquest. Readings in Zionism and the Palestine Problem until 1948*, Beirut: Institute of Palestine Studies, p. 208.

8 The Palestine Mandate was not finally approved until 29 September 1923 as the Council wanted to promulgate it simultaneously with the French Mandate for Syria, which was held up by Franco-Italian differences. The original mandate included what was known as Trans-Jordan, a residual territory in the post-war imperial division of the Arab Middle East. Following extensive and violent Palestinian protests, Britain suggested, in spite of intense Zionist opposition, to exclude Trans-Jordan from the obligation of implementing the establishment of the Jewish National Home as promised to the Zionists in the 1917 Balfour Declaration and incorporated in the preamble of the Mandate for Palestine. The Council confirmed the exclusion of Trans-Jordan in September 1922. See J. J. Zasloff, *Great Britain and Palestine. A Study of the Problem*

before the United Nations (Institut Universitaire de Hautes Internationales, Université de Genève/Verlagshaus der Amerikanischen Hochkommission, München, 1952) pp. 7–9.

9 For the text of the Mandate for Palestine, see, for example, Cherif Bassiouni (ed.) (2005) *Documents on the Arab-Israeli Conflict: Emergence of Conflict in Palestine and the Arab-Israeli Wars and Peace Process, Volume I*, New York: Transnational Publishers, pp. 103–8.

10 UNGA Resolution 181 (1947).

11 On 9 and 10 September 1993 respectively, just a few days before the official signing ceremony for the Oslo agreement, the chairman of the Palestine Liberation Organization (PLO) Yassir Arafat and Israel's prime minister, Itzhak Rabin, exchanged letters of mutual recognition. Israel's recognition of the PLO as 'the representative of the Palestinian people' paved the way for universal recognition of Palestinian national rights also among traditional supporters of Israel. See reprints of the letters for example in Omar Masalha, *Towards the Long-Promised Peace* (Saqi Books, London, 1994).

12 'From its very inception as an entity Trans-Jordan's value [was recognized], not for its own sake but as a buffer and a bridge among lands of inestimably greater importance.' Philip Robins, *A History of Jordan* (Cambridge University Press, Cambridge, 2004), p. 13. Britain ruled Trans-Jordan as a mandate until 1928, from then indirectly under an Anglo-Trans-Jordanian treaty until the country's nominal independence in 1946, all the time closely coordinated with its rule in Palestine. Trans-Jordan occupied the West Bank in the Arab-Israeli war 1948–49 and annexed the territory in 1950, whereupon the country was renamed the Hashemite Kingdom of Jordan. After Israel's occupation of the West Bank in 1967 it was widely believed that Israel and Jordan would divide the territory between them as part of a peace settlement. The Palestinians resisted that solution and in 1988 Jordan's King Hussein renounced his claim to the West Bank, supporting instead Palestinian self-determination. But a Jordanian option in one form or another, whereby Jordan is part of a constitutional arrangement (i.e., con-federation) with Palestine, possibly also with Israel, is still frequently put forward in the debate.

13 Such provisions have been taken from the Ottoman Empire, the Hashemite Kingdom of Jordan (in the case of the West Bank) and British Mandate authority (in the case of the Gaza Strip). See International Commission of Jurists and the Center for the Independence of Judges and Lawyers (1994) *The Civilian Judicial System in the West Bank and Gaza: Present and Future*, Geneva: International Commission of Jurists and the Center for the Independence of Judges and Lawyers, pp. 11–15.

14 See for example, Stephen Bowen (ed.) (1997) *Human Rights, Self-Determination and Political Change in the Occupied Palestinian Territories*, Cambridge, MA: Kluwer Law International; Natan Feinberg (1971), *On the Arab Jurist's Approach to Zionism and the State of Israel*, Jerusalem: Magnes Press, Hebrew University; Paul J. I. M. de Waart (1996), *The Legal Status of Palestine Under International Law*, Birzeit: Birzeit University, Law Centre.

15 The International Court of Justice, *Legal Consequences of the Construc-*

95

tion of a Wall in the Occupied Palestinian Territory, 9 July 2004, available at http://www.icj-cij.org.

16 'The wall' refers to what Israel describes as a 'security fence' to halt infiltration from the West Bank. A plan for this purpose was approved by the Israeli Cabinet in July 2001. On 14 April 2002 it adopted a decision to start construction works; ibid., Paragraph 80.

17 The Israeli government decided not to address ICJ, except for a limited Written Statement, because it did not accept that the Court had jurisdiction to render an advisory opinion as requested. The Court discusses the question of 'sufficient facts' in Paragraphs 55–58.

18 See 'Declaration of Judge Buergenthal', available at the ICJ homepage, *supra* note 3.

19 The Green Line designates Israel's internationally recognized borders and refers to the armistice demarcation line (drawn in green) between Israeli and Arab forces established in the Rhodes Agreement on 3 April 1949.

20 Paragraph 101 (emphasis added).

21 The Court does not discuss the status of territory occupied by Israel in the 1948–49 war and that was allotted to the Arab state or a permanent international trusteeship by the UN Partition Resolution 181 (1947). This includes West Jerusalem, and is why Tel Aviv is the internationally recognized capital of Israel.

22 Emphasis added. Since the publication of the advisory opinion in July 2004 Israel has 'disengaged' from the Gaza Strip, by removing its settlers and withdrawing its military troops. However, since Israel continues to have de facto military control over the territory and its borders and since the Gaza Strip and the West Bank constitute a single territorial unit, '[t]he withdrawal of Jewish settlers from Gaza should be seen as the decolonization of Palestinian territory. This does not affect Israeli control of the territory, which will remain. Consequently, Israel will remain an occupying Power in respect of Gaza, subject to the international humanitarian law applicable to occupied territory.' Report of the Special Rapporteur of the Commission on Human Rights on the situation of human rights in the Palestinian territories occupied by Israel since 1967, Paragraph 10, United Nations A/60/271.

23 Paragraph 86.

24 Paragraph 87, citing GA resolution 2625 (XXV) (1970) pursuant to Art. 2, Paragraph 4, of the UN Charter.

25 Paragraph 118.

26 Paragraph. 88.

27 Paragraphs 102–113.

28 Paragraph 109.

29 Paragraph 112.

30 Paragraph 120. Paragraph 6 of Article 49 of the Fourth Geneva Convention provides that 'the Occupying Power shall not deport or transfer parts of its own civil population into the territory it occupies.' As Judge Buergenthal explains in paragraph 9 of his Declaration (see *supra* note 6), this provision of the Fourth Geneva Convention 'does not admit for exceptions on grounds of military or security exigencies.'

31 Watson, G. R. (2000) *The Oslo Accords: International Law and the Israeli-Palestinian Peace Agreements*, Oxford: Oxford University Press, p. ix.

32 See discussion in ibid., chapters 3–5.

33 Article I of the DOP states that '[t]he aim of the Israeli-Palestinian negotiations ... is ... to establish a Palestinian Self-Government Authority ... leading to a permanent settlement based on Security Council Resolutions 242 and 338.' This gives the impression that the process is based straightforwardly on UN resolutions. However, Israel's interpretation of resolution 242 is that it is not required to withdraw from all territories occupied in 1967, an argument not accepted by the ICJ (see paragraph 78: 'All these territories (including East Jerusalem) remain occupied territories and Israel has continued to have the status of occupying Power.').

34 On the Palestinian side, opposition to the Accords was particularly articulated by the left, represented by the Popular Front for the Liberation of Palestine (PFLP) and Islamic radicals, represented by Hamas and Islamic Jihad. On the Israeli side, opposition was strongest among right-wing (both secular and religious) groups and particularly among the settlers.

35 The Israeli Prime Minister Itzhak Rabin used 'this great victory for Zionism' to convince the Israeli parliament (Knesset) to approve the DOP. See 'Itzhak Rabin, Statement to Knesset on Israeli-Palestinian Declaration of Principles, Jerusalem, 21 September 1993, reprinted in *Journal of Palestine Studies*, Vol. 23, No. 2 (Winter 1994): 138–41.

36 The PNC at this meeting decided to accept the UNGA Partition Resolution of 1947 and the UNSC Resolution 242 implicitly recognizing the state of Israel within the 1949 ceasefire lines. In addition, the PNC declared a Palestinian state in the Palestinian territories occupied by Israel in 1967.

37 For a comprehensive analysis of the history of the PLO up until the Oslo Accords, see Yezid Sayigh (1997) *Armed Struggle and the Search for State: The Palestinian National Movement, 1949–1993*, Oxford: Oxford University Press.

38 Ibid., pp. 447–63.

39 Ibid., p. xi.

40 Nathan J. Brown (2005) *Evaluating Palestinian Reform*, Washington: Carnegie Endowment for International Peace, Carnegie Papers, Middle East Series, Democracy and Rule of Law Project, Number 59, June 2005, p. 6.

41 Ibid.

42 Only later did Israel and the USA consider Arafat to be a major obstacle, and not as the solution.

43 Published in the *Al-Quds* newspaper, 11 May 2006.

44 Excerpts from the press conference at the White House, 23 May 2006:

'*Q*: Mr. President, the Prime Minister just said that the settlement blocks in the major population centers will be part of Israel, annexed to Israel in the future. Do you support that? Would the United States sanction that?

'*President Bush*: My answer to your question is, refer to my April 14th, 2004 letter. I believed it when I wrote it, and I still believe it. [Laughter.]' See www.whitehouse.gov/news/releases/2006/05/20060523-9.html. In the letter Bush stated: 'As part of a final peace settlement, Israel must have secure and

97

recognized borders, which should emerge from negotiations between the parties in accordance with UNSC Resolutions 242 and 338. In light of new realities on the ground, including already existing major Israeli populations centers, it is unrealistic to expect that the outcome of final status negotiations will be a full and complete return to the armistice lines of 1949, and all previous efforts to negotiate a two-state solution have reached the same conclusion. It is realistic to expect that any final status agreement will only be achieved on the basis of mutually agreed changes that reflect these realities.' See: www.mfa.gov.il/MFA/Peace+Process/Reference+Documents/Exchange+of+letters+Sharon-Bush+14-Apr-2004.htm.

45 The platform is basically in line with the resolutions adopted by the Palestine National Council meeting in 1988, see *supra* note 36. Since the signing of the Oslo Accords, Abbas (Abu Mazen) has indicated willingness to compromise on every permanent status issue, as exemplified in the so-called Beilin-Abu Mazen Document from October 1995.

46 There are numerous, but conflicting, signals that Hamas may reconsider its rejection of a two-state solution. However, as things stand today, the PLO and Hamas represent two very different visions for a future Palestinian state and thus a solution to the conflict and it is difficult to know how deep-seated that difference is. The PLO political stand on the solution of the conflict is a two-state solution, a sovereign state with East Jerusalem as capital, armed resistance confined to 1967 areas, the right of return for the refugees and the PLO as sole legitimate representative, as against Hamas's (and Islamic Jihad's) conception with its adoption of an Islamic Palestinian state in all of mandate Palestine, armed resistance to include areas inside Israel, and the PLO, as it stands today, *not* recognized as the sole legitimate representative of Palestinians.

5 | The Bush administration and the two-state solution

HUSAM A. MOHAMAD

During the 2000 presidential election campaign, George W. Bush argued against expanding US involvement in nation-building efforts around the world. But the events of 11 September 2001 and the wars in Afghanistan and Iraq shifted President Bush's approach in support of further involvement in the Middle East. As part of advancing his foreign policy agenda in the region, Bush proposed a new peace plan for resolving the Israeli-Palestinian conflict on the basis of a two-state formula. The plan was influenced by recommendations made by Senator George Mitchell's fact-finding commission, which, along with investigating the causes that led to the outbreak of the Palestinian Intifada in late September 2000, suggested steps for restarting the stalled peace process and restoring confidence between Israel and the Palestinians. In response, the Bush Administration dispatched Secretary of State Colin Powell, along with other envoys to the region, in order to halt the escalating violence and to restart the peace process.[1] Despite delays caused by the September 11 attacks and the war in Afghanistan, President Bush delivered his 24 June 2002 speech in support of the creation of 'a peaceful and democratic Palestinian state alongside Israel.'[2] Within the same speech, Bush asked the Palestinians to reform the Palestinian Authority (PA), dismantle their militant groups and elect new leaders. A year later, in April 2003, Bush then backed the Quartet's Road Map formula (also sponsored by the UN, the EU, and Russia) for resolving the Israeli-Palestinian conflict.

Bush's two-states vision and the Road Map formula are based on understandings formulated at the Madrid Conference in 1991, the principle of land for peace, the UNSC Resolutions 242 and 338 along with other peace efforts, including the Oslo Accords and Saudi Crown Prince Abdullah's plan, which was adopted by the Arab summit held in Beirut in March 2002.[3] Bush's explicit backing of an independent Palestinian state (the first such move by an American president) has been particularly significant. Previous US-backed plans, notably the Oslo Accords, had neither called for the creation of a Palestinian state nor did they consider Israel as an occupying power and never viewed Israel's colonial settlements as illegal.[4]

Although Bush's 'vision' and the Road Map marked a new shift in US policy in the region, both plans failed to exercise US leverage upon Israel to withdraw its forces from the Palestinian territories occupied in 1967. Both initiatives focused instead on complying with Israel's demands while paying little notice to the Palestinians' urgent needs.[5] The failure of the plans to provide details concerning the final status issues, including the future of Jerusalem, the refugees, the settlements and a border solution was also intended to satisfy Israel's objection to package deals that might entail pressure for withdrawal. The leaving of the final status issues for future negotiations between Israel and the PLO was also alarming, given that a repeat of past failures experienced during the Camp David II summit might resurface. Bush's 'vision' and the Road Map formula could, however, be improved if they would rely more on the results that were reached at the Taba and Geneva talks.[6] The Geneva talks, which were conducted between elements of the Israeli opposition and a number of Palestinian officials, were largely removed from public debate after Israel initiated its unilateral 'disengagement' plans for the Occupied Territories.[7]

Israel's concerns with what it considers a demographic threat to its Jewish identity, which is attributed to the natural growth of the Palestinian community within Israel's borders, motivated Israel and the US into backing the two-states idea. In past mediation efforts between Israel and the Arab world, which often included the two-state formula, the US and Israel have expressed their opposition to the notion of a Palestinian state in favour of assimilating Palestinians into surrounding Arab countries. Over the course of its history, Israel, supported by the US, has also rejected Palestinian claims to national self-determination within any part of historic Palestine.[8] Bush's adoption of the two-state solution is, in this regard, considered a significant turning point in handling the Israeli-Palestinian conflict. Yet President Bush continues to advocate the same old US 'frame of reference'[9] that has always sided with Israel against the Palestinians. As a result, Bush's supporters and critics alike have often appeared confused by Bush's explicit support for a Palestinian state while continuing to align himself with extremist Israeli positions regarding the Palestinians.[10]

The rhetoric behind the Bush Administration's adoption of the two-state formula has, among other things, been motivated by policies adopted by Israel towards the Palestinians following the launching of the second Intifada. After taking office in 2001, Ariel Sharon's government sought to isolate the Palestinians from Israel and to confine them within manageable limits that would be strengthened by its separation wall and checkpoints.[11] By effectively confining the Palestinians within the boundaries of their own isolated towns and cities, along with barring them from entering Israel, the Sharon government expressed its readiness to give up control over most populated centres in the Palestinian territories and to abandon its past strategies that entailed the transferring of Palestinians into surrounding countries or leaving them under Israel's indefinite military occupation. To accommodate Sharon's demographic and territorial concerns, Bush assured the Israelis that his support of a Palestinian statehood would not undermine Israel's security and goals.[12]

While exploring factors, events and forces that may have motivated President Bush's efforts to resolve the Israeli-Palestinian conflict, this chapter underlines the main themes of Bush's two-states 'vision' and those of the Road Map formula. It also examines signs of inconsistencies and fluctuations in the Bush Administration's policies towards the Israeli-Palestinian conflict, along with comparing Bush's rhetoric on the Palestinian state to the actual realities on the ground. The purpose of this chapter is to seek a critical understanding of US policy towards the Israeli-Palestinian conflict in general and the Bush Administration's conception of the two-state solution in particular. To contemplate further on the circumstances that may have influenced Bush's 'vision', it is essential to begin with a brief background to the US's political legacy towards Israel and the Palestinians.

US policy towards Israel and the Palestinians

Over the course of its involvement in the Middle East, US policy has largely been formulated in the context of a Zionist/Israeli understanding of, and reference to, the Palestinian Arabs. In order to safeguard its fundamental interests, the US approach to Israel and the Palestinians resulted in double-standard policies that increased anti-American sentiments in the Arab and Muslim world.[13] Faced with new challenges that threatened their long-term interests, US policymakers were often urged to pursue more balanced policies for Israel and the Palestinians.[14]

To appear impartial, the Bush Administration began advocating democracy building in the Middle East along with backing the two-states idea for resolving the Israeli-Palestinian conflict. The administration had hoped that these steps would improve the US's battered credibility and thus minimize anti-Americanism in the region. However, the daily images of the Iraq war, the failure of the administration's democracy project, the continuation of Palestinian suffering, and the unwillingness to bring an end to Israel's military occupation has thrown into doubt Bush's plans and schemes.[15]

The strength of pro-Israeli influence on US policymakers, media outlets, lobbyists, Congress, bureaucrats and the public has, over the years, tilted US policy towards serving Israel's interests, which may consequently have endangered the US's other interests in the region.[16] The absence of a Palestinian and Arab public relations network to counter the pro-Israeli mindset in the US may also have contributed to the Americans' lack of sympathy for Arab causes. The early accounts that have revealed American ignorance about the Palestinian cause are evident in Mark Twain's writings that portrayed Palestinians as 'primitive' and 'beggars by nature.'[17] With little questioning of the accuracy of their research on the Muslim world, Americans have also accepted ethnocentric materials made available by European orientalists about the region.[18] As time went by, the US media and the public at large became more liable to accept Zionist accounts of the Palestinians as either non-existent, homeless refugees or terrorists.[19]

The US and Israel: the special relationship

The special relationship that exists between the US and Israel has been attributed to several factors, including biblical ties that connect Christians with Jews, the guilt caused by the crimes of the Holocaust, the Israeli identification with democracy, the role played by the pro-Israeli lobbyists in the US and other geopolitical and strategic factors that were particularly important during the Cold War era. Essentially, the pro-Israeli lobby has proved to be a major source of pressure on US policymakers.[20] Unlike other pro-Israeli groups, Protestant evangelicals in the US solidified their relationship with Israel on 'theopolitical' grounds that depict the Israeli-Palestinian conflict as a struggle between good and evil and as a reflection of biblical accounts of David and Goliath.[21]

US presidents who have been involved in the region since the turn of the 20th century have, in one way or the other, designed their policies to favour Zionism and Israel. From the start of the Palestine conflict, President Woodrow Wilson not only failed to derail the British and French policies that decided the future of the Arab world without consulting its residents, but also supported the Balfour Declaration that designated Palestine as a Jewish homeland.[22] Franklin D. Roosevelt's lack of interest in the Palestine issue did little to prevent him from objecting to the 1939 British White Paper that intended to limit Jewish immigration to Palestine.[23] By extending US recognition of Israel and in making its birth possible, Harry Truman occupied 'an immortal place in Jewish history.'[24] Despite the destructive effects of the 1948 War on the Palestinians,[25] the US continued to deploy policies that sided with Israel and downplayed Palestinian claims. Presidents Eisenhower, Kennedy and Johnson's policies were formulated in the context of the Cold War environment that treated Israel as a key player in containing the spread of Communism and defending the US's interests in the region.[26] Although Kennedy had called for the repatriation of the refugees, the deeply rooted pro-Israeli politics in the US distanced him from supporting Palestinian claims.[27]

In the post-1967 war era, the US began pursuing policies that were indistinguishable from the Israeli perspective on the Palestinians, including the treatment of the PLO as a terrorist group and a pro-Soviet puppet. Richard Nixon and Gerald Ford squandered all peace efforts that called for the inclusion of the PLO in negotiations, along with those advocating the two-states idea.[28] By excluding the PLO from peace efforts, US Secretary of State Henry Kissinger advanced his step-by-step approach that intended to resolve the conflict between the Arab states and Israel without including the Palestinians. Kissinger, therefore, effectively isolated the PLO from negotiations and placed Palestinian claims on hold for the next two decades.[29] Prior to Jimmy Carter's presidency, the Palestinians were absent from the US dominant discourse on the region, unless they were mentioned in the context of humanitarian issues concerning the refugees or in relation to their conflict with Israel. President Carter is singled out as the first US president to express some empathy with the Palestinians by addressing their need for a homeland.[30] Carter's inability to transform the conventional wisdom in the US on the Palestinian cause was reflective of the strength of the pro-Israeli influence in Washington. Ronald Reagan, who considered the Palestinian territories as disputed, but not occupied, and labelled Israel's settlements on them as obstacles, but not illegal, has been viewed as the most vehement supporter of Israel.[31] Reagan's strong relationship with Prime Minister Menachem Begin has often been viewed as strikingly similar to the strong relationship that existed between George W. Bush and Prime Minister Ariel Sharon throughout Sharon's tenure in office.[32]

The disintegration of the Soviet bloc and the launching of the first Gulf War deepened the first President Bush's involvement in the region.[33] President Bush and his Secretary of State James Baker's lack of empathy for Israel failed to cause any substantial changes in their policy towards the Israeli-Palestinian conflict.[34] The revelation of the Oslo Accords, which gave the PLO a new role to play in negotiations, dominated Bill Clinton's foreign policy agenda.[35] Although President George W. Bush's backing of the Palestinian state has distinguished him from past administrations, his support for Israel remains stronger than his predecessors'. Bush's linkage between the creation of a Palestinian state and the PA's inability to meet his demands serve as a pretext to justify Israel's continued control of the Palestinian territories.[36] By demanding that the PA change its leaders before it can negotiate with Israel, Bush has also, like his predecessors, contributed to placing Palestinian goals on hold. Bush's obsession with ideas articulated by Israeli Knesset member Natan Sharansky, who objected to peace-making efforts with the Palestinians unless they consolidate a thriving democracy, raised scepticism about Bush's rhetoric on the two-states vision. Bush's letter of assurances, of 16 April 2004, to Sharon about demography, borders and settlement further heightened suspicions of Bush's real 'vision' for the Palestinian state.[37] By further promising to support Sharon's unilateral plans, Bush also strengthened the Arab world's scepticism with regard to his intentions.[38] Bush's conception of the Palestinian state became, in this respect, almost indistinguishable from Sharon's policies. Consequently, despite his embracing of the two-states plan and promoting democracy in the region, Bush's policies continue to demonstrate a fundamental connection with the US legacy that favoured Israel. In contemplating the unending US special relation with Israel, one study presented compelling questions and answers:

> Why has the US been willing to set aside its own security and that of many of its allies in order to advance the interests of another state [Israel]? One might assume that the bond between the two countries was based on shared strategic interests or compelling moral impera-

tives, but neither explanation can account for the remarkable level of material and diplomatic support that the US provides. Instead, the thrust of US policy in the region derives almost entirely from domestic politics, and especially the activities of the 'Israel Lobby'.[39]

Deconstructing Bush's two-states 'vision'

During its initial two years in office, the Bush Administration was criticized for not being actively involved in resolving the escalating Israeli-Palestinian conflict. The failure of the Clinton Administration to set up an agreement between Israel and the Palestinians at the Camp David II Summit may have caused Bush's reluctance to risk his prestige in similar mediations. Despite their ability to exert extensive leverage on Israel, President Bush, Vice President Dick Cheney, National Security Advisor Condoleezza Rice, Secretary of State Colin Powell, Secretary of Defense Donald Rumsfeld and Defense Deputy Paul Wolfowitz endorsed the position of Prime Minister Ariel Sharon and adopted a 'hands-off' approach to Israel's handling of the Palestinians.[40] By advancing the use of US military power to promote so-called moral principles expressed by Bush's neo-conservative supporters, the administration was able to justify also Israel's excessive use of force against Palestinians in the territories. The September 11 attacks, which derailed Bush's policy away from peacemaking, had significantly empowered the administration's neo-conservative camp. Only after the support of Arab states was needed to topple Saddam's regime did Bush begin, after consulting with Israel, to reveal his two-state 'vision' for resolving the Israeli-Palestinian conflict.[41] Bush later launched the democracy promotion plan as part of reinventing causes for the Iraq war. In the midst of planning for the war in Iraq, which was launched on 19 March 2003, Bush delivered his June 2002 speech, calling upon Israel and the Palestinians to establish peace between them by accepting his vision of 'two states living side by side in peace and security'. Bush declared:

> This moment is both an opportunity and a test for all parties in the Middle East: an opportunity to lay the foundations for future peace; a test to show who is serious about peace and who is not. The choice here is stark and simple.[42]

Bush's two-state solution was initially revealed on 10 November 2001 in a speech he delivered at the UN, where he invoked, for the first time in US history, the endorsement of a democratic Palestinian state alongside Israel. Bush anticipated 'the day when two states – Israel and Palestine – live peacefully together within secure and recognized boundaries'.[43] Although Bush was critical of the PA and called for the ousting of Arafat and the election of a new leadership, the PA welcomed Bush's support for a Palestinian state. Aware of his dedication to Israel's security, the Israeli government also accepted Bush's call for the creation of a provisional Palestinian state.[44]

In his June 2002 speech Bush identified the basic content and procedures that must be considered in order for the two-states vision to be fulfilled within three years. He stated:

> ... when the Palestinian people have new leaders, new institutions and new security arrangements with their neighbors, the United States of America [will] support the creation of a Palestinian state whose borders and certain aspects of sovereignty will be provisional until resolved as part of a final settlement in the Middle East ... Israel also has a large stake in the success of a democratic Palestine. Permanent occupation threatens Israel's identity and democracy ... So I challenge Israel to take concrete steps to support the emergence of a viable, credible Palestinian state ... Ultimately, Israelis and Palestinians must address the core issues that divide them if there is to be a real peace, resolving all claims and ending the conflict between them.[45]

Accordingly, Bush assumed that once the Palestinians had accomplished their expected duties, and only after Israel responded favorably by carrying out its own tasks, the two-state solution would then be implemented, where Israel and Palestine could coexist peacefully alongside each other. Aside from his rhetoric, Bush's demands have been difficult to implement, in part because of the Palestinians' inability, under Israel's military occupation, to accomplish their expected tasks. They are also difficult to implement because of Israel's unwillingness to end its colonial settlement activities and land confiscation in the territories. Although he justified Israel's use of force against the Palestinians, Bush also expects the PA to de-legitimize the Palestinians' resistance to Israel's military occupation.

Democracy in the region as a necessary condition for Palestinian statehood

Furthermore, Bush's fixation with promoting democracy also places the creation of a Palestinian state on hold until surrounding Arab autocratic regimes also become democratic. Bush's democracy promotion serves not only as a means to prevent Israel's withdrawal from the territories but also to distract attention from Israel's policies. Israel and its supporters have often used arguments suggesting that the future Palestinian state must be democratic and tolerant towards Israel as a pretext to link and determine the creation of a Palestinian statehood with regional democratization:

> A democratic Palestinian state is impossible as long as other Arab countries remain autocratic, if not despotic. The presence of a democratic Arab government would influence the populations of other Arab states and threaten the continuation of some neighboring autocracies. In addition, the rogue states of the region ... would use all of their resources to sabotage a democratic Palestinian state.[46]

As the Bush Administration continues to back autocratic Arab regimes, many of its neo-conservative members continue to portray these same regimes as obstacles to the peace process and democracy promotion in the region.[47] Ironically, in his support for democracy, Bush urged Jordan and Egypt to work with the PA 'to create a new constitutional framework and a working democracy for the Palestinian people'. These mixed messages continue to thwart US credibility in the Arab world.[48] By warning the Palestinians that their state 'will never be created by terror', while providing Israel with the right 'to defend herself',[49] Bush has created a flexible definition of the meaning of success, where Israel and the US can always contest and argue that their demands have not been met. Bush's double-standard approach to Israel and the Palestinians is also reflected in his sympathetic language of support for Israeli victims of Palestinian terrorism that were never uttered to describe the Palestinian victims of Israel's vicious military attacks and operations. This is, in part, caused by the Bush Administration's neo-conservative assumptions that consider Israel's conflict with the Palestinians as similar to the US's conflict with al-Qa'ida.

By calling upon Israel to support the emergence of 'a viable Palestinian state' at the conclusion of his speech,[50] with the knowledge that the Israeli-Palestinian conflict could never be resolved through military means, Bush indicated that Israel's long occupation since 1967 would be expected to end through direct negotiations with the Palestinians. However, given the unequal balance of power that exists between the two, Israel is sure to prevail in direct talks with the Palestinians. The two-states plan, if implemented in its current format and procedures, would aim at forcing the Palestinians to establish isolated 'ghettos' in areas that are proportionally smaller than what the international community would expect from an Israeli withdrawal to the 1967 borders.[51] In this case, Bush's rhetorical backing of a Palestinian state would never be translated into an actual reality of a viable, territorially continuous and contiguous state. Israel's construction of facts on the ground, including its wall that 'is designed to surround a truncated Palestine completely, and a network of exclusive highways [that] cut across what is left of Palestine' is not consistent with Bush's two-states vision.[52] These policies are far more consistent with the creation of a permanent Palestinian bantustan, which Israel has been trying to establish for decades.[53] Irrespective of whether Bush's vision is genuine or meaningful, the actual realities in the occupied territories reveal that it might be impossible to implement the two-state solution, given that the Palestinians in the West Bank are sharing their land with over '180,000 Jewish settlers and a Jewish population of over 200,000 in and around east Jerusalem'.[54]

In the meantime, Bush's low approval rating in most US public opinion surveys[55] has shifted his attention further away from the Israeli-Palestinian conflict and more towards the Iraq war. Bush's plans for democracy promotion in the Middle East also yielded other unexpected results, which raised more doubts about his neo-conservative legacy, namely after 'the election victory of Hamas in Palestine and the rise of the Muslim Brotherhood in Egypt.'[56] The Bush Administration has not yet been willing to accept Palestinian choices, in part due to Israel's rejection of the outcomes of the Palestinian elections, which are also used as a pretext to strengthen the Israeli government's pursuit of more 'disengagement' plans. In rhetoric, however, the Bush Administration continues to support the Road Map formula and its prospect for a two-state solution.

The Quartet's Road Map formula

In support of Bush's two-states plan, the Quartet's Road Map formula has become the latest US attempt to resolve the Israeli-Palestinian conflict. Its disclosure on 30 April 2003 was done on the heels of Sharon's re-election in January 2003 and just before Abu Mazen's appointment as Palestinian prime minister in March the same year. The Road Map formula consists of three phases that are intended to lead to a lasting agreement between Israel and the Palestinians on the basis of the two-state solution.[57] The Road Map has thus far faced similar challenges to those that have confronted Bush's two-states vision, notably with regard to the so-called absence of a Palestinian partner for peace. Although the Road Map could have been pursued following Arafat's death and the Palestinians' presidential elections, the Iraq war and Israel's focus on its unilateral 'disengagement' plans stalled the process.

Similar to Bush's vision, the first phase of the Road Map expected the Palestinians to halt their Intifada, address Israel's security needs and make serious efforts to prevent attacks on Israelis. Before negotiations resumed, the PA was expected to confiscate weapons and dismantle the infrastructure of militias and begin consolidating security forces under a new unified command structure. The PA's inability to provide basic needs and services for its people placed it in a weak and difficult position when attempting to meet such demands. Likewise its inability to guarantee the fulfilment of minimal Palestinian claims also hindered the PA's attempts to meet the Quartet's expectations. With the absence of exact details about the future peace settlement, the PA runs the risk of a low intensity civil war in the territories if and when it tries to disarm militant Palestinian groups. On the other hand, although Israel was asked to remove its settlements and ease travel restrictions on Palestinians, it failed to do so. Despite these challenges, the UN special coordinator, Terje Roed-Larsen, was, in 2003, optimistic in his assessment of the PA's and Israel's tasks to meet the Quartet expectations. He stated:

> On security, we need ... a workable security plan that allows the Palestinian Authority to rebuild its shattered security services into a unified and reliable force. By combating terror and collecting illegal weapons, this force should send a clear message that the PA is now determined to extend its authority over all Palestine ... On settlements, Israel is about to start removing West Bank outposts ... This will send a clear message to the Palestinians that Israel is serious about the peace process ... On the daily suffering of the Palestinian civilians, Israel must ease as soon as possible movement restrictions ... leading to a full military withdrawal to the line of September 2000.[58]

Based on the degree of progress made in the first phase, the Road Map's second phase would entail the formation of a provisional Palestinian state that lacks identifiable boundaries and sovereignty. Palestinians fear that this state might remain permanently provisional.[59] The provisional state is also expected to emerge within a year and a half following the implementation of the first phase. The Road Map would then enter its third and most difficult phase, where the focus would centre on issues such as borders, refugees, settlements, security, and Jerusalem. A major concern at this phase is that there might be a repeat of the collapse of the Camp David II talks, for the failure of which Israel and the US blamed Arafat.[60] Although the PA failed to accomplish its duties as part of the Road Map for the reasons mentioned above, Israel continued to construct its separation wall with no regard for the 1967 boundaries, failed to remove newly erected settlement outposts, which it described merely as unauthorized outposts, and continued to restrict the movement of Palestinians through the enforcement of its existing checkpoints throughout the territories.[61]

The third phase was expected to have finalized an agreement by May 2005, declaring an end to the Israeli-Palestinian conflict. Despite risking disagreements with Bush's 'vision' and the Road Map, Israel pursued its uncoordinated unilateral steps in an attempt to determine its version of the final status negotiations. Although the 2006 election of a Hamas-led government posed a threat to the implementation of the Road Map, Hamas's electoral success was largely caused by the absence of peace between Israel and the Palestinians. Israel, backed by the Bush Administration, chose to use Hamas's election to illustrate the absence of a partner for peace on the Palestinian side, a policy that it employed openly with Arafat and, in effect, with Abu Mazen after his election as president of the PA in January 2005. Although 'Israel has announced a policy of isolating and destabilizing the new [Hamas] government (perhaps joined by the United States)'[62] to force a new leadership upon the Palestinians, the Palestinians have never enjoyed this same luxury of voicing their own objections to Israeli politicians who often hold extremist credentials.

In pointing out the Road Map's mixed features, Harvey Sicherman stated:

... the Palestinians gain a state without having to make final concessions on vital issues such as Jerusalem and refugees; the Israelis presumably gain ... cooperation while also not having to make final concessions on the same issues. But the Palestinians fear that nothing will be so permanent as the temporary. And the Israelis fear that recognition of a Palestinian state, even a temporary one, without resolution of the refugee problem, for instance, will expose them to escalating pressures ... The Road Map simply postponed those fears.[63]

The failing peace process places the Palestinians at a deeper disadvantage than the Israelis, given that the Palestinians continue to live under dire economic, political and social conditions. Although the Road Map expects the Quartet members to monitor both parties' completion of their tasks, the absence of US pressure on Israel does little to hinder Israel's own plans for the occupied territories, including its expansion of existing colonial settlements along with creating new ones. As long as the Bush Administration continues to manipulate all diplomatic manoeuvrings for the Road Map, while excluding the Quartet's other members from playing their part, the realization of the two-state solution will remain difficult. At the same time, the Road Map still enjoys far more international and regional legitimacy than all other US sponsored plans. Aside from the UN's, the EU's, and Russia's backing, Israel, the PA and the Arab League Summit have also endorsed the Road Map. Given the current circumstances, however, and although most Palestinians continue to support the two-state solution,[64] the realities on the ground can only be measured by the Road Map's inability to improve the status quo.

Vision vs. reality in the two-state solution

The outbreak of the Al-Aqsa Intifada came primarily as a Palestinian response to Israel's military occupation along with the failure of the peace process. Until a peace agreement is reached, implemented, and honoured by both sides, the PA will likely remain unable to reform itself and Israeli-Palestinian violence will continue to escalate. Although it has met Israel's demands, Bush's two-states plan has failed to establish the foundation for a successful peace deal that satisfies the minimal claims of the Palestinians. Bush's 'vision' and the Road Map formula continue to suffer from challenges similar to those that confronted past peace efforts. The Oslo process, for instance, can be seen as a setback in peacemaking as it deprived Palestinians of their internationally recognized claims while helping Israel to build its projects of bantustanization in the occupied territories.[65] The failure of the Camp David II summit, accompanied by the absence of other viable alternative peace models from the agendas of the negotiators, also resulted in exacerbating the tensions surrounding Palestinian-Israeli relations. Despite being different from previous peace efforts, Bush's 'vision' and the Road Map's formula continued to expect the Palestinians to settle for incremental gains, and, in this context, the two-states plan is destined to fail. The absence of peace continues to rest on the inequality between Israel and the PLO/PA, along with the lack of impartial third-party mediators. By demanding more from the Palestinians than from Israel, the present peace efforts lay most of the blame for the violence on the victims rather than the perpetrators.

Although the Road Map is viewed as the best US-approved offer for a solution, the absence of essential details about the future and the means of enforcement to create a viable and sovereign Palestinian state along the Green Line boundaries challenge its implementation. Although all parties may share the blame for the failure of the Road Map, the US's refusal to pressure Israel into agreeing to withdraw to the 1967 borders in return for peace and security remains the main cause of the failure.[66] This is, in part, because the Bush Administration continues to approach the Israeli-Palestinian conflict as if it were only a matter concerning Israel's security. However, the continued marginalization of the Palestinians 'by the current politico-economic arrangement that suppresses their freedom' does little to entice the Bush Administration into enforcing the two-states idea.[67]

Reactions to Hamas's victory

Hamas's ability to win 74 out of 132 seats in the Palestinian Legislative Council (PLC) posed new challenges to the US and questioned the Bush Administration's handling of its democracy promotion project. The administration's resentful reaction to Hamas's success fundamentally deviated from the democratic procedures that it continued to advocate. Bush's promotion of democracy in the Palestinian territories contradicted his rejection of the outcomes of the Palestinian electoral choices. By opposing Hamas's success, the US once again repeated past mistakes that were made during the 1991 Algerian elections, when it stood, along with European countries, against Islamists who had won the election.[68] Furthermore, in opposing the inclusion of Hamas in the political process, the administration not only hindered the prospect for the group to moderate itself, but also strengthened authoritarian Arab regimes' arguments warning that democracy promotion in the region only benefits Islamists, given that Islamists are usually the most popular groups in the Arab world.[69] As such, the Bush Administration's policies towards Hamas represent a fundamental continuity to the US's legacy that opposed the choices of the Algerian people – justified at the time on the grounds that Islamists are 'anti-democratic in orientation' and, as US diplomat Edward Djerjian believed, have generally utilized the 'one man, one vote, one time' formula to establish 'legitimately elected Islamist governments'.[70]

In the US, Hamas's victory led many politicians and pro-Israel lobbyists to criticize the Bush Administration's pressures upon the PA to carry out the elections, despite the expectations that Hamas's strength matched that of Fatah.[71] Domestic pressure on the Bush Administration entailed the boycotting of the new PA's government along with reinforcing Hamas as a terrorist organization.[72] Consistent with this, Congress started a process for formulating a new 'legislation that would tighten restrictions on US contacts and aid' with the new Hamas government. The House of Representatives had previously passed resolution 575, 'which asserts that Hamas and other terrorist organizations should not participate in elections held by the Palestinian Authority.'[73] The pro-Israel lobby and the members of Congress feared that pressure on the administration, deriving possibly from Bush's Arab allies, could lead to the build-up of a working relationship between the US and Hamas. These concerns were raised after Russian President Vladimir Putin met with Hamas's representatives in Moscow in March 2006. Congress and the Bush Administration agreed to cut off financial aid to the Palestinian government, and objected to all 'dealings with Hamas unless it renounces violence, disarms and recognizes Israel.'[74] The administration also dispatched Secretary of State Rice to the region in order to discourage Arab countries from providing a Hamas-led government with aid, unless the group were to meet US demands and pursue a moderate strategy acceptable to Israel and the Bush Administration.[75] Bush's insistence that Hamas accept these conditions 'or suffer a cutoff' of aid to the Palestinians, which is reflective of the strength of pro-Israeli lobbyists, was, once again, 'short-sighted', 'dangerous', and a possible further threat to US interests in the region.[76]

In assessing the factors that may have led to Hamas's success in the elections, most US politicians concluded that the failure of the old guard of the PA was the main reason. Although this may indeed have been a prime factor leading to Hamas's unexpected level of success, US

113

policymakers chose to ignore the fact that the continuation of Israel's military occupation, breeding violence and extremism, and the failure of the Road Map formula were strong contributors.[77]

The widening gap between Bush's 'vision' and the reality on the ground

In principle, Bush's 'vision' and the Road Map were intended to bring moderation to the political stance assumed by both sides in order to arrive at a negotiated end to the conflict. However, the content of Bush's vision contradicted such a message. Nicholas Veliotes states:

> The most obvious feature of the Bush vision is that it requires nothing of the Likud government of Israel. Indeed, some Israeli commentators have suggested that the vision is so one-sided that it must have been written by Prime Minister Ariel Sharon. Foreign Minister Shimon Peres is reported by the Israeli press as having listened to the speech in disbelief and despair. This view is shared by the United States' European and Arab friends and allies, whose advice and interests, after extensive consultations, the President simply ignored.[78]

Apparently, Bush's two-states vision, along with his backing of the Road Map formula, continued to be motivated by the established legacies in the US and by new changes in Israel's policies towards the Palestinians. The Bush Administration's initial hands-off approach that allowed Israel to crack down on the Palestinian uprising failed. Unable to crush the Intifada, the Sharon government began pursuing its long-term unilateral plans that complemented Bush's provisional Palestinian state idea, given that Palestine may never become a true sovereign state. The Bush Administration then backed Israel's 'unilateral physical separation from the Palestinians' and accepted Israel's 'building and armed patrolling of a country-long security fence dividing Palestinian areas from Israeli ones'.[79] Bush's conduct, contradicting his stated vision, was obviously inconsistent with attempts to create a Palestinian state. Instead, like Israel, Bush appeared more willing to support the creation of a restricted 'Palestinian entity that falls short of the attributes of statehood.'[80] Although the US president's vision called upon the Palestinians to exercise their democratic right to free themselves from their old leadership, the Bush Administration, following Hamas's election, became engaged in destabilizing the PA and in penalizing the Palestinians for choosing leaders unacceptable to Israel.

Hamas's election was used, in this context, to 'deepen Israelis' inclination toward unilateralism in their relations with the Palestinians'.[81]

Aside from being motivated by its support for Israel's plans, Bush's two-states vision was mainly influenced by the Iraq war. The US's ability to resolve the Israeli-Palestinian conflict in a satisfactory way for both sides would undoubtedly preserve its long-term interests and credibility in the region. As such, Bush realized that he had to support the Road Map as a means to 'contain Arab ferment' over the US war in Iraq.[82] Given his pursuit of unilateralism during the preparation for the Iraq war, Bush believed that the Road Map might provide him with the chance to appear more cooperative with the UN and the EU on the peace process. Bush's two-states conception and his backing of the Road Map have perhaps been used as a means to cover up, justify and rationalize the US's pursuit of its other nationalist objectives in the region, notably its need to succeed in Iraq.

As far as the underlying forces that may have determined the course of Bush's policies towards Israel and the Palestinians are concerned, pro-Israel lobbyists, Protestant evangelicals and the neo-conservative camp remain by far the most important influencers of Bush's foreign policy agenda. Pressures from domestic forces that support Israel and consider Arab claims to be risk-free have guided Bush's policies throughout the region. In a study conducted by John Mersheimer and Stephen Walt,[83] the American Israel Public Affairs Committee (AIPAC) was singled out as the most important pro-Israeli lobby because of its ability 'to divert US foreign policy as far from what the American national interest would otherwise suggest, while simultaneously convincing Americans that US and Israeli interests are essentially identical'.[84] Although the American Jewish community is by no means a homogeneous group, AIPAC has succeeded in pressuring the Bush Administration to follow Israel's lead in peace talks.

Along with AIPAC, Protestant evangelical groups in the US have exerted tremendous influence on the Bush Administration and have succeeded in placing Israel's interests at the forefront of the US foreign policy agenda. The evangelicals' vital political base has motivated many of the Bush Administration's policies towards Iraq, Israel and the Muslim world. Their support for Israel is based on biblical accounts that are reflective of deep affinity with the Jewish state and the Holy Land. Known as Christian Zionists, a majority of them assume that as the world nears its end, the Church, comprised of Christians, will be

115

raptured into heaven leaving behind those who have not been saved. To accelerate this process, they believe that Solomon's temple must be rebuilt in modern-day Jerusalem at the location of the Dome of the Rock (Al-Aqsa Mosque). Aside from having anticipated the creation of Israel, they also believe that the Jewish state will deliver for them their other theological prophecies.[85] While awaiting the second coming of Christ, evangelicals continue to pressure US policymakers to preserve Jerusalem as the unified capital of Israel. They predict more warfare to emerge in the Holy Land, notably on the site of Armageddon (*Megiddo*), where the anti-Christ will be defeated and the Messiah will emerge from heaven to end evil and set up a paradise on earth. Since the evangelicals form a vital electoral constituency, Bush has been influenced by their views that reject the imposition of territorial compromises upon Israel. In assessing their impact on Bush, Martin Durham stated:

> ... the election of George W. Bush has resulted in a new importance for the relationship between evangelicals and US foreign policy. This has become particularly clear following the 11 September 2001 attacks ... Not only were many evangelicals committed to Israel, they were also often drawn to policies that were being advanced by the more hard-line forces within the Jewish state. This involved opposition to the proposed road map for peace.[86]

Although not all Protestant evangelicals subscribe to these beliefs, politicians and religious figures like Ralph Reed, Kay Arthur, Jane Hanson, Gary Bauer, Jerry Falwell, and Pat Robertson, along with many members of Congress such as Richard Army, Tom DeLay, and James Inhoff, to mention a few, have been candid about their religious beliefs and political support for Israel on religious grounds. They believe that any position taken against Israel is a stand against God, who they believe purposefully led the Jews to the Holy Land.[87] They also support Israel's 'expansionist agenda' and they believe that to do otherwise 'would be contrary to God's will.'[88] These followers have also expressed a romanticized view of Israel not just because it was the place where Jesus was born and had been resurrected, but also because their prophecies are believed to be linked to Israel. Although evangelicals continue to support Bush's policies, many of them have opposed his backing of the Road Map. Pat Robertson, for instance, warned Bush that his support for the Road Map defies God:

You know the prophet Joel speaks about those who divided my land, that there is a curse on them. I think I would walk very, very softly if I were George Bush in this regard ... The crunch will come when he tries to divide Jerusalem ... I think he is going to incur the wrath of the Lord if he does that.[89]

However, it is too simplistic to assume that evangelicalism is the only driving force behind Bush's policies towards Israel and the Palestinians. Indeed, the neo-conservatives in the administration have also urged Bush to grant Israel all the freedom it needs to combat Palestinian violence. Following the September 11 attacks, neo-conservatism has widely been identified as the driving force behind Bush's policies worldwide. Supporters and critics of Bush generally consider his democracy promotion project, the Iraq war, his pro-Israel policy and the emphasis on US hegemony in world affairs as integral parts of the neo-conservative strategy motivating Bush's foreign policies. Despite recent disagreements among them on the Iraq war,[90] neo-conservatives have always supported Bush's pursuit of pre-emptive and unilateral exercises of US power in world affairs.[91] Like most Israeli politicians, most neo-conservatives also believe that Arabs understand only the language of force and that they need the US more than the US needs them.[92] Pro-Israel neo-conservative politicians and intellectuals also equate any criticism of Israel with a new form of 'anti-Semitism'.[93]

Bush's two-state solution faces the problem of implementation, especially since it is only one among other, often conflicting, goals that the US is trying to achieve in the region. Bush's style is another challenge that has often hindered his 'vision'. His reference to biblical concepts in scripted speeches has not only led to the construction of Arabs and Muslims as enemies in the minds of Americans, but also increased anti-Americanism in the region.[94] More importantly, the Bush Administration has been engaged in devising policies in the region that have been based less on real knowledge and more on the conventional wisdom and frame of reference favouring Israel.[95]

Despite their setbacks, Bush's two-states vision and the Road Map formula shifted the debate from focusing on whether a Palestinian state could be established, into a debate addressing the size and nature of the state. Scepticism about the viability of the two-state solution also gave rise to discussions on alternative solutions, including those envisioning Jews and Arabs living together in one state. As Israel and

117

the US come to realize that an alternative scenario to the two-states formula would be the formation of a single democratic state, their rhetorical backing for the two-state solution continues. The one-state solution, known as bi-nationalism, entails political equality between Arabs and Jews.[96] Although it is perhaps the most just scenario for a political settlement, bi-nationalism remains an unlikely approach for conflict resolution for both sides. Although most Palestinians continue to support coexistence with Israel within a two-state setting,[97] almost a quarter of the adult population in the West Bank and Gaza support a bi-national state.[98] In the end, no matter what political settlement is pursued, the Palestinians have succeeded in cancelling out plans that aimed at transferring them out of their historic homeland.[99] However, the upcoming Israeli government, supported by the US, will likely maintain its commitment to Sharon's legacy, which Baruch Kimmerling has referred to as 'politicide' – an attempt to liquidate Palestinian national existence.[100]

Notes

1 'Powell to Issue a Plan for Easing Middle East Conflict,' *New York Times*, May 21, 2001, p. A1.

2 See, 'President George W. Bush's Speech Calling for New Palestinian Leadership' at the White House Rose Garden, June 24, 2002, in White House Records, the Bush Presidency, June 24, 2002.

3 'The Mideast Road Map,' *New York Times*, December 24, 2002, p. A22.

4 See the Oslo documents in Geoffrey R. Watson (2000) *The Oslo Accords: International Law and the Israeli-Palestinian Peace Agreement*, Oxford: Oxford University Press.

5 Robert Malley, 'Playing into Sharon's Hands,' *New York Times,* January 25, 2002, p. A23.

6 Jeremy Pressman, 'Visions in Collision,' *International Security*, Vol. 28, No. 2 (Fall 2003): 5–43.

7 Khalil Shikaki (2004) 'The Geneva Accord and the Palestinian Response,' *Palestine-Israel Journal*, Vol. 11 Issue 1, p. 60.

8 Avi Shlaim (2000) *The Iron Wall: Israel and the Arab World,* New York: W. W. Norton and Co.

9 See, Kathleen Christison (2001) *Perceptions of Palestine: Their Influence on US Middle East Policy*, Berkeley: University of California Press.

10 Marek Arnaud, 'The Israeli-Palestinian Conflict: Is There a Way Out?' *Australian Journal of International Affairs*, Vol. 57, No. 2, (July 2003), p. 249.

11 Jeremy Pressman (2003) 'The Primary Role of the United States in Israeli–Palestinian Relations,' *International Studies Perspectives*, 4, 191–4.

12 White House Records the Bush Presidency, November 2004.

13 Harold Saunders, 'Arabs, Jews and Peace: Back to the Basics,' *Christian*

Science Monitor, 4 August 1981, p. 23; See also, Jimmy Carter, 'A Jerusalem Settlement Everyone Can Live With,' *New York Times*, 6 August 2000, p. WK15.

14 See reference to Howard Dean's idea of an 'even-handed role' in John Mersheimer and Stephen Walt, 'The Israel Lobby,' *London Review of Books*, Vol. 28, No. 6, 23 March 2006, p. 8.

15 'Plans for Mideast: Capsule Summaries of Past Proposals,' *New York Times*, 9/11 1982, p. A10.

16 See George Moffett III, 'Israeli Lobby Virtually Unmatched,' *Christian Science Monitor*, June, 28, 1991, p. 3.

17 Kathleen Christison (2001) *Perceptions of Palestine*, p. 16

18 Edward Said (1980) *The Question of Palestine*, New York: Vintage Books.

19 Ilan Pappé (2004) *A History of Palestine: One Land, Two Peoples*, Cambridge: Cambridge University Press.

20 Shmuel Rosner, 'Study: US Middle East Policy motivated by Pro-Israel Lobby,' *Ha'aretz*, Friday, March 17, 2006, Internet edition.

21 Robert Smith, 'Between Restoration and Liberation: Theopolitical Contributions and Responses to US Foreign Policy in Israel/Palestine,' *Journal of Church and State*, pp. 833–60.

22 'Adopts Palestine as Jews' Homeland,' *New York Times*, December 18, 1918, p. 24.

23 'Roosevelt urged to act for Jews,' *New York Times*, May 19, 1939, p. 6.

24 Kathleen Christison (2001) *Perceptions of Palestine*, p. 62

25 Nadav Saran, 'The Number One World Problem Today,' *New York Times*, April 7, 1974, p. 368

26 'The News of the Week in Review,' *New York Times*, January 5, 1958, p. E.1

27 'Shukary Attacks Johnson,' *New York Times*, February 8, 1964, p. 4.

28 Daniel Southerland, 'Prospects for Geneva Talks Recede,' *The Christian Science Monitor*, August 4, 1977, p. 3.; see also, Jason Morris, 'Dayan Takes Peace Plan to Israel,' *The Christian Science Monitor*, October 12, 1977, p. 3.

29 'Kissinger Flies to Cairo to Assess Talks Outlook,' *New York Times*, November 6, 1974, p. 3.

30 Palestinian reaction, in 'Palestinians in Cairo Welcome Carter's Stand on Need for Homeland,' *New York Times*, March 18, 1977, p. 11.

31 See Husam Mohamad, 'Palestinian Politics on the Defensive: From Camp David to the Uprising,' *Scandinavian Journal of Development Alternatives and Area Studies*, Vol. 16, Nos 3 and 4, (September/December 1997): 185–214.

32 David Domke (2004) *God Willing? Political Fundamentalism in the White House, the War on Terror and the Echoing Press*, London, Pluto Press, p. 8.

33 See Husam Mohamad, 'Long Conflict, New Rules,' *Palestine–Israel Journal of Politics, Economics and Culture*, Vol. IV, Nos 3 and 4, (1997–98): 66–71.

34 William Safire, 'Baker's Four Blunders,' *New York Times*, July 13, 1989, p. A23.

35 'From Clinton, Arafat and Rabin: Hope, Dreams and Now Peace,' *New York Times*, September 29, 1995, p. A12.

36 See, Michael C. Desch, 'Sharansky's Double Standard,' *The American Conservative*, March 28, 2005.

37 James Bennet, 'Sharon Coup: US Go-Ahead,' *New York Times*, May 14, 2004, p. A1.

38 See Commentary by Mahmoud Abbas, 'Is the Road Map at a Dead End?', *The Wall Street Journal*, October 20, 2005. Online Edition.

39 See John Mersheimer and Stephen Walt, 'The Israel Lobby,' *London Review of Books*, Vol. 28, No. 6, 23 March 2006, p. 22.

40 Robert O. Freedman, 'The Bush Administration and the Israeli-Palestinian Conflict: A Preliminary Evaluation,' *American Foreign Policy Interests*, 25: 505–11, 2003, p. 505.

41 Roane Carey, 'Palestine Besieged: The Threat of Annihilation,' *The South Atlantic Quarterly*, 102: 4, (Fall 2003), p. 694.

42 The text of 'President George W. Bush's Speech on Palestinian State-hood,' June 24, 2002.

43 See *New York Times*, November 12, 2001.

44 See Ali Jarbawi, 'After Elections, Prepare for a new Springtime Intifada,' *The Daily Star*, December 13, 2005, Internet edition.

45 Text of President's Speech, June 24, 2002.

46 'For the Record: The Two-States Solution,' *American Foreign Policy Interests*, 24: 451–8, 2002, p. 452.

47 See 'The Two-States Solution,' *American Foreign Policy Interests*, 24: 451–8, 2002.

48 See John Kifner, 'US Allies in Mideast Voice Doubts on Bush Peace Plan,' *New York Times*, July 2, 2002, p. A11; see also Jane Perlez, 'Bush Hammers Arafat: Takes Softer Tone With Israel,' *New York Times*, March 30, 2001, p. A1.

49 See President George W. Bush Speech, June 24, 2002.

50 Ibid.

51 Haim Bresheeth, 'Two States, Too Little, Too Late,' *Al Ahram Weekly*, (March 15, 2004), Internet.

52 Jimmy Carter, 'Colonization of Palestine Precludes Peace,' *Ha'aretz*, Friday, March 17, 2006.

53 See, Husam Mohamad, 'Palestinian Politics on the Move: From Revolution to Peace and Statehood,' *Nationalism and Ethnic Politics*, Vol. 7, No. 3, (Autumn 2001): 46–76.

54 See Ghada Karmi, 'A Secular Democratic State in Historic Palestine: An Idea Whose Time Has Come,' *Al-Adab*, July 2002, Lebanon, Internet edition.

55 Bush job approval rate, below 35% (March 2006) Gallop Poll http://poll.gallup.com/content/?ci=21745

56 See Fareed Zakaria, 'Islam and Power,' *Newsweek*, 2/13/2006, Vol. 147, Issue 7, pp. 34–7.

57 See 'Mideast Road Map,' *New York Times*, December 24, 2002, p. A22; See also 'US Still Trying to Unfold Mideast Road Map,' *New York Times*, November 15, 2002, p. A13.

58 Terje Roed-Larsen, 'Explaining the Road Map,' *Palestine-Israel Journal*, 10, 2 (2003) pp. 88–9.

59 Jamil Hilal (Arabic) 'Questions about the Aftermath of Israel's Withdrawal from Gaza,' *Majalat al-Dirasat al-Filistinyeh*, Beirut, Lebanon: IPS (Summer 2005): pp. 5–12.

60 See Robert Malley and Hussein Agha, 'The Palestinian-Israeli Camp David Negotiations and Beyond', *Journal of Palestine Studies*, Vol. 31, No. 1 (Autumn, 2001), 62–85.

61 Paola Rizzuto, 'Buttu assesses Road Map, Israel's Roadblocks,' *Washington Report on the Middle East,* October 2003, Vol. 22, Issue 8, p. 67.

62 See Jimmy Carter, *Ha'aretz*, Friday, March 17, 2006.

63 See Harvey Sicherman, 'Peace facts: The Road to Palestine,' a briefing on the Middle East Peace process at the Foreign Policy Research Institute, Volume 10, No. 1 (June 2003) Internet site.

64 See Office of Research, Department of State, 'Opinion Analysis: Hamas and Fatah Neck and Neck as Palestinian Elections Near,' January 19, 2006.

65 See Nicholas Guyatt (1998) *The Absence of Peace: Understanding the Israeli-Palestinian Conflict,* London: Zed Books.

66 Stephen Zunes, 'The US Role in the Collapse of the Peace Process,' *Peace Review*, 15: 1, 2003, pp. 11–18.

67 Erwin S. Fernandez, 'The United States and the Arab-Israeli Conflict: (UN) Forging Future Peace,' *International Social Science Review*, Vol. 80, Nos 1 and 2, p. 48.

68 See Husam Mohamad, 'US Policy Towards Islamists: a Review of Recent Debates,' *Third World Quarterly*, Vol. 21, No. 3, June 2000: 567–78.

69 Chris Zambelis, 'The Strategic Implications of Political Liberalization and Democratization in the Middle East,' *Parameters* (Autumn 2005), p. 92.

70 Quoted in Tamara Cofman Wittes, 'The Promise of Arab Liberals,' *Policy Review*, (June/July 2004), p. 64.

71 Office of Research, Department of State, 'Opinion Analysis: Hamas and Fatah Neck and Neck As Palestinian Elections Near,' January 19, 2006.

72 Steven Weisman, *New York Times*, March 17, 2006, Vol. 155 Issue 53521, pp. A1–A8, 2p.

73 Shirl McArther, 'First Session of 109th Congress Adjourns With Mixed Results,' *Washington Report on the Middle East*, March 2006, Vol. 25, Issue 2, pp. 32–3, 2p.

74 Paul Richter, 'Hamas Poll Victory Tears at a Key Bush Alliance,' *Washington Report on Middle East Affairs*, Vol. 25, Issue 3 (April 2006): 18–19.

75 'How will Hamas Rule?', *Time*, Vol. 167, Issue 9, pp. 44–5.

76 *Nation*, March 13, 2006, Vol. 282, Issue 10, p4–4, 1/2pp.

77 See Robert Malley and Hussein Agha, *New York Review of Books*, March 9, 2006, Vol. 53, Issue 4, pp. 22–4, 3pp.

78 Nicholas A. Veliotes, 'The Bush Vision for Palestine: Realistic or Apocalyptic,' *Mediterranean Quarterly*, (Fall 2002), pp. 11–12.

79 David C. Unger, 'Maps of War, Maps of Peace,' *World Policy Journal*, (Summer 2002), pp. 1–2.

80 Ibid., p. 6

81 Michael Herzog, 'Can Hamas Be Tamed?,' *Foreign Affairs*, March/April 2006, Vol. 85, Issue 2.

82 Daniel Mandel, 'Try, Try, Try Again: Bush's Peace Plans,' *Middle East Quarterly* (Summer 2004), p. 3.

83 See the full text of their study at, John Mersheimer and Stephen Walt, 'The Israel Lobby,' *London Review of Books*, Vol. 28, No. 6, March 23, 2006, pp. 22.

84 Quoted from Shmuel Rosner, 'Study: US Middle East Policy Motivated by Pro-Israel Lobby,' *Ha'aretz*, Friday, March 17, 2006.

85 See Clare Amos, 'Text, Tribulation and Testimony: The Bible in the Context of the Current Middle East,' *Political Theology*, 4: 2, (2003): 175–91.

86 Martin Durham, 'Evangelical Protestantism and Foreign Policy in the United States after September 11,' *Patterns of Prejudice*, 38, No. 2, 2004, pp. 145, 151.

87 Marjorie Hyer, 'Fundamentalists Join Jews in Strong Support for Israel,' *Washington Post*, November 13, 1982. p. B6; See also, William Claiborne, 'Israelis Look on US Evangelical Christians as Potent Allies in Battle with Arab States,' *Washington Post*, March 23, 1981, p. A11.

88 John Mersheimer and Stephen Walt, 'The Israel Lobby,' *London Review of Books*, p. 6.

89 Martin Durham, 'Evangelical Protestantism and Foreign Policy in the United States after September 11,' *Patterns of Prejudice*, 38, No. 2, 2004, p. 152.

90 Rupert Cornwell, 'Neo-con Dream of New World Order in Tatters,' *The New Zealand Herald*, March 10, 2006, internet edition.

91 Steven Hurst, 'Myths of Neoconservatism: George W. Bush's Neo-conservative Foreign Policy Revisited,' *International Politics*, 2005, 42, pp. 42–3.

92 Especially during the Dubai Port deal, many expressed these and similar comments on news channels, including one conducted on CNN with William Bennett, the former secretary of education who is usually identified as a neo-conservative, in February 2006.

93 See John Mersheimer and Stephen Walt, 'The Israel Lobby,' *London Review of Books*, p. 12.

94 See Debra Merskin, 'The Construction of Arabs as Enemies: Post September 11 Discourse of George W. Bush,' *Mass Communications and Society*, Vol. 7, No. 2, 2004, pp. 157–75.

95 See Kathleen Christison, *Perceptions of Palestine*, 2001.

96 Edward Said, 'The One-State Solution: Why the only answer to Middle East Peace is Palestinians and Israelis living as equal citizens under one flag,' *New York Times*, January 10, 1999, p. 31.

97 Saeb Erekat, 'Saving the Two-State Solution,' *New York Times*, December 20, 2002, p. A39.

98 See Cynthia Johnston, 'Palestinians Talk of Scrapping Call for State,' *Reuters*, July 8, 2004. Internet edition.

99 See Norman Finkelstein, *Image and Reality of the Israel-Palestinian Conflict*, London: Verso, 2nd revised edition, April 2003.

100 See Baruch Kimmerling, *Politicide: Ariel Sharon's War against the Palestinians*, London: Verso, 2003. See also Baruch Kimmerling, 'Politicide: Ariel Sharon and the Palestinians,' *Current History*, Vol. 104, Issue 678, pp. 25–9.

6 | The economics of an independent Palestine

SUFYAN ALISSA

Since 1967, Israeli policies have shaped the nature of economic development in the West Bank and Gaza Strip (WBGS). These policies have been directed coherently and consistently to secure military, economic, and political control over the WBGS and, as will be demonstrated in this chapter, to undermine the viability of the Palestinian economy in the WBGS and to weaken its indigenous economic base. Since the establishment of the Palestinian Authority (PA) in 1994 as a result of the Oslo Accords signed by the Palestine Liberation Organization (PLO) and Israel in 1993, these policies have taken new dimensions. The Accords stipulate the PA's mandate over the WBGS and its ability to determine political and economic policies. In addition, they set out the nature, structure and capacity of the PA institutions. The Accords also allow the government of Israel to exercise political and economic power over the territories, both directly through controlling more than half of the WBGS and indirectly through the type of PA institutions constructed as a result of the Accords. Many Palestinians built their hopes on the Oslo Accords believing that they would lead to the creation of the future Palestinian state within the 1967 borders. This project unfortunately ended with the failure of the Camp David negotiations and the outbreak of the second Intifada in September 2000. Since this Intifada, Israeli policies in the WBGS have taken yet another dimension: to control the WBGS and to destroy its economy.

Although Israel is the dominant power in the WBGS and its policies are the primary factor shaping the nature of economic development, it is not the only actor with that role. The PA and international donors' community also have a significant impact on these issues. The main focus of this chapter, therefore, is on the implications of these policies for the establishment in the WBGS of a viable Palestinian state within the 1967 borders both in general and with regard to the viability of the economy in particular.

In this chapter, a viable national economy is considered to possess two main characteristics: the ability to function as a normal economy, and to generate economic prosperity for the population. A functioning economy is defined as having geographical linkage between all areas of the country, free movement of labour and capital, its own currency, the possibility of determining its own fiscal and monetary policies, control over its own natural resources, rights to develop its own productive base, the capacity to determine economic relations with other countries, and the ability to make the necessary legal arrangements to regulate and protect the economy. The ability to generate economic prosperity is defined in this chapter as having the capacity for the economy to create employment, and to develop and deliver sufficient services to the people.

Israeli policies towards the WBGS economy

Since 1967, Israeli policies towards the WBGS have been the driving force of a process of 'de-development'[1] in the WBGS. These policies have been shaped by political and ideological considerations but also have economic realities. They have been directed coherently and consistently towards securing, on the one hand, military, economic, and political control over the WBGS and to protect Israel's national interests, and, on the other hand, to destroy the Palestinian economy and weaken its indigenous economic base in a way that diminishes national aspirations.

Israel's economic policies in the WBGS were intended to achieve two contradictory ends: improving the standard of living without achieving any structural change in the WBGS economy and progressively weakening the indigenous economic base. The guidelines for these policies from the Israeli point of view were that Israel should prevent any genuine development of the economy of the WBGS, while allowing improvement in the standard of living. Successful economic development in the WBGS would generate competition with Israeli products and would strengthen Palestinian society. This would further the Palestinian objective of achieving a Palestinian state and would therefore put the Israeli state at risk. A reasonable standard of living can be achieved by employment in Israel, which on the one hand would increase dependence on Israel and on the other hand could damp down national aspirations. These policies were enhanced by interconnecting all Palestinian grids (roads, electricity, communication, water) to the Israeli infrastructure and by forcing the WBGS to use only Israeli ports for import and export; they were implemented by the military administration in the WBGS (Benvenisti 1984).

According to Meron Benvenisti, former deputy mayor of Jerusalem, Israeli economic policies were implemented in the WBGS through a complementary and discriminatory system of integration and segregation producing a dual outcome. This is what Benvenisti characterized as individual prosperity and communal stagnation. Individual prosperity is based mainly on the purchasing power earned by Palestinian labourers in Israel, providing the Palestinians with higher income and a better standard of living. Communal stagnation is caused by discriminatory trade practices, lack of production, credit, infrastructure, or subsidization, and by administrative restrictions (Benvenisti 1984).

While the Israelis view this process as full integration, evidence suggests that it is a selective integration aimed at the marginalization, isolation, exploitation and the dependency of the WBGS economy on the Israeli one. It is selective integration since admitting only unskilled (cheap) labour and limiting production in the WBGS are its dominant aspects. Israel never allowed the employment of professional and middle-class Palestinians in Israel. In addition, Israel never allowed equal commercial exchange or faster processess of industrialization in the WBGS.

Marginalization and isolation mean here the systemic destruction of the WBGS economy and its production base and the segregation of this economy from the international market. This process has been consolidated by policies of closures. Exploitation in this context refers to the use of the WBGS as a cheap source of labour and raw material and as a supplementary market for Israeli goods. Dependency in this context refers to the deliberate and systematic process of making the separation of the WBGS from the Israeli economy an impossible task.

By the early 1990s, Israeli policies towards the WBGS economy had begun to take a new form. The shift took place through introducing several restrictive policies and measures towards the WBGS economy.[2] In 1991 (particularly after the second Gulf War), the Israeli government institutionalized policies of collective punishment and restrictions on the movement of people and goods. Like other policies, closure policies were shaped by political considerations, but they had an economic rationale and reality. Accompanied by settlement building, bypass construction, a separation wall and control over natural resources, these policies not only completed the process of marginalization, isolation, exploitation and dependency, but also created much more complex political and economic realities in the WBGS. The next section illustrates these issues in more detail.

Closure policies

Closure policies were first imposed by the Israeli government on the Palestinians during the Gulf War in 1991, and since 1993 have become more systematic and intensive. According to the Israeli view, these policies have been institutionalized to prevent or minimize the threat of Palestinian attacks on Israeli security forces or citizens. For the Palestinians, they have meant new forms of collective punishment and of securing control over the WBGS. However, they had a tremendously negative impact on the WBGS economy and represented a shift away from Israeli dependence on Palestinian low-skilled labour. According to the Office of the United Nations Special Coordinator (UNSCO), the main economic effect of these policies has been to diminish the geographical scope of economic activities in terms both of production and employment, and of access to markets. These policies reduce the income of Palestinian producers and workers who cannot reach their places of employment, or who are unable to obtain inputs and/or sell their goods and services. The effect of income loss has been a decrease in the demand for goods and services produced in the domestic economy, generating a further decline in production and employment (UNSCO 2001).

Three major forms of closure can be distinguished: general, comprehensive and internal. General closure aims at restricting the interaction between the populations of the WBGS and Israel, between the WBGS and Jerusalem, and between the populations of the West Bank and Gaza Strip. Comprehensive closure aims at completely blocking personal, vehicular and merchandize mobility. Internal closure aims at restricting the movement of people, vehicles and commodities within the West Bank (UNSCO 1997). In addition, the Israeli authorities implemented policies of border closures between the West Bank and Gaza Strip, and Jordan and Egypt.

The policy of collective punishment (economic, political and social) has coincided with the harsh procedure of land confiscation for the purpose of building colonial settlements and bypasses, control over natural resources and, in 2002, with starting to build the separation wall. Such measures were intended to extend control over the WBGS by increasing the size and number of colonial settlements and and to fragment the WBGS areas into many enclaves. This o. can only destroy the possibility of building a viable Palestinian stau and economy in the WBGS, as will be illustrated in this chapter.

Building settlements, bypasses, and the separation wall, and control over natural resources

Despite the fact that the Palestinian Authority assumed power over part of the WBGS in 1994, Israel has maintained its control over large parts of the WBGS through various procedures. By the end of 2000, Israel still fully controlled over 60% of West Bank land and 26% of the Gaza Strip. The number of Israeli colonial settlements reached 150 in the West Bank and 17 in the Gaza Strip. Israel also constructed 65 bypass roads with a length of 652 km, in addition to the military positions. As a result of these constructions, Israel uprooted more than half a million trees, the majority of which (70%) were olive trees (Tofakji 2001). Moreover, having taken control of all water sources after 1967, Israel still controls more than 80% of WBGS water (Palestinian Independent Commission for Citizens' Rights 2001).

Since 1967 Israel has been implementing deliberate policies not only to control water resources in the WBGS, but also to achieve supremacy over its neighbours.[3] Colonial settlements have served to protect Israel's control over water. This can be summarized by the very rhetorical question that former Israeli Prime Minister Ariel Sharon posed in April 2001, when he responded to the *Ha'aretz* newspaper interviewer's question about his willingness to withdraw from the settlements: 'Is it possible today to concede control of the hill aquifer, which supplies a third of our water? ... you know, it's not by accident that the settlements are located where they are ...' (*Ha'aretz* 12 April 2001: unpaged).

These policies of land confiscation and control over natural resources have resulted in grossly undermining and marginalizing the agricultural and industrial sectors and their ability to absorb Palestinian labour. The prices of land and water have increased, thereby increasing the cost of agricultural production. This has restricted the opportunities for Palestinian agricultural produce to compete in Arab markets with products from Spain, Morocco and Turkey. As for the industrial sector, among other factors, rising prices for a diminishing supply of land and water have constrained the capacity to develop or expand.

In 2002, Israeli policies took a new turn with the start of the building of the separation wall. According to Israel, it is a security fence, but this claim lacks credibility since, in reality, a true security fence would have been built on Israel's 1967 pre-occupation border (the 'Green Line'). It is clear that the objective of this wall is two-fold. The first objective is to confiscate more land to expand the colonization in the West Bank and redraw the geopolitical borders between the WBGS and Israel. The second is to displace the Palestinians by denying them access to their land and to adequate water resources, and by restricting freedom of movement to such an extent that remaining in the town or village becomes an unviable option (Negotiation Support Unit, March 2004).

The projected length of the wall is 788 km, double the length of the Green Line (approximately 320 km). The land enclosed and thus de facto annexed into Israel will be 43.5% of the West Bank, and the projected number of Palestinians to be trapped between the wall and the Green Line is 343,300 (14.9% of the Palestinian population in WBGS). The projected number of Palestinians who will be separated from their land by the wall is 522,000 (Negotiation Support Unit, March 2004).

In brief, it is quite evident that the economic, political and closures policies alongside policies of building settlements, bypasses and the separation wall, and control over natural resources constitute a process of 'bantustanization'[4] of the WBGS. This relationship is summarized clearly in Figure 6.1. The term was first used by Azmi Bishara (1995 and 1999) and Meron Benvenisti (April 2004) to refer to the territorial, political and economic fragmentation model that the Israeli government has created in the WBGS. Azmi Bishara defines the Palestinian Bantustan as 'a place that lacks sovereignty and at the same time is not part of Israel. It's neither one thing nor the other. Its people do not have right of entry to ... neighbouring countries. In this respect, they are more restricted than in the bantustans of South Africa, where at least you could travel to work' (Bishara 1995: 44–5).

Four Bantustan models have been created by Israel in the WBGS. One is already fully complete in the Gaza Strip and reinforced by the implementation of Sharon's 'disengagement plan'. The other three will be finalized with the completion of the separation wall: first Jenin-Nablus; second, Bethlehem-Hebron; and third, Ramallah.

The term 'cantonization' also has been used by Graham Usher (1999), Salim Tamari and Rema Hammami (2000) to describe the territorial fragmentation of WBGS as an outcome of the Oslo agreement. However, the term bantustanization is more relevant to explain the

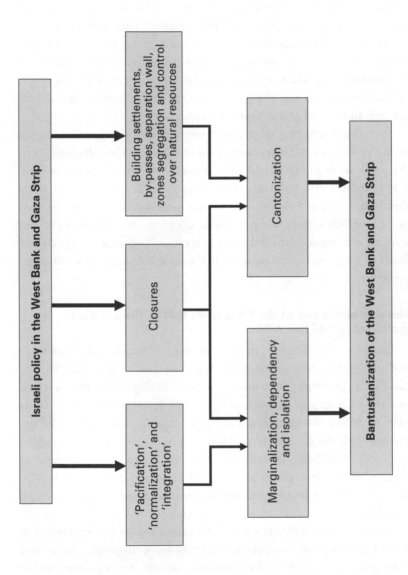

Figure 6.1 Key elements of the bantustanization of the WBGS

current development in the WBGS for two main reasons. First, the term 'bantustanization' considers the economic realities and the facts created on the ground by this fragmentation (four entities will be totally separated from Israel and each other, yet totally dependent on Israel economically) unlike the term 'cantonization', which describes only the territorial fragmentation of the WBGS. Second, the term 'bantustanization' centres on the political and power relations between the Palestinians and Israel. An emblem of this power is the fact that each of the four entities has one gate controlled by the Israelis that can be opened and closed at any time Israel chooses.

The assessment presented above suggests that the overall outcome of the process of bantustanization in the WBGS is the demolition of the basis for building a viable Palestinian state and economy by creating economic and political facts on the ground, and the continuous destruction of the Palestinian economy and institutions. As the next section will illustrate, this process is rooted in the Oslo Accords that were signed between the Palestine Liberation Organization (PLO) and Israel in 1993, and which resulted in the establishment of the Palestinian Authority (PA).

The establishment of the PA and its role in the economic development of the WBGS

Since its establishment in 1994, the PA has faced many challenges and constraints in relation to its mandate and responsibilities, the conditions governing its work, its role in serving Palestinian society, and the relationship between political and developmental work in its plan of action. As indicated above, the establishment of the PA coincided with the acceleration of Israel's policies of land confiscation, settlement building, water control, and restriction on movement of persons and commodities and on economic activities in the WBGS. Thus PA has only limited control over land and water and none at all over borders.

Despite these challenges, to a large extent the PA has succeeded in building a range of government institutions, delivering services and managing the daily life of the Palestinian people. An assessment of the impact of the PA on the economic development of the WBGS requires, among other things, an examination of the nature, structure and characteristics of this Authority. Then the way in which the PA has strengthened or weakened development capacity needs to be examined.

The nature, structure and capacity of the PA

The Oslo Accords specified the PA mandate over the WBGS and its ability to determine political and economic policies. They also set out the institutional nature, structure and capacity of the PA institutions. A brief assessment of the 1994–2006 period provides valuable evidence about the specific implications of the Oslo Accords, the obstacles and challenges created by these agreements, and the strengths and weaknesses of the PA. Assessing the main implications of these issues for the viability of the Palestinian state and economy requires paying special attention to the colonial context (the Israeli policies in the WBGS), which has been explained in the previous section, to the objective of the Oslo Accords, and to the internal arrangements made by the PA concerning the development of the WBGS economy.

As we have seen in the previous section, the Israeli policies in the WBGS create a process of 'bantustanization'. In this section I argue that the nature and implications of the Oslo Accords rooted this process in the WBGS and made the possibility of challenging it or mitigating its negative effects very difficult. In addition, the Accords institutionalized the dependence of the WBGS on Israel. They gave the PA full control of only 18% of the WBGS and divided the WBGS into three zones: A, B and C. Zone A (the 18%) is under full control of the PA; Zone B is under the administrative control of the PA and the security control of Israel; Zone C is under the full control of Israel. Zone A is divided into many enclaves, effectively divided one from another. These enclaves are surrounded by areas B and C, which gives Israel effective control over the whole WBGS. However, since 2000 the PA no longer even controls Zone A, since Israel reoccupied most of it. Moreover, Israel has abrogated the Oslo Accords by frequent invasions of the WBGS and the construction of the separation wall.

In addition, the Oslo Accords left the PA with no control over borders and natural resources, no currency, and no power over determining fiscal and monetary policy, or foreign policy. It also left the PA with no power over determining citizenship and forced it to be highly dependent on and restricted and regulated by the government of Israel.

From the outset, the Oslo Accords were not aimed at creating a full sovereign state in the WBGS, but rather at creating a 'client state'. The term client state is used by Jamil Hilal and Mushtaq H. Khan to characterize the transfer of selective responsibility by Israel to the

131

PA to ensure political compliance by this authority in the security-first route to Palestinian statehood in the WBGS. The viability of this state depends in the first place on the external power (Israel) that has both the intention of dominating policy-making in the client state and the ability to control the allocation of financial resources necessary for the state's survival (Hilal and Khan 2004). Many conditions observed in the WBGS since the establishment of the PA appear to support the consolidation of a client state.[5] For instance, the PA has played the policing role in the WBGS to protect Israel and the settlers inside the WBGS, and to oppress opponents to the Oslo Accords. In addition, Israel has controlled the finances of the WBGS. This has been achieved through two main mechanisms. First, Israel has the right to collect all taxes on commercial transactions between the WBGS and Israel and between the WBGS and the rest of the world. Under the Oslo Accords and Paris Economic Protocol, signed between Israel and the PLO in 1995, Israel should remit the proceeds of these taxes to the PA, but frequently Israel has suspended or delayed the transfer of money to the PA under the pretext of security concerns (Fjeldstad and Zagha 2004) or as a form of direct pressure on the Palestinian government, as indeed happened when a Hamas government was elected in March 2006. Since the beginning of the second Intifada Israel has suspended (often, now and then, and occasionally) the transfer of all the proceeds from tax collected on behalf of the PA. Second, Israel has the right to interfere in the flow of aid to the WBGS. In many cases Israel has refused to let donors finance the development of agriculture since this would contradict the Israeli policies in the WBGS and require more land to be given to the PA (Alissa and Hilal 2001).

Under the Oslo Accords the PA accepted the principles of a client state. However, it attempted to challenge the realities created by these Accords and to build a developmental state – a goal made impossible by the policies of closure, settlement building and expansion, bypass construction, erection of the wall and control over natural resources. While there are many reasons for the PA to be criticized with regard to the WBGS economy, many of its internal arrangements concerning the development of the economy have been highly constrained by the severe external context. There are three fundamental aspects that need to be assessed in this regard: the development vision of the PA, the management of the PA institutions, and the relationship with the private sector. An assessment of these aspects will serve to illustrate the complex relation between the internal and external contexts and the implications of both of them for the WBGS economy.

Palestinian development plans

There are three fundamental problems that should be taken into consideration in relation to the internal and external contexts. These problems have restricted the PA in managing the development process effectively. First, as mentioned above, PA sovereignty over the WBGS is very limited and the external constraints (represented by Israeli policies) hamper any development arrangements in the WBGS. Second, the political situation has not been stable in the WBGS since the establishment of the PA. Third, the institutional capacity to design and manage the process of development is very constricted in the WBGS and restricted by the ramifications of the Oslo Accords. This problem will be illustrated in more detail in the next section.

Since its establishment, the PA has adopted two main approaches to deal with the economy in the WBGS (see PA 1997, 1998). The first development approach was applied from 1994 to 1999. It was thought that during that period a full sovereign state would emerge in the WBGS as a result of the Oslo Accords. The PA started to design its developmental policies according to this view and different attempts were made to accelerate development. As we will see in the next sections, the outcome of the PA efforts was not satisfactory. On top of the obstacles mentioned above, there was inadequate developmental intervention.

While the development plans designed by the PA included important objectives such as employment generation, building infrastructure, rural development and promoting exports, they suffered from several structural weaknesses. These mainly related to the planning methodology, the assessment of the priorities of the Palestinian people, and implementation procedures. It is argued by the plan designers that they were comprehensive plans developed through a consultation process with the private sector and Non-Governmental Organizations (NGOs) (see PA, 1997, 1998). However, the design of a comprehensive development plan requires more than consultation; it needs an assessment of the real needs and priorities of the society and research on how these issues can be met efficiently. Many studies have addressed these issues and emphasize that the Palestinian Development Plans (PDPs) do not constitute a comprehensive strategy with a long-term development vision. They were not developed through a process of dialogue between

133

different sectors of society, especially the private sector and NGOs; nor were they based on an assessment of the real needs of Palestinian society (DSP 2000; Alissa and Hilal 2001).

The PDPs further lacked specific mechanisms and tools for implementation and monitoring. It seems that the PDPs were merely a list of projects designed to obtain financial assistance from the donor community, and not development plans with long-term vision. This can be seen quite clearly in the Five Year Plan (1999–2003), which replaced the Three Year Plan (1998–2000) (PA 1998). In addition and more importantly the major objectives of the plan were not fully implemented during the planning period. As the next sections will show, whether due to internal or external factors, PA practices during the period were in contradiction with the objectives of these plans, especially in terms of public expenditure and managing the Palestinian economy.

The second approach adopted by the PA in the WBGS has been implemented since the outbreak of the second Intifada in 2000. This approach shows a structural shift in PA policies from promoting development towards a survival strategy to avoid economic, political and institutional collapse. The outbreak of the second Intifada indicated clearly that the national struggle against occupation was far from over. From the outset Israel implemented well thought-out, coherent and systematic policies to destroy the PA and its institutions. This was due to the fact that the PA challenged the role designed for it (client state) in the WBGS by engaging in the national struggle against occupation. Israel's policies forced the Authority to use money extracted from rent and monopoly – which was mainly deposited in secret accounts – not to promote development in the WBGS, but to finance the operation of the PA institutions in order to avoid political and economic collapse.[6]

The PA approach in managing the WBGS economy

There is much evidence to support the argument that the role of the PA in managing the WBGS economy has been characterized by two contradictory policies. On the one hand, the PA adopted an approach to promote investment and to give the lead role to the private sector in encouraging economic development in the WBGS. On the other hand, it maintained a heavy-handed presence in the economy, mainly through state-dominated monopolies personally controlled by individuals high up in the PA bureaucracy.

The promulgation of the Investment Promotion Laws in 1995 and

1998 was one of the major attempts by the PA to promote investment in the WBGS. These laws give tax exemptions for investment projects on the basis of the amount of capital invested and number of workers employed. The Investment Promotion Laws are considered one of the major factors behind the increase in the number of registered companies in the WBGS after 1997. There were 1,841 registered companies in 1999, compared with 1,517 in 1994. New registrations witnessed a decline in 1996 and 1997 (1,269 and 1,198 companies respectively) before rising again in 1998 (1,370). As a result of the second Intifada and policy of closures, investment in the Palestinian economy declined as the number of newly registered companies fell to 1,603 in 2000, compared with 1,841 in 1999.[7]

As for the role of the private sector, the period following the establishment of the PA saw an open dialogue between the public and the private sectors. The objective of this dialogue was to activate the participation of the private sector in developing economic policies and procedures to improve the working environment in the sector. The dialogue between public and private sectors reached a peak in May 2000 through the National Economic Dialogue Conference, which made numerous recommendations for improving the role of the private sector in the Palestinian economy, improving PA efficiency, and strengthening the principles of accountability and transparency (Paltrade 2000).

The real question here is whether these recommendations have been translated into concrete practical steps to have a positive effect on the Palestinian economy and Palestinian people or whether the division of roles between public and private sectors in the economy remain unchanged. Assessment of the extent to which these recommendations have been implemented is beyond the scope of this chapter. Up to 1999 there were no indications that PA involvement in the economy through state monopolies had changed. Despite the fact that it has initiated legislation for promoting investment and creating dialogue with the private sector to give the latter the lead role in the economy, it continues to create trade monopolies over certain essential goods through PA-dominated companies controlled by individuals in the upper of echelons of the PA bureaucracy working in collaboration with Israeli suppliers (Roy 2001a).

These companies have the monopoly over the importation of at least thirteen essential commodities, such as flour, sugar, oil, frozen meat, cigarettes, live animals, cement aggregate, steel, wood, tobacco, and

135

petroleum.[8] These monopolistic practices have hindered free competition in the WBGS economy; weakened the private sector (especially small companies) and resulted in increased prices of basic commodities. For example, between the summer of 1995 and the summer of 1996, the price of a six-kilogram sack of flour rose from NIS 45 to NIS 120. According to Roy, the largest increase from NIS 70 to NIS 120 occurred during the last four months of this period and was directly attributed to the flour monopoly (Roy 2001b).

Using data from the US State Department, Roy indicates that the PA and individuals in senior positions in the Authority have earned hundreds of millions of dollars per year from these monopolies. This revenue effectively constitutes a transfer of income from poorer groups to a new political class with considerable economic power (Roy 2001b). For instance, Mohammed Nasr reported that the Palestinian Telecommunication Company (Paltel), a PA-sponsored monopoly, does not collect telephone bills from governmental institutions and compensates for this loss by overpricing private consumers (Nasr 2004).

Because of internal and external pressures, the PA accepted a reform process to restructure its institutions to reduce monopoly and to prepare for privatization in the WBGS and reduce rents extracted by individuals in senior positions in the PA (IMF 2003). As the next section will show, there is no doubt that the PA institutions need reform in order to increase efficiency in managing the WBGS economy and in meeting the needs and requirements of the Palestinian people in WBGS. However, the objective and motivation behind this forced reform is highly questionable. It has been viewed as a method to restrict the PA's ability to support the national struggle against occupation. The effectiveness of this process is also questionable, since it has been taking place at a time when the WBGS is still under occupation and the PA institutions are on the way to collapse.

Public sector performance

As indicated above, despite the challenges and constraints facing the PA since its establishment and its limited experience as a new authority, it has taken important steps in a number of areas relating to public institutions. It succeeded in establishing the infrastructure of executive institutions, at both national and local level. These institutions provide important services to the public, such as education and health, assistance to poor families and the implementation of infrastructure projects. In addition, following the Palestinian presidential and legislative elections in 1996, the Palestinian Legislative Council (PLC) assumed its role in legislation and supervision. The PLC has passed many social, political and economic laws for organizing the daily life of the Palestinian people and the structural work of different institutions, both governmental and civil.

Despite these achievements, and taking into account the constraints imposed on the PA, the period between 1994 and 2006 provides much evidence of structural weakness and imbalance in the performance of the Authority in terms of what can be achieved. An assessment of this is beyond the scope of this chapter, but two interlinked examples – the management of public employment and the allocation of public expenditure – will serve as illustration.

The PA has relied on public sector employment to alleviate the loss of jobs and the decline in income resulting from the difficult economic conditions in the WBGS (including the restriction on employment of Palestinian workers in Israel). In addition, it has used recruitment in the public sector to integrate those returning from the diaspora into Palestinian society. From 1995 to 2000 the number of employees in PA bodies and ministries more than doubled, equivalent to an annual growth rate of 12.3%. Since 2000, employment in the public sectors has grown at an annual growth rate of 2.6%. By 2003, around 128,000 employees were on the PA budget (World Bank 2004).

The rapid expansion of public sector employment resulted in an increased weight and cost of employment in the PA. The government payroll increased from $304.3m in 1995 to $519m in 1999 and to $871m in 2004, accounting for 61% of total PA current expenditure during that period (World Bank 2004).

This policy of public recruitment is not a healthy solution to the unemployment problem and the decline in income in the WBGS. There are long-term costs associated with creating permanent jobs in the public sector, such as recruitment costs and future pension costs. Efficiency may also suffer through overstaffing and ineffective distribution of jobs (World Bank 1999). In addition, and more importantly, this strategy has reduced policy choices for budget allocation. For instance, the Ministry of Education Plan for the academic years 2000/2001–2004/2005 shows that it needs $1,894m in governmental expenditure. This plan aims to provide primary education to all Palestinian children, improve the quality of formal and informal education, develop education management,

137

and develop the human resources needed for the education sector in the coming years (Ministry of Education, PA, 1999).

The Role of International Aid

Since the signing of the Oslo Accords between the PLO and Israel in 1993, the international donor community has committed itself to supporting the peace process. The central purpose of this support is to deliver a 'peace dividend' to the Palestinian people and boost the public support for the peace process. This support took two main forms. The first has been to promote reconstruction and social and economic development in the WBGS. The second has been to build the capacity of the Palestinian Authority to deliver services and manage the daily lives of the Palestinian people.

This support was viewed by the international donor community as the first step towards the establishment of a Palestinian state through negotiations between Israel and the PLO. The real question is, to what extent were its purposes served, and what is the track record of this aid? What are the challenges that have been facing the international donor community, and what went wrong in the process of assistance to the Palestinian people?

Evidence from the period 1993–2005 reveals that international aid to the Palestinians played a very limited role in both promoting economic development in the WBGS and maintaining the peace process. Up to 2000, the donor community could claim a limited success in promoting economic growth and maintaining the negotiations between Israel and the Palestinians, but without any structural changes in the WBGS economy or in the process of building a viable Palestinian state. An aid effectiveness study conducted by the World Bank, assessing the role of aid in the WBGS since 1993, concluded that 'donor support slowed the overall economic decline, contributed to economic growth, and strengthened key institutions and local capacities. In doing so, donors have contributed to political stability, thus helping to sustain continued Israeli-Palestinian negotiation.' (World Bank 2000: xx).

The main reason for this limited role is twofold. The first is that donors' assistance to the Palestinian people has coincided with severe punishments, policies and measures against the Palestinians in WBGS, including closures, the building of colonial settlements, control over natural resources, and the erection of the separation wall. As shown above, these policies have had a severe socio-economic and political impact on Palestinian society. They have also undermined the development effort of both the PA and the international donor community. More recently the emphasis of international donors and aid agencies has been increasingly directed towards emergency and short term projects to mitigate the impact of the socio-economic and humanitarian crisis in the WBGS and to permit the survival of the PA, instead of towards developmental and institutional building programmes and projects.[9] In 2000, donors' commitments of assistance to the WBGS were US$973m of which 87.5% was allocated to development programmes and projects, and 12.7% to emergency assistance and budget support. By 2002, 83% of total commitments (US$1,527m was allocated to emergency assistance and budget support, and only 13% (US$261m) was allocated to regular development support[10] (World Bank 2004).

In addition, Israeli collective punishments and restrictive policies and measures in the WBGS have complicated the work effort of international aid agencies in the field and their ability to implement projects and deliver assistance in a predictable, timely and cost-effective manner (Le More 2005).

Donors have not taken action or exercised pressure to challenge Israeli policies and to protect the process of state building and economic development in the WBGS. The main excuse for this is that such pressure or action could undermine the peace process. Therefore, no pressure should be exercised on the government of Israel to change their policies and measures. In his assessment of foreign aid and the mistakes of the 1990s, Nigel Roberts, the director of the World Bank in the WBGS, has concluded that 'it is time for a more forthright donor approach to the conflict – one in which the parties are held accountable for the promises they have given to the international community. Today's status quo is not tenable: the large and complex aid effort already in place is unable to halt Palestinian economic and social decline, and only makes strategic sense if seen as a bridge to a period of serious change.' (Roberts 2005: 26).

The history of aid assistance to the Palestinians is notable for its lack of achievement. This evidence suggests that aid cannot be used as a substitute for the political will. In the absence of a viable political settlement, aid has proved a limited tool in promoting fundamental changes in the WBGS economy. The experience of the WBGS indicates that using aid, without having clear mechanisms to achieve its objectives, could even play a counter-productive role (keeping the economy static and maintaining the occupation).

Conclusion

The process of bantustanization has destroyed the possibility of constructing a national economy in the WBGS. In fact it has sliced the economy into different segments, increasing its vulnerability and dependency on Israel. This has led to insufficient growth and to a severe fragmentation of the labour market. The inadequate developmental intervention, mismanagement of the economy and public sector, and centralization of economic and political power have all had a significant impact on development in the WBGS. These features have restricted the ability of the PA to allocate the financial resources for developing strong institutions, build sufficient infrastructure, and deliver efficient services to the Palestinian people. The role of the international donor community in promoting economic development (structural change and economic reform) has been very limited.

Talk about a viable Palestinian economy is irrelevant in the presence of occupation, closures, and the bantustanization process; yet it is imperative to build a national economy in the WBGS in order to provide prosperity for the Palestinian people. The main political and economic arrangements and the viability of the WBGS, in terms of land and natural resources needed for building such an economy, have been shown to be problematic. This also raises questions about the viability of the current Palestinian national project; that is, the two-state solution, where the Palestinians establish their state within the 1967 borders of the occupied territories.

Notes

1 The term 'de-development' is used by Sara Roy, to represent the systematic destruction of an indigenous economy by a dominant power (Roy 2001).

2 It is important to mention that policies of collective punishment such as curfews, restrictions on movements of people and goods and closing public institutions, especially schools and universities, have been taking place since 1967, but since the 1990s these policies have been more systematic and institutionalized.

3 Israel has taken three main steps to gain control over water sources. In 1965 it destroyed the joint Syrian-Jordanian water project on the Yarmouk River. In 1967 Israel achieved control over the Sea of Galilee and implemented the Israeli water law in the occupied territories. Under this law, no wells may be dug without Israeli approval. From 1967–1995 a number of measures/laws were

passed by Israel, which aimed at developing West Bank water use in accordance with Israeli state interests. A total of only 23 new Palestinian wells have been dug in the WBGS since 1967, while the growth of settlement building has continued essentially unabated (Becker, Tabari and Zeitoun January 2004).

4 The term 'bantustanization' was originally used in the South African apartheid literature to refer to the development of the reserves set aside for African occupation into self-governing states, colloquially known as 'bantustans'. In this system, the whites retained exclusive rights in their own part of the country, where any native African (officially known as 'Bantu') was regarded only as a visitor and could only enter the white areas with a permit (National Land Committee 1990: 2 and Hill 1964: 1; see also Posel 1991). The permit policy in South Africa was similar to that of Israel, which has been imposed on the Palestinians since 1991 with the start of closures. Although the motivation behind the Israeli policy in the WBGS is different from that of white South Africa, the economic outcome is similar. While the objective of the Israeli policy in the WBGS is primarily political (particularly control over land and displaced Palestinian people) but has severe economic realities, the aim of white South Africans was to enforce economic control and then achieve political supremacy over the blacks. The main economic outcome of the bantustans in South Africa was the destruction of the indigenous economy and freeing of native Africans to be a source of cheap labour for white areas; the main economic outcome of the Israeli policy in the WBGS since 1967 has also been the destruction of the Palestinian economy and the use of the WBGS as a cheap source of labour as well as of raw material (see Chapter 2: 20–41 in Hill 1964 for more details on the economics of the bantustans).

5 Hilal and Khan suggest that in addition to the client state, there are other types of state such as 'predatory', 'fragmented clientelist' and 'developmental' that can be used to characterize the outcomes of the Oslo Accords (Hilal and Khan 2004). There is some evidence in the WBGS that supports the consolidation of these categories, but the client state has better explanatory value than other types of state. Assessing the nature and viability of these states in the WBGS is beyond the scope of this chapter.

6 A comprehensive assessment of state formation in the WBGS (Hilal and Khan 2004) shows that rent seeking and monopoly are outcomes of the Oslo Accord.

7 The sources of information for the number of registered companies in the WBGS for the period 1994–2000 is the General Unit for Policies and Statistics (Ministry of Trade and Commerce, PA) for the number of companies registered in the West Bank, and the Registration Unit (Ministry of Justice) for the number of companies registered in the Gaza Strip.

8 According to the US State Department these commodities are as many as 25.

9 For comprehensive assessments of the impact of Israeli policies and measures on donor community efforts and programmes in the WBGS, see Le More 2005.

10 These amounts exclude support to UNRWA's regular budget.

141

References

Alissa, S. and J. Hilal (2001) *Development Environment in the West Bank and Gaza Strip*, Background Paper for Palestine Human Development Report 2000/2001, Ramallah, Development Studies Programme at Birzeit University (Arabic).

Becker, A., S. Tabari and M. Zeitoun (2004) *Water in Palestine – Scarcity, Inequality, Conflict*, Jerusalem, Applied Research Institute.

Benvenisti, M. (1984) *The West Bank Data Project: A Survey of Israel's Policies*. Washington, DC, American Enterprise Institute for Public Policy Research.

Bishara, A. (1995) 'Bantustanisation or Binationalism?' An interview with Azmi Bishara by Graham Usher, *Journal of Race and Class*, Vol. 37, No. 2, pp. 43–9.

— (1999) 'Bantustanisation or Binationalism?', in Usher, G. (ed.), *Dispatches from Palestine: The Rise and Fall of the Oslo Peace Process*, London: Pluto Press.

Development Studies Programme (DSP) (2000) *Palestine Human Development Report (1998/1999)*, Ramallah: Birzeit University.

Fjeldstad, O. H., and A. Zagha (2004) 'Taxation and State Formation in Palestine 1994–2000', Chapter 6 in M. Khan, G. Giacaman and I. Amundsen (eds), *State Formation in Palestine: Viability and Governance during a Social Transformation*, London: RoutledgeCurzon.

Hilal, J., and M. Khan (2004) 'State Formation under the PNA: Potential Outcomes and their Viability', Chapter 2 in M. Khan, *State Formation*.

Hill, C. R. (1964) *Bantustans: The Foundation of South Africa*, London: Oxford University Press.

IMF (Internal Monetary Fund) (2003) *West Bank and Gaza: Economic Performance and Reform Under Conflict Conditions*, Washington DC: IMF.

Keating, M., A. Le More and R. Lowe (eds) (2005) *Aid, Diplomacy and Facts on the Ground: The Case of Palestine*, London: Chatham House.

Khan, M., G. Giacaman and I. Amundsen (eds) (2004) *State Formation in Palestine: Viability and Governance during a Social Transformation*, London: RoutledgeCurzon.

Le More, A., (2005) 'Are "Realities on the Ground" Compatible with the International State-Building and Development Agenda?', Chapter 3 in M. Keating, A. Le More and R. Lowe (eds) (2005).

Ministry of Education, Palestinian National Authority (1999) *The Five-Year Education Development Plan 2000/2001–2004/2005*, Ramallah: Ministry of Education.

Nasr, M. (2004) 'Monopolies and the PNA', Chapter 5 in *State Formation*.

Negotiation Support Unit, Adam Smith Institute (2004) 'Israel's "Security" Wall: Another Land Grab', Fact Sheet, Ramallah: Adam Smith Institute.

Office of the United Nations Special Co-coordinator (UNSCO) (1997) *Economic and Social Conditions in the West Bank and Gaza Strip: Quarterly Report (April 1997)*. Gaza, UNSCO.

Office of the United Nations Special Co-ordinator (UNSCO) (2001) 'The Impact on the Palestinian Economy of Confrontation, Border Closures and Mobility Restrictions', 1 October 2000–30 September 2001, Gaza: UNSCO.

Palestinian Authority (PA) (1997) *Palestinian Development Plan 1998–2000*, Ramallah, Palestinian National Authority.

— (1998) *Palestinian Development Plan 1999–2003*, Ramallah: Palestinian National Authority.

Paltrade (Palestine Trade Centre) (2000) 'Conference Conclusions and Private Sector Recommendations', Ramallah: National Economic Dialogue Conference.

Roberts, N. (2005) 'Hard Lessons from Oslo: Foreign Aid and the Mistakes of the 1990s', Chapter 2 in M. Keating.

Roy, S. (2001a) 'Palestinian Society and Economy: The Continued Denial of Possibility', *Journal of Palestine Studies*, Vol. 30, No. 4 (Summer 2001), pp. 5–20.

— (2001b) *The Gaza Strip: The Political Economy of De-Development*, Washington, DC: Institute for Palestine Studies.

Salim, T., and R. Hammami (2000) *Beyond Oslo: The New Uprising*, Ramallah: *Middle East Report*, No. 217.

Shavit, A., *Ha'aretz* (April 2001) 'An Interview with Ariel Sharon', Jerusalem: *Ha'aretz*, 5/12/2004.

The Palestinian Independent Commission for Citizens Rights (PICCR) (2001) *Seventh Annual Report*, Ramallah, PICCR.

Tofakji, K. (2001) 'Israeli Settlement in Palestinian Territories: Reality and Problems', Jerusalem: Arab Studies Society.

Usher, G. (ed.) (1999) *Dispatches from Palestine: The Rise and Fall of the Oslo Peace Process*, London: Pluto Press.

World Bank (1999) *West Bank and Gaza: Strengthening Public Sector Management: Social and Economic Development Group*, Middle East and North Africa Region, World Bank.

— The Secretariat of the Ad Hoc Liaison Committee (2000) *Aid Effectiveness in the West Bank and Gaza*, Washington, DC: World Bank.

— (2004) *Four Years – Intifada, Closures and Palestinian Economic Crisis: An Assessment*, Washington, DC: World Bank.

7 | The transformation of the Palestinian environment

JAD ISAAC AND OWEN POWELL

Introduction

The two-state solution envisages a sovereign Palestinian state living in peaceful coexistence with Israel and remains widely accepted as the necessary means to resolve the Palestinian-Israeli conflict. This outcome, however, is arguably dependent on the ability of a Palestinian state to be viable. The notion of 'viability' can be defined as a state's ability to exist, function and to be sustainable while possessing enough resources to cater for the needs of its people. According to Bossell (2001), viability can be assessed by analysing the different system components that contribute to society's overall function. These components are complex and dynamic and represent the broad spectrum of human and physical resources. Institutions, social organizations, the economy, financial resources, infrastructure, human factors and the physical environment are some of them. Bossel indicates that these components vary in their overall contribution to the wider system and that viability emerges from the interactions of the component systems, which contribute to the whole by being individually viable.

This rhetoric of a viable Palestinian state does not indicate, for example, the size, or political and socio-demographic parameters of such an entity. The PLO resolutions define the Palestinian state as comprising all the Palestinian areas that were occupied by Israel in 1967: that is, the Gaza Strip and the West Bank including East Jerusalem. However, Israeli governments have come up with a wide range of scenarios and options for defining what could constitute, from their perspective, a Palestinian state, which comprises 40%–70% of the Palestinian area mentioned. In any case, the available environmental resources and their management constitute a critical factor in determining the viability of the two-state solution.

The environment plays an important role in determining viability as it provides the physical context in which society exists and determines the extent to which society is sustainable. Environmental properties constrain development possibilities on all spatial scales limiting the extent of physical, technological and biological processes (Bossel 2001). Possibilities are further limited by the resource constraints of the environment: available space, waste absorption capacity of soils, rivers, atmosphere and oceans; and the availability of renewable and non-renewable resources (Bossel 2001; Ayala-Carcedo and Gonzalez-Barros 2005).

The status of the environment in Palestine has received less attention in the continuing debate regarding the Palestinian-Israeli conflict despite its fundamental role in the successful realization of the two-state solution. Limited resources, poor management and unsustainable practices have resulted in the radical transformation of the Palestinian environment, degradation of its natural ecosystems and depletion of its resources (Isaac et al. 1997; Isaac and Ghanayem, 2002; Isaac et al. 2004). This, however, has been exacerbated by unilateral policies conducted by the state of Israel to exploit and exert complete control over Palestine's natural resources for its own purposes and benefits.

To assess the viability of a Palestinian state it is necessary to consider the fundamental and co-dependent relations that exist between the environment and society, and their capacity for sustainable development. This chapter will discuss the major characteristics of environmental change in Palestine, analysing them in relation to their potential impact on the viability and sustainability of a Palestinian state. It will seek to illustrate that the current environmental, socio-demographic and geo-political conditions will render any Palestinian state unviable, highly unstable and serving the geo-political interests of Israel, and thus emphasizing the need for Palestinian leadership to re-evaluate the negotiation process to ensure a lasting peace.

The transformation and status of the Palestinian environment

The power imbalances between Israel and Palestine have enabled Israel to appropriate Palestinian land and other resources virtually unchallenged and according to its own narrow interests (Morag 2001; Falah 2004; Jarbawi 2005; Schnell 2005). The borders of a future Palestinian state and the status of its environment will most probably be determined by Israel's unilateral actions over the coming years as it continues its occupation and unilateral 'disengagement' or 'convergence'. Subsequently, the viability and sustainability of a Palestinian state will

145

be profoundly influenced by the geo-political and environmental conditions Palestine will inherit.

Data concerning the current status of the environment in the West Bank and Gaza indicates that there are a number of core environmental and socio-economic issues that will affect the viability of a state. These include population growth, lack of space, depletion of water resources, solid waste disposal, deterioration in water quality, land degradation and the level of geographical continuity between Palestinian areas determined by the segregation wall, checkpoints, settlements and bypass roads (Isaac et al. 1997; Falah 2004; Isaac et al. 2005, 2005a; Isaac and Hrimat 2005; ARIJ Monitoring Settlements and GIS Units 2005). Many of these issues intersect and influence each other in terms of their impact on viability and sustainability.

Population growth is widely recognized in the literature in terms of its impact on global environmental sustainability (Salwasser 1990; Dilworth 1994; Hinterberger 2001). The case is no different in Palestine whereby population growth is placing additional pressures on the environment to absorb waste and support the existent population. Developing countries such as Palestine face major dilemmas as industrial and social development necessitate additional environmental pressures (Spangenberg 2004).

Under present growth rates the Palestinian population can be ex-

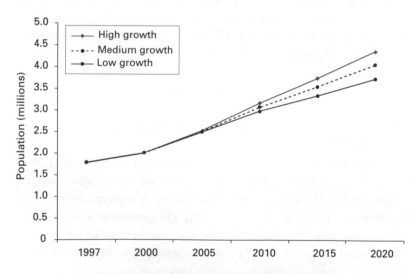

Figure 7.1 Population growth in the West Bank
(*source:* Isaac et al. 2005a)

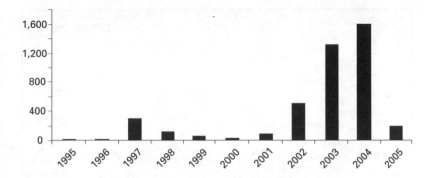

Figure 7.2 House demolition in the occupied territories
(*source*: Isaac et al. 2005a)

pected to expand considerably over the next decades with resultant environmental impacts. Figure 7.1 indicates three projection models of population growth in the West Bank for the coming decades: low, medium and high.[1]

Current population growth contributes to Palestine's chronic lack of space due to Israeli land restrictions and annexation. In the West Bank, over 50% of the land is closed or has been confiscated by Israel. Population density varies greatly from one region to another. However, urban areas which are the focal point for a large sector of the population suffer the most (Isaac et al. 1997). The limited area for urban expansion, the high land prices and the difficulty of obtaining a building licence from the Israeli authorities, especially in the areas planned for colonization activities, have forced many Palestinians to build on their own land without having building licences. These houses are then subjected to demolition by the Israeli authorities in attempts to control Palestinian demographics (ARIJ 2005; Isaac et al. 2005a). Figure 7.2 indicates the number of house demolitions between 1995 and 2005.

In regions such as the Gaza Strip, population density has reached critical levels. In 2005 Israel withdrew from this region as part of its unilateral disengagement strategy; however, it still maintains effective control over the Gaza Strip through control of its borders and vital infrastructure. The Gaza Strip is entirely enclosed by Israeli fences and security buffer zones, preventing the urban expansion and out-migration necessary to relieve the population density crisis (Isaac et al. 2004; Falah 2005). Under the three growth rate projection models, population densities will continue to rise.

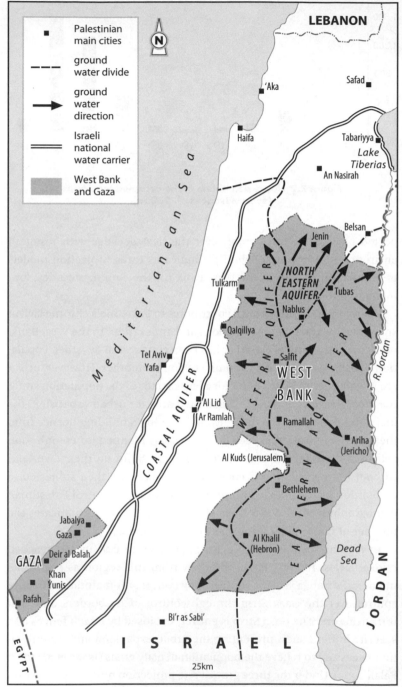

Figure 7.3 Palestinian ground and surface water resources (adapted from ARIJ GIS Unit 2006)

TABLE 7.1 Comparison of natural resources accessible to Israelis and Palestinians

Indicator	Israel	Palestine	Ratio
Population (millions)	6	3	2:1
Total area (million dunum)	21	6	3.5 :1
Accessible area (m dunum)	24.6	2.4	12:1
Irrigated area (m dunums)	2.18	0.2	11:01
Contribution of agriculture to GDP	1.80%	12%	1:7
Water consumption (MCM)	1960	286	11:1

Source: ARIJ Database 2005.

Water resources in Palestine consist of both surface and ground water. Surface water in Palestine consists of the Jordan River and intermittent streams. The Jordan, however, is the only source of permanent surface water in Palestine. The majority of ground water in Palestine is in the West Bank and can be divided into three major aquifers: the western, eastern and north-eastern aquifers. Ground water in Gaza is derived from the western coastal aquifer. Figure 7.3 indicates ground and surface water resources in Palestine.

Unsustainable utilization and management of both surface and ground water in Palestine have led to their depletion and deterioration in quality (Isaac et al. 1997; Isaac et al. 1998; Froukh 2003; Isaac et al. 2005). Current extraction from ground water is exceeding recharge, and ground water levels are decreasing rapidly. Similar conditions exist for the Jordan river where upstream extraction has dramatically reduced flow. Depletion of water resources is largely due to Israeli consumption, which utilizes more than 80% of Palestinian ground water and denies Palestinians their rightful utilization of the Jordan river (Isaac et al. 1997). Israel allocates Palestinians 93 million cubic metres per year for industrial use, and 153 million cubic metres per year for agricultural use, leaving per capita consumption for domestic use at less than 30 cubic metres per year. Settlers in the Occupied Territories are consuming Palestinian water at the rate of more than 100 million cubic metres per year. On an annual per capita basis Israelis consume more than four times as much water as Palestinians (Isaac et al. 1997, 2004). Table 7.1 indicates the ratio of population and water consumption between Israelis and Palestinians. Agriculture contributes a higher level of GDP to the Palestinian economy but does not receive equitable water allocation owing to the Israeli occupation.

Water quality in Palestine has deteriorated owing to a number of factors. Management of waste water has been neglected throughout Palestine, and in many cases it is discharged into the environment without prior treatment (Isaac et al. 1997, 2004, 2005). Municipal and industrial waste water contains a variety of nutrients, chemicals and heavy metals which contaminate ground and surface water. Israeli settlements exacerbate this problem as they generate large amounts of untreated waste water which is discharged into Palestinian areas (Isaac et al. 2005). Ground water contamination in Palestine is further associated with agriculture. The widespread and excessive use of fertilizers, pesticides and other farm chemicals contaminate aquifers during heavy rains, where they are leached from the soil (Isaac et al. 1997, 1998). Unless action is taken soon, major health problems for the Palestinian population can be expected.

Water quality in the Gaza Strip has reached critical levels due to high population densities, subsequent environmental impacts and extraction of ground water. In Gaza, ground water has been over-pumped, which has resulted in lowering the water table below sea level and saline water intrusion in many areas (Isaac et al. 1997). In addition to this, waste water from deficient sewerage networks has contaminated ground water. Nitrate concentrations provide an insight into the water quality crisis in the Gaza Strip. Concentrations have reached high levels exceeding the rates internationally recommended by the WHO for drinking purposes (50 mg/ l). Nitrate levels are typically above recommended levels reaching in excess of 400 mg/l.

The disposal of solid wastes in Palestine is a major environmental hazard as it is generally not controlled, allowing dumping sites to accumulate a variety of hazardous chemicals which contaminate soil and ground water (Isaac et al. 1997, 2005). Military operations and curfews in Palestinian areas have contributed by denying citizens freedom of movement, forcing them to dispose of wastes in illegal open sites. Israeli settlers living in the West Bank exacerbate Palestine's solid waste problem. The 450,000 Israeli settlers living in the West Bank, including East Jerusalem, generate 471 tonnes of solid waste a day, 80% of which is dumped on Palestinian land and dumping sites (Isaac et al. 2005). Urbanization and population growth has made solid waste disposal a significant environmental concern highlighting the need for recycling and solid waste facilities. Lack of available space for municipal planning due to Israeli land restrictions dictates that dumping sites are invariably close to wells and urban centres.

Land degradation may be attributed to a variety of factors which have arisen from unsustainable land management. The most significant factors include soil erosion, desertification, salinization and soil contamination (Isaac et al. 1997). Soil erosion is the most destructive phenomenon to soils as it involves the loss not only of valuable nutrients but soil particles themselves. Soil erosion is predominant in regions of intensive field cultivation where the removal of biomass and ploughing exposes the soils to erosive processes (Isaac et al. 1997). Soil erosion is most common in the mountainous regions of the West Bank, where, in addition to steep slopes, soils are subjected to heavy rainfall. There is a wide variety of means to reduce soil erosion in cultivated areas, including contour ploughing, digging grassed cut-off drains, planting wind breaks, retaining biomass residue after cultivation, and utilizing sloped pastures for other agricultural activities (Isaac et al. 1997; Kort et al. 1998) These practices are often not implemented in Palestine due to lack of council initiative and community awareness.

Overgrazing by goats and sheep is one of the principal causes of soil erosion and desertification in Palestine (Isaac et al. 1997). Available pastures are severely limited, due to the growth of Palestinian cities as well as land restrictions imposed by Israel, leading to the concentration of grazing in particular areas. Intensive grazing reduces plant cover and trampling compacts the soil, increasing rates of erosion. Salinization is a major factor contributing to the degradation of agricultural land. Due to their dependence on ground water, Palestinian farmers must irrigate their crops with water that often contains high levels of minerals. Salinization occurs when water containing minerals is carried to the root zone. Most of the water returns to the atmosphere through transpiration, while salts remain in the soil. Salinity and toxic build up in irrigated areas can cause lands to be entirely unproductive (Isaac et al. 1997; Isaac et al. 1998).

The presence of checkpoints, settlements, the segregation barrier and bypass roads constitute perhaps the greatest transformation of the Palestinian environment. Many of these activities have led to the destruction of Palestinian assets such as orchards and arable land. Until 2004, up to 45,000 fruit trees were uprooted for the segregation wall alone (ARIJ Monitoring Settlements and GIS Units 2005). However, by far the greatest impacts have been related to socio-economic factors deriving from the fragmentation of the environment and the compartmentalization of Palestinian areas into isolated cantons.

The construction of the Israeli infrastructure in the Palestinian areas occupied in 1967 requires the confiscation of land through 'legal proceedings'. The primary military order used to legitimize the confiscation of Palestinian land is Military Order 58 of 1967, known as the Absentee Property Law. The Military Order transfers lands and properties of absentee Palestinians to the Civil Administration. In addition to this, in 1969 the Civil Administration issued Military Order 321, which gave the military the power to confiscate land for public services. Thus 'public' works in the Palestinian territory are inevitably those that benefit the Jewish colonies and bypass roads. Figure 7.4 indicates rates of land confiscation under the Israeli occupation.

The growth of colonies is mainly geared to the formation of blocks; i.e. they grow outwards and towards each other. Successive Israeli governments have encouraged the development of specific blocks more than others, which enables the linking of Israeli colonies and the enclosing of Palestinian areas (Isaac et al. 2004). In June 2004, the Israeli authorities announced the construction of a new Israeli settlement in Al Walaja village north-west of Bethlehem. The plan will involve the construction of Givat Yael settlement on 2,000 dunums (1 dunum = 0.1 hectares) of Palestinian land. Combining with other expanded colonies,

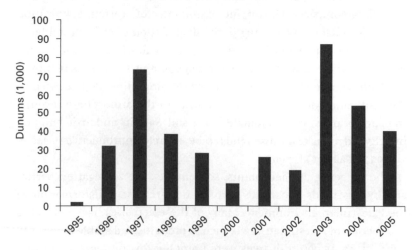

Figure 7.4 Israeli land confiscation in the occupied territories
(*source*: Isaac at al. 2005a)

TABLE 7.2 Checkpoints, roadblocks, wall gates and trenches in the West Bank 2006

District	Check-point	Earth mound	Observation tower	Permanent checkpoint	Planned tunnel	Road gate	Road block	Tunnel	Agricultural gate	Sum
Al Khalil (Hebron)	8	123	11	2	3	18	16	1	0	182
Al Quds (Jerusalem)	8	13	0	0	0	2	4	2	0	29
Ariha (Jericho)	5	4	4	0	0	0	2	0	0	15
Bethlehem	6	15	8	1	2	3	2	7		44
Tulkarm	2	11	2	1	0	1	3	1	11	32
Tubas	2	0	0	0	0	1	0	0	1	4
Salfit	3	8	3	0	1	2	2	5	1	25
Ramallah	5	20	9	3	1	11	15	6	0	70
Qalqiliya	1	2	1	0	0	1	2	1	15	23
Jenin	3	0	5	0	0	3	0	0	10	21
Nablus	7	40	7	0	4	7	7	0	1	73
Sum	50	236	50	7	11	49	53	23	39	518

Source: ARIJ Monitoring Settlements Unit 2006.

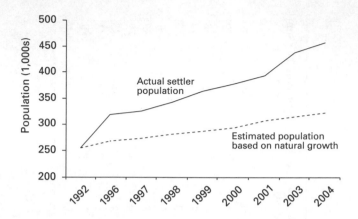

Figure 7.5 Population growth in Jewish colonies (*source:* ARIJ Monitoring Settlements Unit 2005)

this settlement will physically complete the ring of settlements that separates Jerusalem from the rest of the West Bank and encircles Bethlehem (ARIJ Monitoring Settlements and GIS Units 2005).

Since the Oslo Accords, construction of housing units has increased in both existing and new Israeli colonies in the Occupied Palestinian Territories (OPT). The Israeli government offers significant tax incentives to Israeli settlers and this has contributed to the growth of colonies in the West Bank. Figure 7.5 indicates the population growth of settlers in the West Bank compared to levels which could be expected under natural population growth within Israel.

Checkpoints constitute another form of fragmentation and often consist of permanent or temporary road blocks placed in Palestinian areas to control or restrict the flow of movement. Many checkpoints, such as Kalandia checkpoint outside Ramallah, are similar to international borders, whereby Palestinians must have identification cards in order to pass through. In addition to checkpoints, Israeli authorities utilize a wide range of other methods by which to restrict and control movement of Palestinians, including roadblocks, observation towers, earth mounds, trenches, and agricultural gates (Table 7.2).

Bypass roads were created by the Israeli government to link colonies with each other and with Israel proper. The Israeli army controls the bypass roads and enforces a 50–75 metre buffer zone on each side of the road, in which no Palestinian construction is allowed. The construction of bypass roads commonly occurs along the perimeter of Palestinian

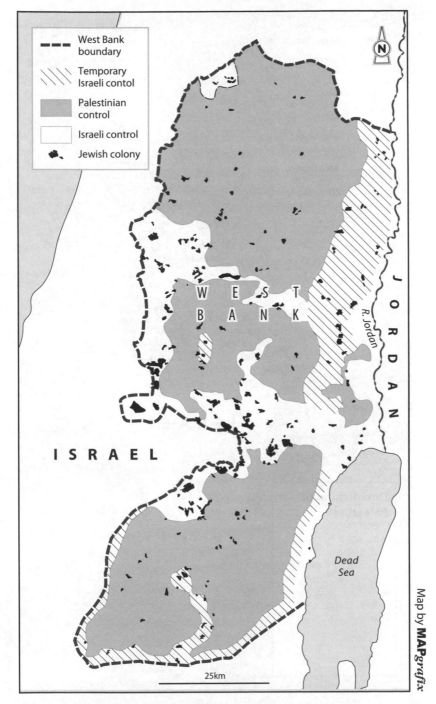

Figure 7.6 Final status solution proposed by Israel 2000
(*source*: *Al-Quds* Newspaper 2000)

Figure 7.7 Physical dismemberment of the Palestinian territories
(*source*: ARIJ GIS Unit 2006)

built-up areas (Isaac et al. 2004). In the major towns bypass roads form asphalt boundaries that limit the expansion and development of Palestinian communities.

Construction of the segregation barrier is a fundamental component of Israel's geo-political strategy. While the Israeli government declared the barrier a security measure, its construction has clearly been shown to be part of Israel's 'land grab' policy. In 2005, the Israeli government published a revised plan whereby the wall will run for 683 km in the West Bank. Only 138 km (20.2% of the total length) runs on the Green Line (ARIJ Monitoring Settlements and GIS Units 2005). The wall dips significantly into Palestinian territory dividing Palestinian communities, annexing land and appropriating vital resources. The segregation wall encloses 98 Israeli settlements accommodating 83% of the Israeli settler population and 55 Palestinian localities (ARIJ Monitoring Settlements and GIS Units 2005). The wall has effectively become the de facto boundary of Israel/Palestine.

The impact of fragmentation on a future state was already apparent during the 2000 Camp David talks. Palestinian negotiators were offered approximately 65% of the West Bank on a discontinuous land mass. The proposed state would be enclosed by Israel and have no international boundaries. The resulting Palestinian enclaves would be completely surrounded by Israel and movement to and from these areas would be dependent upon Israeli approval. The bulk of Jerusalem would remain under Israeli control, with the exception of a few peripheral Palestinian neighbourhoods (Figure 7.6).

Since the failure of the Camp David talks the Israeli government has been increasingly moving away from a negotiated settlement with the Palestinians towards unilateral actions. The broad elements of the Israeli ambitions as stated recently are: no return to 1967 borders; Jerusalem remains under Israeli control; the segregation wall becomes the new border for Israel; and six settlement blocks within the West Bank will be retained and annexed to Israel (Ariel, Modiin, Givat Zeev, Gush Etzion, Maleh Adumin and Hebron blocks). According to the Israeli statements up to 45% of the West Bank can be expected to be annexed by Israel. Figure 7.7 indicates the likely fragmentation of a Palestinian state as well as the significant loss of the Jordan valley, which is a major source of Palestine's agricultural production.

Requirements for viability

In terms of viability, a Palestinian state should be as large as possible, to incorporate enough natural resources to serve its population. Ideally it should consist of the entire West Bank (including Jerusalem) and Gaza Strip. While the final outcomes of the two-state solution are unknown, unilateral actions by Israel creating facts on the ground have effectively made this an unlikely scenario. The 2006 elections in Israel brought to power Kadima, whose main political platform is to define the final borders of the state of Israel taking in and annexing as much Palestinian land as possible. This will leave the Palestinian population with as little land as possible, and living in fragmented 'bantustans' connected by a complex system of roads and tunnels.

Assuming a two-state solution is implemented, an independent Palestinian state will exist in a unique political and social context presenting unique challenges, which it must face, and highlighting certain requirements for viability. Requirements for viability may be reduced to the following issues: environmental sovereignty, sustainable development, economic viability, sufficient natural resources, improvements in social infrastructure and stable democratic government.

Environmental sovereignty will be a necessary requirement in order to achieve effective social planning. Without control over natural resources Palestine will be unable to implement the comprehensive environmental management necessary for sustainable development. The capacity to foster economic growth and social development, while preserving the environment and natural resources, will be crucial for the long-term success of a Palestinian state.

Economic viability will be necessary to ensure genuine independence as well as the ability to adapt to changing social and political conditions. Since its occupation of the West Bank and Gaza, Israel has partially integrated the Palestinian economy with its own. While Palestinians initially benefited from this, the economic relationship has been characterized by an overwhelming Israeli dominance of the Palestinian economy. The majority of Palestinian goods and services are currently provided by Israel, including vital infrastructure such as water. Palestinians pay inflated prices for these products not representative of their current level of development (Allen 2001).

Prior to the second Intifada, unskilled Palestinians further relied upon Israel for employment. This benefited Israel greatly as a source of cheap labour. However, the inherent risk of this dependency has been shown by the current conflict, whereby the Israeli authorities have been effectively able to shut down the Palestinian economy by preventing access to Israel and imposing internal travel restrictions. Dependence on monetary contributions from donor states also creates economic uncertainty in the Palestinian economy. The recent Hamas victory and subsequent threats by the international community to cut funding has further shown the unsustainability of Palestine's lack of economic independence.

For economic growth, relative self-sufficiency and food security, the availability of natural resources will be a key factor. The availability of land and water, for instance, will be critical in determining the viability and success of all sectors of the economy. For example, providing greater access to water would have significant benefits for the rural economy. This process would increase GDP, help to alleviate the current employment crisis and assist in promoting self-sufficiency, reducing dependence on Israeli and other food imports. The rural economy could also assist in the absorption of refugees likely to return following the establishment of a state. Economic viability in Palestine will also be greatly assisted by sovereignty over borders to engage in foreign trade as well as access to both sea and airports in Gaza.

Tourism has high potential for growth in Palestine and could further contribute to economic self-sufficiency. However, access to the Dead Sea and holy sites will be necessary. Dead Sea tourism and beauty product manufacture have generated large amounts of revenue for Israeli tourism, which needs to be shared with a Palestinian state. Palestinian holy sites, such as the Church of the Nativity, the Haram Al Sharif and Jacob's Well in Nablus, also have major tourism potential that have been impeded by the continued Israeli occupation.

A viable Palestinian state will need to improve social infrastructure as a modern state requires a robust, healthy and adaptive society with the necessary skills base for development (Bossel 2001). Public infrastructure needs upgrading, particularly municipal waste disposal, telecommunications, water, health, education and electricity, as well as roads and public transport. A Palestinian state will also need to address major aspects of inequality in its society, including the alleviation of poverty which is disproportionately experienced by refugees and citizens living in the Gaza Strip region. An independent Palestinian state will also need to address the potential for domestic political fragmentation arising from the geographical separation between the West Bank and Gaza. The existing geographical division could have the potential to widen the social and economic gaps that already exist between the two regions, risking national division.

The return of displaced persons and refugees from the diaspora who choose to return to Palestine once a state is established will place additional strain on the already over-stretched resources and ability to process waste. The influx of refugees will also require the massive task of providing employment, services and housing. The ability to improve the social well-being of Palestinians will rest largely on the availability of natural resources and sustainable economic growth to pay for services and provide job opportunities. The current lack of job opportunities has significant impact on the Palestinian economy and society as it encourages the immigration of skilled Palestinian workers who will be vital for the functioning of a successful state.

Effective democratic governance will be necessary to provide security which is considered a central component for viability (see Brinkerhoff 2005; RAND 2005). Following the establishment of a Palestinian state significant distrust between the Israeli and Palestinian leaderships is likely to continue. Subversive action taken by Palestinians opposed to Israel's unilateral impositions will have the real potential to derail the peace process. Given Israel's historical stance on security, any actions taken by Palestinians will be likely to provoke retaliation and resurrect the conflict.

Discussion

The capacity for a Palestinian state to be viable will be affected by a variety of environmental constraints which have arisen due to environmental mismanagement and Israeli unilateralism. The Palestinian Authority has not focused enough attention on the environment due to the immediate political challenges it faces from the second Intifada and Israeli occupation. Limited public funds, destruction of infrastructure and the lack of environmental sovereignty have all impeded efforts towards environmental sustainability. Israeli unilateralism exacerbates environmental constraints towards viability and sustainability through exploitation and appropriation of vital Palestinian resources.

The geo-political ambitions of Israel can be analysed in direct relation to Zionist aims to secure strategic advantage, provide high standards of living for Israelis, as well as to accommodate large numbers of immigrants for the purposes of creating an ethnically Jewish state

(Morag 2001; Falah 2005). The policy of 'unilateral disengagement' has come to be adopted following two violent Intifadas which have forced the Zionist political elite to rethink its strategies in the 1967-occupied territories. Prior to the first Intifada the Israeli government was opposed to the concept of an independent Palestinian state (Reuveny 2005). However, with the increasing costs and difficulties associated with the occupation, the two-state solution has been assimilated into the Zionists' strategy to maximize their control over Palestinian land. The demographic realities on the ground further make this necessary. Israel cannot continue to deny equal rights and services to a portion of its territory's population on the basis of ethnicity, without this appearing as a system of apartheid (Yiftachel 2005). The only way for Israel to resist both democratizing pressures and the moral dilemma of racial discrimination is to exclude Palestinians physically and declare that they have a 'state' of their own.

Falah (2005) further supports the view that Israel has been using the second Intifada to dismantle the public and private Palestinian space vital for building territorial continuity and sovereignty (see also Graham 2003). Such spatial engineering is geared towards ensuring an outcome to Israel's overwhelming advantage in future negotiations over the outstanding permanent status issues and to eliminate any potential for state viability and polity.

Effective management of the environment and capacity for sustainable development will be impeded by a variety of factors. Primarily population growth is likely to exceed Palestine's ability to absorb and process waste, which is already at a critical level. The imperative for industrial development and improving standards of living will also place additional pressure on an already over-stretched environment on the verge of collapse. Fragmentation of the Palestinian environment will further prevent effective environmental management. Israeli and Palestinian cooperation will be vital to promote sustainable development, however; the division of Palestine into numerous cantons separated by Israeli territory will create a complex matrix of bureaucratic structures and functions that will be difficult to coordinate.

The capacity for a viable and sustainable Palestinian economy will be primarily impeded by deficient resources, lack of space, compartmentalization and Israeli control of national borders. Lack of water and urban space will constrict the development of Palestinian industry on all levels. Furthermore, lack of water resources will maintain the

161

dependence of a Palestinian state on Israeli infrastructure; increasing water scarcity may also increase water rates, placing an additional burden on the Palestinian economy.

Deficient water resources coupled with the scarcity of farming land will restrict the options of the rural economy. Fragmentation of land in Palestine will ensure the high cost of transport and the free flow of goods, while Israeli control of borders will prevent the Palestinian state from engaging in independent trade. The loss of the Jordan valley as both Palestine's agricultural heartland and access to Dead Sea tourism will be another factor hindering economic potential. Denying Palestinians access to Jerusalem as both their economic and cultural centre will further undermine the potential for viability, statehood and polity.

The ability to improve social infrastructure will be determined primarily by the high probability of economic failure. Vital areas such as health and education are likely to remain underfunded, while the lack of job opportunities will encourage the continued emigration of skilled Palestinians. Increased population growth will place further pressure on the central authority to provide basic services and manage human waste. It can be expected that increased population densities, coupled with an inability to manage waste solid and water, will lead to significant population health risks similar to the current situation in Gaza. In addition to this, population density and unemployment will further contribute to an already unstable and volatile society.

The effectiveness and development of political democracy will be impeded by fragmentation, the eradication of the possibility for statehood, and stagnation of the economy. Geographical fragmentation will have profound social impacts, dislocating communities and impeding public administration, while economic stagnation will limit public funds and the ability to invest and assist in economic development.

The current scenario clearly indicates that under current conditions a Palestinian state cannot be viable or sustainable. Such a state would require the indefinite support of donor countries to prevent a major humanitarian crisis. This raises questions as to the fundamental credibility of the two-state solution. As the issue stands now, the two-state solution will ensure that the Palestinian 'state' will be independent in name only and effectively exist as a client of the Israeli state. The outcome may be similar to what occurred following the Israeli withdrawal from most of the Gaza Strip. By enveloping Palestinian areas and maintaining control of vital infrastructure, Israel can maintain effective occupation while avoiding the problems associated with direct occupation.

This scenario, whereby the two-state solution will clearly serve the interests of one party, requires Palestinian political leaders and the international community to rethink the negotiation process. For some time, there has been growing awareness among intellectuals that the two-state solution is not credible and that a single Arab-Israeli state might be the only means to ensure peace (see Lappin 2004, Moughrabi 2005, Reuveny 2005, Sayigh 2005). Annexing Palestine entirely into Israel will arguably compel the Israeli government to dismantle its Civil Administration, designed to discriminate against non-Jewish minorities, and provide to Palestinians equal rights denied to them under occupation. However, Israeli unilateralism and the Kadima Party's policy to maintain Israel's 'Jewish' character may effectively eliminate this possibility. Given the indicated outcomes of a two-state solution, the point to consider is that the Israeli-Palestinian conflict cannot be solved within the traditional context of ethnic nationalist identity, which apparently necessitates the existence of two separate states (Moughrabi 2005). Such a paradigm will only perpetuate the conflict and the dominance of one ethnicity over another.

Conclusion

The two-state solution is widely accepted as the means by which to bring an end to the Israeli-Palestinian conflict. However, the success of the two-state solution rests on the fundamental viability and sustainability of a Palestinian state. As has been indicated, the transformation of the Palestinian environment has been profound in the last four decades. This chapter has indicated key environmental factors which will be significant in terms of the viability and sustainability of a Palestinian state. These include the depletion of water resources, solid waste disposal, deterioration in water quality, lack of space, land degradation and the level of geographical fragmentation between Palestinian areas.

We argue that an independent Palestinian state will face a variety of challenges. These include improving services for Palestinians, including returning refugees, building a society that is adaptable and skilled, creating a viable economy, and building democratic institutions to govern effectively, provide security and manage the environment. However, the transformation of the physical environment will place massive restrictions on available resources and the capacity for sustainable development, rendering a Palestinian state unviable and highly unstable.

Israel's unilateral withdrawal indicates that Israel wishes to continue its occupation of Palestinian land while avoiding responsibilities to provide equal rights and services. Cantonization of Palestinian territory will ensure that Palestinians live in manageable-sized ghettos that the Israelis may monitor and control while exploiting them as open markets. The physical environment is the very foundation of human society in its ability to function and exist. A prosperous and viable state cannot logically arise from unviable conditions. Environmental justice and equitable allocation of resources remain the focal point of the Palestinian-Israeli conflict. Until these are addressed a lasting peace will be unlikely, and we shall see a continuation of the current pattern of Palestinian resistance and Israeli repression.

Note

1 The low growth scenario assumes population growth will slow down as a result of long-term trends in declining fertility rates and net out-migration. The medium growth scenario assumes population growth will remain constant in the future. Any long-term fertility rates will be offset by a net increase in immigration from refugees from outside the West Bank. The high growth scenario assumes that population growth will be faster in the future. The scenario is based on the assumption that a large number of refugees will return to the West Bank between 2006 and 2020 after the declaration of a Palestinian state. The fertility rates are assumed to decrease to a percentage which will still be higher than the fertility rate in the medium scenario. The nature of this influx will depend on the outcome of negotiations which will lead to a permanent peace agreement. The scenario also assumes a very low rate of out-migration as a result of improved economic condidtions.

References

Allen, T. (2001) *The Middle East Water Question: Hydro-politics and the Global Economy*, London: I.B. Taurus.

Al-Quds newspaper, 20/5/2000.

Applied Research Institute Jerusalem (ARIJ) Monitoring Settlements and GIS Units (2005) *Geopolitical Conditions in the Bethlehem Governorate*, Bethlehem: ARIJ.

ARIJ Database, 2005.

ARIJ GIS Unit, 2006.

ARIJ Monitoring Settlements Unit, 2006.

Ayala-Carcedo F., and M. Gonzalez-Barros (2005) 'Economic Development and

Sustainable Development in the World: Conditioning Factors, Problems and Opportunities', *Environment, Development and Sustainability*, 7, pp. 95–115.

Bossal H. (2001) 'Assessing Viability and Sustainability: A Systems-based Approach for Deriving Comprehensive Indicator Sets', *Conservation Ecology* 5 (2):12. URL: http://www.consecol.org/vo15/iss2/art12

Brinkerhoff, D. (2005) 'Rebuilding Governments in Failed Sates and Post-Conflict Societies: Core Concepts and Crosscutting Themes', *Public Administration and Development*, 25, 3–14.

Dilworth, C. (1994) 'Two Perspectives on Sustainability', *Population and Environment: A Journal of Interdisciplinary Studies*, 15, 441–67.

Falah G. W. (2004) 'War, Peace and Land Seizure in Palestine's Border Area', *Third World Quarterly*, 25, 955–75.

— (2005) 'The Geopolitics of "Enclavisation" and the Demise of a Two-state Solution to the Israeli-Palestinian Conflict', *Third World Quarterly*, 26, 1341–72.

Froukh L. (2003) 'Trans-boundary Groundwater Resources of the West Bank', *Water Resources Management*, 17, 175–82.

Graham, S. (2003) 'Lessons in Urbicide', *New Left Review*, 19, Jan–Feb, 2003.

Hinterberger, F. (2001) 'Introduction to Special Issue on Sustainability', *Population and Environment*, 23, 137–8.

Issac J., V. Qumsieh, M. Owewi, N. Hrimat, W. Sabbah, B. Sha'lan, L. Hosh, R. Bassous, D. Al Hodali, N. Al Dajani, M. Abu Amrieh, F. Al Junaidi, F. Neiroukh, O. Sleibi, A. Al Halaykah, N. Quttosh, I. Al A'raj and I. Zboun (1997) *The Status of Environment in the West Bank*, Bethlehem: ARIJ, 1997.

Isaac, J., S. Walid, M. Abu Amrieh, F. Al Juneidi, Y. Abu As'ad and M. Owewi (1998) *Water Resources and Irrigated Agriculture in the West Bank*, Bethlehem: ARIJ, 1998.

Isaac, J. and M. Ghanayem (2002), 'Environmental degradation and the Israeli-Palestinian Conflict', *Voci dal conflitto: Israeliani e Palestinianesi a confronto*, Rome: Ediesse.

Isaac J., K. Rishmawi and A. Safar (2004) 'The Impact of Israel's Unilateral Actions on the Palestinian Environment', *Palestinian and Israeli Environmental Narratives*, 5–8, December 2004, Toronto: York University.

Issac J. and N. Hrimat (2005) 'Assessing the Impact of Israel's Segregation Wall on the Palestinian Biodiversity', International Conference: Promoting Community-Driven Conservation and Sustainable Use of Dry-land Agro-biodiversity, International Center for Agricultural Research in the Dry Areas (ICARDA).

Isaac J., A. Safar, K. Rishmawi, G. Darwish, S. Sbieh, A. Qabajah, T. Weinroth, A. Nassar and E. Bannourah (2005) *Analysis of Waste Management Policies in Palestine*, Bethlehem: ARIJ, 2005.

Isaac J., N. Salam, N. Hrimat, E. Viarosnes and F. Abed-Latif (2005a) *The Impact of Urban Activities on Land Use and Palestinian Communities in the West Bank*, Bethlehem: ARIJ, 2005.

Jarbawi A. (2005) 'Remaining Palestinian Options', *Middle Eastern Studies*, 8, 118–21.

Kort K., M. Collins and D. Ditsch (1998) 'A Review of Soil Erosion Potential Associated with Biomass Crops', *Biomass and Bioenergy*, 14, 351–9.

Lappin S. (2004) 'Israel/Palestine: Is there a Case for Bi-Nationalism?' *Dissent Magazine*, Winter, 2004.

Morag N. (2001) 'Water, Geopolitics and State Building: A Case for Israel', *Middle Eastern Studies*, 8, 179–98.

Moughrabi F. (2005) 'Waiting for the Barbarians: When Palestine Becomes Finland', *The Arab World Geographer*, 8 130–2.

RAND (2005) *Building a Successful Palestinian State*, RAND Corperation URL: http//www.rand.org

Reuveny, R. (2005) 'The Binational State and the Colonial Imperative', *The Arab World Geographer*, 8, 109–17.

Salwasser H. (1990) 'Sustainability as a Conservation Paradigm', *Conservation Biology*, 4 213–16.

Sayigh Y. (2005) 'Closing the Window of Opportunity for the Two-State Solution', *The Arab World Geographer*, 8, 122–4.

Schnell I. (2005) 'A Route Leading to Separation and Peace', *The Arab World Geographer*, 8, 147–52.

Spangenberg J. (2004) 'Reconciling Sustainability and Growth: Criteria, Indicators and Policies', *Sustainable Development*, 12, 74–86.

Tilley, V. (2005) 'From "Jewish State and Arab State" to "Israel and Palestine"? International Norms, Ethnocracy, and the Two-State Solution', *The Arab World Geographer*, 8, 140–46.

Yiftachel O. (2005) 'Neither Two States or One: The Disengagement and "Creeping Apartheid" in Israel/Palestine', *The Arab World Geographer*, 8, 125–9.

8 | Hamas: from opposition to rule

ZIAD ABU-AMR

The making of a mass movement

The Islamic Resistance Movement (Hamas) was established as a wing of the Muslim Brotherhood Society (MB) in Palestine in the aftermath of the outbreak of the first Palestinian Intifada in December 1987. The formation of Hamas marked a clear shift in the ideological and political attitude of the MB in Palestine towards the Israeli occupation. Until December 1987, the public MB position was that the time was not yet ripe for 'Jihad', or violent resistance against the occupation, although the movement was at that time engaged in some sort of preparation for this phase.[1]

The formation of Hamas, then, was an act of transformation within the MB, dictated by pressing and changing circumstances. In the light of a rising number of acts of resistance by other Palestinian groups, such as the Fatah movement and the Palestinian Islamic Jihad, the Society could no longer justify its reluctance to engage in the struggle against the occupation. Since it was difficult for the MB to make an immediate and radical shift in its ideological stand, it decided to create a body from within the Society to undertake that role and to engage in the struggle against Israel: that body was the Islamic Resistance Movement (Hamas). Creating Hamas to engage in the Palestinian popular Intifada that erupted in December 1987, on behalf of the MB, was less risky than engaging the Society directly in the Intifada with whatever that might entail in terms of liabilities for the Muslim Brothers in Palestine.[2]

As the Intifada progressed, the mother MB organization in Palestine defined its relationship with Hamas in pragmatic terms. When Hamas became popular, the MB was willing, and saw fit, to be unofficially linked to the movement. Very little mention of the Brotherhood was made during the years of the two Intifadas, in 1987, and in 2000. Only when Hamas was at a low ebb and needed broader Islamic patronage did the name of the Brotherhood become involved apparently to provide legitimacy and support.[3]

By creating Hamas, the MB had gone through another process of ideological and political transformation. Hamas, as its charter indicated, projected a national Islamic expression of the MB vis-à-vis its pan-Islamic character, which at some point lent priority to other Islamic issues such as, for example, that of Afghanistan when it was under Soviet occupation.

Transformation in a reformist Islamic movement such as the MB was not unusual since it could find cover in the Islamic doctrine or tradition, as long as it served the interests of Muslims, as defined by the leaders of the MB themselves. According to the teachings of Hasan al-Banna, the founder of the MB in Egypt, and other Islamic ideologues, it was incumbent upon the MB to work within existing political frameworks and transform (i.e. Islamicize) society and its leadership gradually (through phases) by legal and peaceful means. Transformation was not peculiar to the mother organization of the MB; later years have shown that Hamas itself was prone to transformation, if only to emphasize that it was a legitimate child of the MB.

The rise of Hamas as an actor in the national struggle triggered serious rivalry and competition between Hamas and factions within the Palestine Liberation Organization (PLO), especially the Fatah movement. While that rivalry and competition were taking place between the MB and other PLO factions in the social and political spheres, they were also extended with the establishment of Hamas, to the national and armed struggle against the Israeli occupation. This rivalry amounted in due course to a clear struggle over the leadership of the Palestinian people and the direction of Palestinian society – a long struggle that went through several phases and culminated in the fierce competition over the municipal and legislative elections in Palestine in 2005 and 2006.

When the Oslo agreement was signed between the PLO and the Israeli government in 1993, Hamas opposed it; it also opposed the Palestinian Authority (PA), which had been established on the basis of Oslo. This opposition was both ideological and political, and was based on the premise that the agreement violated Hamas's Islamic vision for Palestine and prejudiced Palestinian national rights. Hamas urged that the PA was merely a tool to implement an Israeli-American scheme against the interests of the Palestinian people; it decided, therefore, to resist the Oslo agreement and to oppose and undermine the PA. It exercised this opposition through violent attacks against Israel, and through an official boycott of the presidential and legislative elections that took place in 1996.[4] It was natural for Hamas to try to undermine an authority from which it was excluded, in addition to the fact that the Oslo agreement required the PA to put an end to all acts of violence and armed resistance directed at Israel. Hamas rejected this PA commitment and continued its activities against Israel, bringing the wrath of the PA upon itself. Hamas militants and political leaders were periodically put in jail.

The eruption of the second Intifada in September 2000 marked the beginning of a dramatic shift in the rise of Hamas's strength and popularity vis-à-vis the PA, which for its part suffered from a systematic Israeli campaign of siege and the destruction of its security infrastructure. Hamas's social and political power base was diversified. It gained adherents from 'impoverished young men, who took part in the armed resistance, the devout middle classes, and Islamist intellectuals in the region and in the West'.[5] Up to the eruption of the second Intifada and even afterwards, Hamas's popularity, as indicated by repeated public polls, never exceeded that of Fatah, the ruling party of the Palestinian Authority. A number of factors accounted for the new but persistent rising popularity and strength of Hamas:

1. With the eruption of the second Intifada, Hamas could easily claim that the peace process was failing, that the Palestinian Authority and its ruling party, the Fatah movement, were wrong in wasting time and effort investing in futile negotiations and a peace process, and that Hamas was right in rejecting the peace process and in resorting to armed resistance in fighting the Israeli occupation. This Hamas claim was substantiated by the sheer fact that Fatah itself and the PA security services were key partners in the Intifada and in the acts of violence and resistance which broke out at a later stage of the Intifada.

2. Hamas's spectacular suicidal attacks inside Israel and its other resistance tactics captured the imagination and admiration of large sectors of Palestinians. Scores of Palestinian youth joined the movement to become martyrs. In light of an excessive Israeli use of military power against a civilian population under occupation, which included the use of advanced jet fighters, Apache helicopters, and rockets, there was the risk of shaking the will and determination of the Palestinians. With its lethal suicidal attacks inside Israel, Hamas

may have provided Palestinians with a national projection of force to restore their psychological balance or equilibrium. In addition, these attacks satisfied a desire for revenge for the heavy human losses the Palestinians sustained.

3. Hamas's popularity during the second Intifada had risen in the aftermath of the Israeli assassination of its founder and leader, Sheikh Ahmad Yasin, while in his wheelchair. Yasin suffered from quadriplegia. Israel also assassinated his successor, Dr Abdel-Aziz al-Rantisi, together with several other prominent Hamas leaders. These assassinations earned the movement a great deal of popular sympathy, as a movement which was prepared to sacrifice its top leaders, while PA and Fatah leaders were perceived to be enjoying wealth and lives of luxury. Sheikh Yasin and other Hamas leaders have been reputed for their extreme modesty and simple way of life.

4. Hamas's claim, that the Israeli withdrawal (unilateral disengagement from Gaza) came mainly as a result of the Palestinian resistance championed by Hamas, found resonance in the Palestinian street. If Hamas were empowered, people thought, it could do more.

5. Through its expropriation of the Islamic religious and spiritual discourse, and its use of an extensive network of mosques, Hamas provided religious, spiritual, and psychological shelter to a people whose ongoing suffering and hardship have put them in dire need of this sort of support. To cope with the loss of people and property, individuals and society were in need of intervention. Hamas was always ready to step in. With the rise in the intensity of the Intifada and in the level of violence, more and more people went to the mosque to hear Hamas or other Islamic preachers glorifying resistance and sacrifice, and providing solace.[6] In the words of Nayef Rajoub, a Hamas leader from the city of Dura in Hebron: 'Twenty years ago when I was working in the mosque, around 150 to 200 people came on Friday (prayer). Now it's a few thousand. At that time, there was only one mosque in Dura. Now there are twelve'.[7]

6. Hamas's extensive social and charity network of services has won many Palestinians to its side. These Palestinians admired the organization for engaging in the resistance against Israel, and at the same time extending help to the needy and the poor among the Palestinians. So Hamas managed to fill a vacuum in this regard which the Palestinian Authority, with its comparatively huge resources, was

supposed to fill, but did not. In addition to controlling and running its own institutions, Hamas was competing for the control of other Palestinian civil society organizations, and was making long strides.

7. Hamas's reputation and image of integrity and clean conduct vis-à-vis the image of corruption and inefficiency that tarnished the Palestinian Authority may have been the most immediate and direct reason for its popularity. Its austerity was usually compared to stories of extravagance and corruption of PA leaders and officials. It is suggested in this regard that the deep desire for change and reform was the primary factor for Hamas's wide popularity.

Making the transition: taking part in elections

Hamas's transformation and its strategic decision to participate in municipal and legislative elections are embedded in a number of factors and changing circumstances. Since the beginning of the second Intifada, the organization had lost a large number of its top political and military leaders and cadres as well as part of its infrastructure. These included founders and leaders of the political and military wings of the movement. Hamas was also sensitive to the various types of losses sustained by the Palestinians as a result of the continuation of its attacks against Israeli targets, especially after the return of the Israeli occupation to the West Bank in 2002 and the tight siege imposed on the Gaza Strip with its resulting deteriorating economic conditions, which caused rising poverty and high unemployment.

Salvaging itself as well as the Palestinian people from hardship required a review of Hamas's strategy and tactics. Hamas, and the Palestinians as a whole, needed time, a breathing space, to recuperate and restore their power and ability to maintain the cohesion of Palestinian society, to defend themselves, and continue the struggle against the occupation.

Additionally, and in the minds of the Hamas leaders, participating in and winning the elections was a source of empowerment for the movement and its programme of resistance, change and reform.[8] Hamas, as a democratically and popularly elected force in the PLC, would achieve legal and political legitimacy.[9] In this capacity it could prevent any future oppression, arrest or harassment of its leaders and cadres by the PA security services – contrary to what happened to the movement in the aftermath of the signing of the Oslo agreement – especially

171

in the likelihood of any attempt to implement the Road Map, which stipulates the dismantling of the military infrastructure of Hamas and other Palestinian armed groups.

More on the positive side for Hamas, its victory in the elections and concomitant control of PA institutions promised to provide the movement with the opportunity and access to implement its programme and undertake a process of Islamic transformation, with the objective of establishing an Islamic order. However, following the capture of some Israeli soldiers by Hamas, a number of Hamas ministers were arrested in August 2006.

Hamas was also fully aware of regional and international developments such as the war in Iraq, the threats to Iran and Syria, the US international war against terrorism, the United States' and European Union's listing of it as a terrorist organization, the restrictions imposed on money collection and transfer to the movement, and the pressures exerted on countries and institutions willing to help Hamas, to stop extending this help. For all of these reasons, Hamas found it necessary to weather the storm and seek an alternative path to maintain itself and its agenda. Hamas's agreement to a period of calm (*tahdi'a*), a halt to its violent attacks against Israeli targets in 2003 and 2005, its public demand for political partnership with Fatah and the PA, and its participation in the elections should be viewed in this context.

Hamas's decision to participate in municipal and legislative elections is consistent with the doctrinal and political stands of the movement. There is nothing in the Muslim Brotherhood's doctrine (Hamas included) that forbids or prevents the movement from political participation with the purpose of seizing power. As a matter of fact, the movement is required from a doctrinal point of view to seek and seize power to promote its Islamic agenda. Hasan al-Banna, the founder of the mother MB Society in Egypt in 1928, had himself entered the parliamentary elections in 1945. Ever since, MB societies elsewhere have participated in elections whenever possible. Furthermore, MB societies were and are willing to form Islamic political parties to overcome obstacles in the way of their participation in elections. Jabhat al-Amal al-Islamia (Islamic Action Front) in Jordan is a case in point. Hamas itself formed a political party (Islamic Salvation Party) after the establishment of the PA.[10]

Hamas's apathy toward seeking power and authority was only relevant to the Palestinian Authority itself because of the former's opposition to the agreements with Israel which produced this authority, and because of its rejection of the commitments and obligations to which the Palestinian Authority was bound. Therefore, when Hamas openly declared that it was ready for power-sharing in the Authority, its leaders made it clear that they were talking about a different type of authority, an authority not shackled by the Oslo agreement. In the words of Mahmoud al-Zahar, a prominent and outspoken Hamas leader, 'Hamas is entering the elections to smash what has remained of the Oslo agreement.'[11]

When Hamas decided to participate in the municipal and legislative elections, it believed that it could form a strong opposition or win these elections and redefine the commitments and functions of the Palestinian Authority and its institutions. These institutions, of course, include the government and the Legislative Council. It is premature at this point to determine whether Hamas will be able to redefine the commitments and functions of these institutions beyond the parameters of the signed agreements between the PLO and Israel, and the conditions and parameters that were established between the Palestinian Authority and the Israeli government.

Hamas's decision to participate in the elections also came as a result of the increasing size, power and popularity of the movement, which required it to act as more than an opposition movement operating from outside the system; people joined or supported Hamas because they wanted change, reform, better governance, and delivery. There is a limit to what Hamas as an opposition movement can achieve in these areas. In order to have open possibilities for delivery, Hamas has to enter the system. The legitimate alternative, then, was free and democratic elections, which would guarantee it a fair chance. Based on clear indicators and assessments, Hamas believed that it had good prospects for a strong showing in these elections.

Hamas scored well in the different rounds of municipal elections that took place in the West Bank and Gaza. It won most of the councils in the big cities and in the heavily populated areas. The most impressive victory in the municipal elections was in the city of Nablus, where Hamas won all 15 seats in the council. This sweeping victory came as a prelude to the landslide victory in the legislative elections of 25 January 2006. Hamas's victory can be attributed to its reputation and performance, and to its sophisticated election campaign. It entered the elections as a united and disciplined movement and was able to bring all of its followers to

173

the ballot box – it prepared for these elections for over a year. All of the factors that contributed to the rising influence and expansion of Hamas in Palestinian society contributed also to its electoral victory.

Fatah, on the other hand, suffered from a number of misfortunes. On the eve of the elections the movement was in a state of disarray, fragmented and entangled in an internal struggle. Fatah tried to organize internal primary elections before the legislative elections. These primaries were cancelled because of fraud and violence. Their failure tarnished the image of Fatah in the Palestinian street and deepened divisions within the movement. Even worse, Fatah decided to enter the elections with two competing lists before President Mahmoud Abbas had managed to unite the two into one. Scores of Fatah leaders and cadres entered the elections as independent candidates, challenging the orders of the leadership of the movement, scattering the vote, and causing the loss of about 20 seats, according to Rawhi Fattouh, a Fatah leader and the former Speaker of the Palestinian Legislative Council.[12] Up until two weeks before the elections, Fatah was hoping to have them postponed; consequently it started campaigning seriously only shortly before they took place.

In the Legislative Council elections Hamas won 74 out of the 132 parliamentary seats, comprising 44% of the popular vote and 56% of the seats, while Fatah won 45 seats, comprising 42% of the popular vote and 34% of the seats in the Council. The outcome of these elections, and Hamas's landslide victory, came as a surprise to almost everyone, including the Hamas movement itself.

The victory of Hamas in the municipal and legislative elections does not in fact reflect its actual strength in Palestinian society. A large number of the votes Hamas won was a protest vote against the ineptitude of the Fatah-appointed municipal councils. Inefficiency and corruption were important reasons for Fatah's poor performance; but the lack of material resources was an important factor as well, especially during the last five years of the Intifada during which normal life was paralysed, due to the ongoing conflict and the restrictive and punitive measures imposed on the Palestinian areas by Israel. The same could be said about the departing Fatah-controlled Legislative Council, which failed to exercise responsibility and accountability over the executive branch of the PA. Voters in the PLC and municipal councils' elections in all likelihood decided to punish Fatah and its candidates, and indeed the Palestinian Authority as a whole.

Hamas in power: prospects and challenges

Now that Hamas is in power, controlling the government, the Legislative Council, and many municipal councils at local government level, what are its prospects for success or failure? It is important to remember here that the logic, dynamics, and imperatives of a resistance and opposition movement are radically different from those of a movement that is not only in power, but also the ruling party. Being in opposition was convenient, since Hamas did not have to bear the responsibilities of political rule under very adverse conditions.

Opposition was also convenient since Hamas could capitalize on every failure of the Palestinian Authority and turn it into a gain or a credit for itself. With Hamas as incumbent, the situation and the roles are reversed. Hamas's failures are likely to translate into gains for the opposition. Fatah is now the main opposition party. It is not yet certain how a convenient majority in the Legislative Council and a Hamas government will help Hamas, with its very limited experience of political rule, international politics, and foreign relations, to overcome a set of tremendous challenges at the political and internal levels.

Hamas: the challenges from without

Politically, Hamas inherits an authority defined and bound by the Oslo Accords, which it refuses to recognize. The terms of reference for establishing the Palestinian Authority inherited by Hamas include the PLO and PA recognition of Israel, the renunciation of violence, and a commitment to resolve the Palestinian-Israeli conflict through peaceful negotiations. If Hamas is to be recognized as a partner by Israel and the international community, it is required to endorse the Oslo agreement, to accept the Road Map, and declare its commitment to these terms of reference. To become eligible for donor community money, Hamas is required to meet three conditions that were set by a Quartet meeting in London on 30 January 2006 that was held following the Hamas victory in the elections: ' ... the Quartet concluded that it was inevitable that future assistance to any new government would be reviewed by donors against that government's commitment to the principles of non-violence, recognition of Israel, and acceptance of previous agreements and obligations, including the Roadmap'.[13]

Israel on its part has reiterated similar demands, and even more, in order to continue its relationship with the Palestinian Authority. It has demanded that Hamas should disarm. Israel's security concerns may force its government to embrace extreme positions and undertake aggressive policies towards Hamas. It can be expected to be watchful and vigilant over Hamas's attempts to develop its military capabilities by smuggling advanced weapons into the Gaza Strip, which would threaten the Israeli heartland. According to the Israeli government, with Hamas in power, the above scenario is not very far-fetched. There is also a concern by Israel's security establishment about 'a possible relationship between Hamas and the Islamic regime in Tehran, which may attempt to engulf Israel with Islamist fundamentalist "terror" groups on the border: Hizbullah in Southern Lebanon and Hamas in Gaza and the West Bank.'[14] [Indeed, after this chapter was written, Israel launched its attack on Lebanon in August 2006, and kidnapped some Hamas leaders.]

Israeli officials are also keen to dramatize their concern with regard to Hamas taking control over Palestinian security services in Gaza and the West Bank: 'If Hamas takes control of the Palestinian armed forces and police, that means it will establish an armed threat right near Jerusalem, Tel-Aviv, and Ben Gurion airport'.[15] The message is very clear: Israel cannot tolerate such a situation.

A counter view argues that it is in the best interests of an Olmert Israeli government to have Hamas in power. In this case the Israeli government can argue that there is no Palestinian partner, and as such it can proceed with its unilateral plans for the West Bank, continue with the construction of the separation wall, and draw its final borders with the Palestinians. If the Israeli government were to adopt this policy, it would only be temporary until it implements its longer-term plans. But in the long run, Israel cannot live with a potential security threat in its backyard. Israel's experience of Hamas does not make it easy for it to co-exist with a militant armed movement.

Israeli sources argued that the Israeli occupation had empowered the Islamic movement in the 1970s and 1980s to create a counter force to that of the PLO. Contrary to the PLO, Hamas was not at that time engaged in any resistance to the occupation. Later on, and after the eruption of the first Intifada, Hamas did become engaged in violent resistance against Israeli targets, which later included suicidal attacks. The Israeli government is unlikely to make the same mistake again by allowing Hamas to grow stronger and use its strength at some point once more against Israel.

There is also a broader Israeli concern that Hamas plans to establish an Islamic 'fundamentalist' political entity in Gaza and the West Bank; Israel is not likely to allow such an entity to emerge. Other countries, such as the US and perhaps the European Union, may support this Israeli position.

Hamas's dilemma

It is clear that Hamas is faced with a huge dilemma, and has to make choices, each of which entails a high price. As a precondition for international and regional recognition, acceptance and support, Hamas is required to meet the specific demands set by the Quartet. Accepting these demands is bound to undermine its credibility since its programme demands the liberation of the whole of Palestine. Hamas is willing to accept a state in the 1967-occupied territories – the West Bank, Gaza and East Jerusalem – only as an interim solution.

The Islamic movement knows that if it accepts the conditions set by the Quartet, it will lose its credibility and popularity. Acceptance would be unlikely to end the occupation, halt Israeli settlement expansion, stop the construction of the separation wall, or prevent Israel from undertaking unilateral disengagement steps in the West Bank.

By accepting the demands of the Quartet, Hamas will find itself in a situation similar to that of the Palestinian Authority. By rejecting them, it will make itself a 'legitimate' target for Israeli reprisals, and a target for restrictive and punitive international measures. If Hamas pursues a middle way, Israeli demands on the movement are not likely to cease. Indeed, Israel is likely to insist on an unequivocal recognition of its right to exist, renunciation of violence and the dismantling of the military wing of Hamas. Hamas's margin for bargaining will then be limited.

Major political concessions by Hamas could also cause a split in the movement between a radical wing (including the armed militants), and a moderate wing. Moreover, such political concessions are likely to spoil Hamas's relationship with its traditional allies in Iran, Syria, and Hizbullah in Lebanon.

Sensitive to these challenges, Hamas began immediately after its victory in the elections to make gestures indicating a readiness for moderation. Khalid Meshal, head of the Hamas Politbureau, declared that Hamas was willing to negotiate with Israel on day-to-day issues.[16] Ismail Haniya, Hamas's prime minister, announced, for his part, that his government would deal with those PA commitments of high national responsibility, referring here to the agreements concluded between the PA and the Israeli government. Haniya also indicated that his government was ready to start a dialogue with the Quartet to discuss the conditions it had imposed on Hamas.[17]

It is not likely, however, that these gestures will be considered sufficient by Israel and the Quartet to lift the ban on Hamas and its government. The American Administration rejected Haniya's offer for dialogue with the Quartet immediately. There are, however, limitations on the exercise of excessive pressure on the PA or the Hamas government. Cutting financial support to the PA and driving the Palestinians close to starvation is likely to create internal turbulence and cause a collapse of the social and security order. This collapse will not only undermine the stability of the Palestinian Authority, but could also disturb that of the region as a whole. Heavy-handed Israeli policies may create a situation that is not very much different from a situation of virtual Israeli occupation, which will force the Palestinians to question the utility of the continued existence of the PA. Some Palestinians are already arguing that the PA is becoming a façade hiding an actual Israeli occupation, and a tool to help Israel regulate its occupation policies. Hamas may also realize that it is left with little choice but to go back to its previous role as a resistance movement, before it loses its legitimacy, credibility and popularity.

Hamas: the challenge from within

Internally, Hamas faces challenges that are no less serious than the external challenges. It will find it extremely difficult to implement its programme of reform in the complex existing reality, especially if the idea is to dismantle one order and replace it with another, and not just to patch up the old system or undertake some superficial measures here or there.

It is not clear how Hamas can revive the economy and, for example, create jobs for a large army of unemployed workers, university graduates, engineers and doctors under the continuing Israeli restrictions on movement between Gaza and the West Bank and Jerusalem in the absence of the necessary resources and investment. It is also not clear how Hamas will handle the extensive day-to-day business with the Israeli side in civil affairs, travel, health, economy, and other spheres.

One of the areas that requires immediate attention is administrative corruption in the Palestinian bureaucracy. Hamas has not made it clear how it would deal with an army of employees, many of whom were arbitrarily appointed. Any serious attempt to dismantle this bureau-cracy will be met with tough resistance by the Fatah movement since the majority of the employees are Fatah affiliates.

The serious internal challenges that Hamas faces are numerous. During the Fatah rule (1994–2005), Hamas constantly complained that exclusion and the one-party rule did not allow for meaningful account-ability and responsibility, and hence created an environment for corrup-tion and inefficiency. After its victory in the elections, Hamas ended up forming a government mainly of Hamas members. None of the other political groups or parliamentary blocs agreed to join its government. Hamas argued that it had made the required effort and concessions to include other political groups in the government, while these groups, for their part, argued that Hamas was not willing to embrace a national consensus political programme. The net result was that the Palestin-ian political system ended up with a Hamas government and a Hamas majority in the PLC, which will make the process of accountability and government rather vague and superficial. Hamas may end up monopo-lizing power to the detriment of democratic and pluralistic politics.

Another challenge facing the movement is its ability to define and forge a functioning relationship with the PA in light of its refusal to recognize the PLO and the PA's Basic Law (constitution). One of the ironies of the situation is that Hamas refuses to recognize the PLO as the sole legitimate representative of the Palestinian people, when more than one hundred countries around the world (including Israel) have granted this recognition. There is also the challenge of making a peaceful transition of authority from one party (Fatah) to another (Hamas), which may prove to be more difficult than concluding free and democratic elections. Fatah is likely to make the transition very difficult since this would consolidate Hamas's political control over the PA, its ministries, institutions, and security services. Fatah has no interest in facilitating the success of the Hamas government, since it has refused to participate in it. In the PLC, Fatah is the main opposition group, and it is only natural that it will try to undermine the efforts of Hamas in the legislative body. Fatah will resist conceding power or control to Hamas, invoking in this regard the memories of the recent past when Hamas undermined and obstructed, whenever it could, the policies and activities of the Fatah-controlled PA.

Two other challenges lie in the area of internal security and in estab-lishing a good working relationship between the Palestinian presidency,

179

on the one hand, and the Hamas government and Legislative Council, on the other.

With regard to internal security, those who voted for Hamas expect it to end the disarray and the lawlessness in the Palestinian street, and to collect the weapons of armed groups and local gangs, in addition to weapons that are widely used in family feuds. Hamas is also required to preserve the truce with Israel. In order to succeed in achieving any one of these goals, or all of them, Hamas needs, as a necessary condition, the genuine cooperation of the Fatah movement, if not that of other groups that have military wings, such as the Islamic Jihad. Fatah is not likely to cooperate, given the heavy defeat it sustained at the hands of Hamas in the legislative elections. Furthermore, Fatah is not united, and cannot yet speak with one voice, especially the armed groups of the movement that operate on the ground. Finally, Fatah recalls bitterly how Hamas acted when in opposition; it construed Hamas's conduct then as a deliberate policy of undermining the movement and the PA.

Of equal significance at the security level is the challenge which could come from inside Hamas itself. It has socialized thousands of its followers on militancy, and has built a military wing of several thousand fighters who made resistance a career. It will face the problems first of having to convince its militant constituency of the dramatic political transformation it needs to undergo, and second of integrating its armed wing and other armed groups belonging to other political factions in the security services. It is not clear if, and in what way, Hamas can accomplish this objective in the near future, or whether it can prevent splits within its military wing. The Islamic movement would be in a very odd position if it found itself forced to arrest militants belonging to its military wing, or that of Fatah's, or that of the Islamic Jihad's, for carrying out attacks against Israel or firing home-made or other rockets across the border. Such an undertaking is likely to cause internal friction and perhaps violent confrontations. The incumbent Hamas government may be required to condemn such attacks. If Hamas complies with the international demands that are required from the movement, such as the renunciation of violence, it would then turn against its own raison d'être as a resistance movement.

The internal tension of a presidential-parliamentary system

As for the future relationship between President Mahmoud Abbas and Hamas, this relationship is open to a number of possibilities.

Abbas was popularly elected on a programme that advocated peace negotiations with Israel and internal reform. Hamas, on the other hand, advocated in its election programme resistance to the Israeli occupation and internal reform. It is not yet clear how to reconcile the two programmes with regard to these two political agendas. The Basic Law gives the president the power to appoint the prime minister and to fire him and his cabinet. Hamas has a majority in the Legislative Council to topple any government or cabinet minister through a no confidence vote. The Council has the power to legislate but does not have the two-thirds majority to override the president's veto of any legislation. Both the president and the Hamas-controlled Legislative Council have tremendous negative power to create political paralysis in the Palestinian Authority. The president and the Hamas Prime Minister, Ismail Haniya, have overlapping responsibilities in the PA, especially in key ministries such as foreign affairs, interior, finance, information and civil affairs.

The alternative to exercising negative power is to forge a good working relationship between the two sides. It is not yet clear how this constructive and cooperative relationship can be established in the light of a history of mutual competition and mistrust between Hamas, on the one hand, and Fatah, on the other, and in the light of two political programmes (Hamas's and Abbas's) which seem to be, at least initially, irreconcilable.

When Hamas was in opposition, the movement created a 'parallel authority' to the Palestinian Authority. There is always the risk that, in case cooperation between the president and the prime minister fails, Hamas would operate the Legislative Council and the government as a parallel authority to that of the president. This is also bound to create serious friction and probably political paralysis.

Hamas and the Islamic one-state vision

Different views are expressed about the future of the democratic process following the victory of Hamas in the legislative elections. There is the view which suggests, following the impressive results in the municipal and legislative elections, and the demonstrated acceptance and respect for the outcome of these elections by all parties, that the democratic process in Palestine may be irreversible. Implicit in this is the assumption that Hamas will be committed to routine and periodic elections and to the principle of a peaceful transfer of power.

181

On the other hand, there is an expressed concern that the ascendance of Hamas to power may mark the end of the democratic process within the Palestinian political system. Once in power, Islamic movements are not in the habit of being easily removed, and Hamas may be no exception. As an incumbent, Hamas may try to transform society and define its permanent nature in a way that would guarantee it a victory in any future elections. Furthermore, it is argued that Hamas may be able to turn against democracy through democratic means.

The future of the democratization process in Palestine is also linked to the resilience of political opposition. Hamas was the main opposition party before the January 2006 legislative elections, and these elections were held at that point in time upon the insistence of Hamas, but more so, upon the insistence of President Mahmoud Abbas. Hamas resisted huge pressure from Fatah to postpone the elections. It is still uncertain whether Fatah, which has moved to the opposition seats for the first time, is able to turn itself into an effective opposition that can force Hamas to respect the democratic rules of the game. Only Fatah qualifies to have a formal parliamentary bloc in the Legislative Council. A parliamentary bloc requires that any political group has at least 5% of the total number of the seats in the Council. None of the elected groups, apart from Hamas and Fatah, has this percentage. It is possible, however, for these smaller groups to unite in order to become eligible to register as a parliamentary bloc; as yet, it is not known whether these groups can unite, or have an effective opposition role inside or outside a coalition.

The Fatah movement remains, therefore, the only viable opposition movement if it manages to unite itself, adjust to the new reality, adopt a political and social programme that is capable of changing the image of Fatah among the Palestinian population at large, and restore the confidence and trust of the people in the movement. Fatah may also be able to rally smaller political groups in the Council behind it in an opposition coalition. Such opposition is likely to crystallize only after Hamas gets deeply involved in national politics and leadership and when it has to make serious decisions under the existing adverse conditions in the Palestinian areas. It would be possible then to find out whether new political party formations are viable or likely to emerge.

After winning the elections and forming the PNA government, Hamas may strive to embrace the Lebanese Hizbullah model in politics and resistance. Its participation in the elections accorded the movement the legal and political legitimacy it always wanted. This legitimacy provided the movement with some sort of protection. Hizbullah claimed the credit for forcing Israel to withdraw from Southern Lebanon. Hamas made a similar claim to the unilateral Israeli disengagement from the Gaza Strip. More importantly, Hamas wishes to emulate Hizbullah in defining its internal status in the Palestinian system. It hopes to establish itself as an integral part of the legitimate political system, but also maintain its resistance option, which runs counter to existing agreements between the PLO and the PA on the one hand, and with the Israeli government on the other.

If Hamas insisted on adhering to this strategy, a clash with Israel would become inevitable. Alternatively, Hamas could evolve in just the same way that Fatah evolved from a revolutionary movement working outside the Arab and international systems into a movement that would gradually get sucked into these systems with whatever that entails. After the Karama battle in 1968 in Jordan between the Fatah and other Palestinian guerrilla fighters on the one hand and Israel on the other hand – which was labelled as a victory for the Palestinian resistance – the doors of the Arab system were opened for Fatah. Fatah then took over the leadership of the PLO and Arafat was invited to Cairo, which marked the beginning of the integration of the Palestinian movement into the Arab system. In 1968 in Moscow, President Nasser of Egypt introduced Yassir Arafat to the Soviet leadership.

Similarly, after Hamas's victory in the legislative elections, its leadership was invited to Cairo and to some other Arab capitals; it was also invited to Turkey and Russia. History could repeat itself, but in a radically different international and regional setting. In these Arab and foreign capitals, Hamas was asked to renounce violence, to abide by international norms, and to recognize Israel. Tremendous pressure has been exerted on the movement to conform, including the deprivation of financial assistance and diplomatic contacts from the Palestinian Authority. It is not yet known for how long Hamas can resist these pressures.

While Hamas and other Islamic movements wish to establish an attractive Islamic model of political rule in Palestine, the integration of Hamas in the Arab and international systems is likely to undermine such a model. Resistance to the rise of such a model is not only Israeli or international, but also Arab. While certain segments of the Arab population may sympathize and support this Hamas desire, Arab governments find it detrimental to their legitimacy and to the stability of their regimes and societies.

Since in the months following its election Hamas was not likely to recognize Israel or negotiate with its government, the movement and its government were more likely to turn their attention to domestic matters, since they could not afford the price of recognition or negotiations. It would be to their advantage, therefore, to stick to the state of calm (*tahdi'a*) existing with Israel at the beginning of 2006. It remains to be seen how much the Israelis' invasion of Lebanon and Hizbullah's stance affect Hamas's policy.

The immediate objective in domestic matters would be the implementation of Hamas's programme of change and reform in the internal situation: security, finance, bureaucracy, economy, education, etc. The long-term objective would be gradually to transform and organize society along Islamic lines, through a carefully designed and implemented process of Islamic socialization and engineering in the areas of legislation, education, culture, economy, and social conduct, among others. The more this intention and trend become evident, and the Hamas grip over the government and society is consolidated, the more the risk that some members of the elite and of the middle class, fearful of Hamas's conservative social agenda, would begin to emigrate or seek residence outside the Palestinian areas. This may be similar to what happened in Iran in the aftermath of the Islamic revolution against the Shah.

Immediately after the Hamas victory in the elections, the Islamic University in Gaza, a Hamas-controlled institution, organized a conference on Islamic legislation. When Ismail Haniya, then prime minister designate, addressed the conference, he announced that he planned to establish an Islamic legislation department in the prime minister's office.[18] In its final statement the conference recommended the adoption of a moderate approach in Islamic *ijtihad*, reviewing Islamic *fiqh* (Islamic jurisprudence) in light of contemporary developments, and establishing an Islamic money market.[19] Hamas's shift from political matters to domestic issues can be justified on an Islamic doctrinal basis. The preparation of society is a prerequisite for both its Islamicization and for the engagement in jihad.

Beyond doctrinal justification, Hamas may use this approach to buy time until more opportune conditions materialize. The concept of a long-term truce (*hudna*), which Hamas offered, is consistent with this approach. Related to this is another possible shift in Hamas's politics which may undermine national achievements at the international level. Because of its Islamic orientation, and the rejection it is facing from the US and Europe, Hamas is likely to focus on Arab and Islamic relations, as its government programme indicates. This programme stresses the Arab and Islamic dimension of the Palestinian cause. It promises to mobilize Arab and Islamic support for the Palestinian people. On the face of it, this position does not harm Palestinian national interests. But if mishandled, there is the risk of Israel successfully downgrading the Palestinian issue from an international question to a controversial issue linked to Islamic and international terrorism – a constant Israeli objective. There is also concern that the Palestinian people would lose international support for their struggle to end Israeli occupation and establish their independent state.

Finally Hamas faces the challenge of articulating and defining a position on Palestinian statehood. The traditional Muslim Brotherhood Society position on this issue is that Palestine, all of Palestine from the River Jordan to the Mediterranean Sea, is Muslim land, and it should constitute a part of the larger Islamic state whose boundaries go beyond the boundaries of any nation state. The Palestinian state in the minds of Palestinian Islamists, as illustrated in the Hamas Charter, means a state in the entire area of mandate Palestine that allows no room for Israel or for Zionist Jews in it. Only non-Zionist Jews can live in this state as Palestinian citizens. This Hamas Islamic position is another version of the 'one-state solution' which was first embraced by the PLO in the late 1960s and early 1970s and which called for the establishment of one democratic secular state in Palestine where Muslims, Christians and Jews could live as equal citizens. The understanding was that the Jews who wished to live in this state should renounce their Zionism. This one-state proposal was rejected by Israel. At a later stage, the PLO replaced it by the two-state solution.

In recent years and in the light of persistent Israeli efforts to create new facts on the ground, and to make the two-state solution non-viable and unattainable, the 'one-state solution' has returned as a relevant item in political debate. But this latest version of the one-state solution talks about equal citizenship between Palestinians and Israelis and does not require Jews to renounce their Zionism. Furthermore, there has been no official Palestinian position, secularist or Islamist, supporting this. While Hamas has not abandoned its objective of liberating

185

Palestine and establishing one Islamic state there, it has begun – over the last few years, and especially in the later years of the second Intifada – to entertain the idea of a Palestinian state in the territories that were occupied in 1967. However, the Islamic movement has made it amply clear that this solution is only interim and would not end Hamas's further claims, or end the conflict with Israel. It would only mean a long-term truce for ten or twenty years, which is covered doctrinally by the Islamic tradition.

The Palestinian state that Hamas is willing to accept, as an interim solution, would have Jerusalem as its capital, be free of all Jewish settlements, and ensure the return of Palestinian refugees to their homes and property in mandate Palestine.

With the persistent Israeli effort to create new facts on the ground, such as the separation wall and the declared intention by Ehud Olmert to draw the final borders of Israel – an undertaking which may swallow over 50% of West Bank land – the two-state solution becomes merely an academic option. If the one-state solution were to become a realistic option, it would do so only by default and not by design, although any Israeli government would fight this option by all possible means. A one-state solution would undermine the Zionist dream and the idea of the Jewish state. In this sense, the two-state solution is less objectionable to Israel. Past and present governments of Israel seem to have a different idea about any future resolution of the Palestinian problem. This does not encompass the concept of the two-state solution as proposed by the PLO; at the same time it excludes the one-state solution. What seems to be in the mind of the Israeli political class is 'a Palestinian state' in Gaza and *parts* of the West Bank, a state that cannot be truly independent, sovereign or viable.

Notes

1 Ziad Abu-Amr, *Islamic Fundamentalism in the West Bank and Gaza: The Muslim Brotherhood and the Islamic Jihad*, Indiana: Indiana University Press, 1994, p. 68.

2 Ibid., p. 67.

3 When Sheikh Yasin, the founder of Hamas, was assassinated and morale in the movement was low, the strong image of Hamas was shaken; graffiti on the walls of Gaza linked the name of the Muslim Brotherhood to that of Hamas.

4 Despite the official boycott, Hamas followers voted for a number of pro-Islamic independent candidates. Without this vote, these candidates were not likely to win. A number of Hamas leaders asserted this argument to the author.

5 David Remnick, 'The Democracy Game: Hamas Comes to Power in Palestine', *The New Yorker*, 27/2/2006, p. 62. Repeated public polls in Palestine have also shown the socially diversified power base of Hamas.

6 Many more people frequented the mosque because of unemployment. Since they had nothing else to do, they went to the mosque to pray. Frequenting the mosque was not necessarily a sign of genuine rising religiosity since the social and moral conduct and dealings among people have not changed in any visible or tangible way.

7 Remnick, ibid., p. 63.

8 Personal interview with Dr Mahmoud al-Zahar, a prominent Hamas leader, Gaza, December 2005.

9 Personal interview with Ismail Haniya, a prominent Hamas leader, Gaza, December 2005.

10 This party is still registered as a political party, but after the eruption of the second Intifada, it submerged itself once again in Hamas.

11 Personal interview with Dr Mahmoud al-Zahar, Gaza, December, 2005.

12 Personal interview with Rawhi Fattouh, former Speaker of the PLC, Gaza, 30 January 2006.

13 Quartet statement, London, 30 January 2006.

14 Remnick, 'The Democracy Game', p. 63.

15 Ibid., p. 68.

16 *Al-Ahram Al-Arabi*, Cairo, 18 February 2006.

17 These points were included in the government programme which Haniya submitted to the PLC confidence vote session in his government, held in Gaza on 27 March 2006.

18 *Al-Quds* newspaper, 16 March 2006, p. 12.

19 Ibid.

9 | Hamas and Palestinian statehood

ARE KNUDSEN AND BASEM EZBIDI

The Islamic Resistance Movement's (Hamas's) big win in the elections to the Palestinian Legislative Council (PLC) in January 2006 marks the end of Fatah's political hegemony. Having trumped Fatah in the elections, Hamas faced several domestic and foreign challenges; and having inherited the ruins of the Oslo agreement, including the beleaguered Palestinian Authority (PA), a Hamas-led government could not deliver on its election promises of rooting out corruption and reforming the Palestinian Authority without massive funding from foreign donors. Unless Hamas were to renounce violence, acknowledge the right of Israel to exist, and accept previous agreements between the PLO and Israel, it would be politically isolated by Western countries (USA, EU), ignored by most Arab states, and shunned by Israel. The organization was thus placed at a crossroads: it must either comply with the demands of renouncing violence and accept a process of political 'integration' or defy political and economic sanctions that would isolate the new leadership and inflict damage on its people and economy. This chapter examines the prospects before Hamas and the political options facing the new leadership in the quest for Palestinian statehood.

Introduction[1]

Hamas's landslide victory in the January 2006 elections has made it one of the most prominent Islamist movements in the Middle East today and it now holds the key to the political future of Palestinian statehood.[2] The election victory ended the political hegemony of the Fatah-led Palestine Liberation Organization (PLO). More importantly, the election victory and the formation of a Hamas cabinet (sworn in on 30 March) plunged the Palestinian Authority (PA) into a political and economic crisis. As a listed terror organization, listed by both the EU and the USA, Hamas's election victory put immediate pressure on the movement to (1) acknowledge the right of the Israeli state to exist, (2) renounce violence (i.e., resistance in all its forms), (3) disarm and (4) complete the transition to a political party. Accepting conditions (1) and (2) are preconditions for a resumption of the stalled 'Road Map' process (US Department of State 2003), including bilateral talks with Israel, and for the continuation of international aid to the PA. Knowing that it took the PLO about 30 years to amend its charter and acknowledge the state of Israel, it can be expected that Hamas will not comply with any of the international community's demands in the short term, even when faced with the threat of bankruptcy. Hamas has offered Israel a long-term conditional ceasefire if Israel pulls back to the pre-1967 borders and accepts the establishment of a Palestinian state on the West Bank and Gaza Strip with East Jerusalem as its capital. There are no signs that Israel would even deign to reply to such an offer.

There is now extensive scholarship dealing with several aspects of Hamas as an organization (see overview in Knudsen 2005), but no attempts have yet been made to analyse the choices before the organization following its election victory (but see ICG 2006; Malka 2005). In this chapter, we attempt to analyse the challenges and pitfalls facing the new Hamas government and the implications for a 'two-state' solution to the Israel-Palestine conflict. Due to the deepening political and economic crisis in the Occupied Palestinian Territories, a more nuanced understanding of Hamas's quest for Palestinian statehood is now urgently needed.

Election victory

In 1994, the Oslo Accords led to the establishment of the Palestinian Authority (PA), at the time the most visible success of the PLO and the highpoint of Yassir Arafat's secular nationalism. The same year, Hamas carried out its first suicide attack, killing several Israeli civilians. A decade later, the Palestinian Authority was in ruins. During the same period Hamas had grown from a fringe Gaza-based group to a mainstream Islamist movement, and presented itself as the mouthpiece for dispossessed Palestinians. In 2004, both Hamas and the PLO lost their long-time leaders and founders: Sheikh Yasin and Yassir Arafat. Hamas quickly recovered but Fatah began to show clear fractures. One reason for Hamas's popular appeal was its social outreach programmes and its duality as 'worshippers' and 'warmongers' (*mujahedeen* to use Hamas's own term), which made the organization extraordinarily popular among dispossessed Palestinians and a political challenge to the secular nationalism of the PLO (Knudsen 2005).

In 1996 Hamas boycotted the elections to the Palestinian Legislative Council (PLC), primarily due to the organization's opposition to the Oslo Accords. In the decade since, the large majority of the 88 seats in the old parliament were controlled by Fatah. Nonetheless, in the same decade, Hamas won several university elections and even trumped Fatah at the student elections to Birzeit University in Ramallah, traditionally a PLO bastion. In the 2005 local elections in Gaza, Hamas won 75 out of 118 seats. The latter showed that Hamas could beat Fatah in open elections and, in mid-2005, Hamas announced that it would participate in the upcoming parliamentary elections slated for January 2006, the first of their kind since 1996 when Hamas did not participate. The January 2006 elections to the Palestinian Legislative Council (PLC) proved a watershed in Palestinian politics: Hamas obtained 42.9% of the votes and won 74 of the 132 seats in the new parliament.[3] The Hamas victory in the elections to the PLC ended the political hegemony of the Palestine Liberation Organization (PLO) and there was now an emerging two-party system in Palestine (Hilal 2006).

Factors leading to Hamas's electoral victory

Hamas was hoping to achieve a significant but not a sweeping success in the legislative elections. It was eager simply to reach the legislative council in order to enjoy enough power to influence the decisions and policies articulated by the government.[4] This situation would have been ideal for Hamas since it would be held accountable only for the achievements, while avoiding blame for the failures. Instead, Hamas won a sweeping election victory. This strong showing was due to a number of factors: popular discontent with the lack of meaningful and tangible results in the political 'peace process'; the support that armed struggle against the Israeli occupation has among Palestinians, and which has become one of Hamas's trademarks; a popular protest against Fatah's poor performance and the misrule of the PA, a body widely seen as inefficient and corrupt. Fatah failed to meet not only the Palestinian people's national aspirations, but also their daily needs.[5] By comparison, Hamas benefited from its strong social programmes and its coherent performance in the election campaign as compared to the disorganized approach by Fatah (Usher 2006a).

However, the view that considers the vote for Hamas as mainly a rejection of corruption fails to grasp the full picture, because Palestinians have much less tolerance for occupation than for corruption.

In fact, corruption has always been considered a phenomenon that is profoundly related to the conditions triggered by the absence of statehood (i.e. the Israeli occupation). To most Palestinians, corruption is an outcome of the practices that limit their abilities to realize independence and statehood. The vote for Hamas therefore, should not necessarily be understood as support for its platform per se; rather it should be understood as an expression of resentment towards the Oslo process, which started in 1994, achieved very little, and virtually converted Palestinians into helpless actors in the political process. This view has been articulated by Hamas's spokesman in the West Bank, who saw in the election results an indication of popular support for Hamas's line of resistance and not only as a cry against the PA's corruption and inefficiencies.[6] In sum, the vote for Hamas can be seen as an 'act of self-determination' (Agha and Malley 2006). Thus Hamas feels a deep – although challenging – sense of pride regarding its achievement and it is unlikely that the Hamas-led government would comply with the demands imposed by the international community in the short term, even when faced with the threat of bankruptcy.

Economic collapse

Every month the PA needs, about US$ 170 million to meet its financial obligations (CFR 2005). The payment of salaries to government employees requires US$ 115 million per month (CFR 2005).[7] In 2005, the total budget of the PA totalled about US$ 1.7 billion, with an accumulated debt of about the same amount (CFR 2005). About half of the PA's annual budget came from aid, and amounted to US$ 1 billion, shared between the EU (US$ 600m) and USA (US$ 400m).[8] There was also substantial aid coming from non-EU member states. In 2004, Norway's bilateral aid to the Palestinian Territories amounted to about US$ 60m (NOK 368m) (MFA 2005).[9] Israel's decision to withhold about US$ 55m in monthly tax revenues it collects on behalf of the PA added to the acute shortage of funds. At the same time, there was a consensus that the major recipient of this aid, the Palestinian Authority, badly needed reform and concerted efforts to root out corruption. President Abbas made repeated calls for a resumption of aid to the beleaguered PA. The lack of money, for example, exacerbated the security problem since the PA was not able to pay the salaries of its security personnel (ICG 2006: 31).

But more urgently, the weakness of the Palestinian economy and its strong aid-dependence have meant that the current political stalemate will have serious repercussions for the Palestinians in the West Bank and Gaza Strip who, at the time of writing in 2006, are sinking deeper into poverty. A large number of poverty-stricken Palestinian families – two-thirds of Palestinians are now below the 'poverty line' – survive on a mix of informal assistance (remittances, local credit facilities and religious charity, *zakat*) and formal aid (food distribution, cash assistance, donations) administered by UNRWA (providing to refugees), Palestinian NGOs and the PA's Ministry of Social Affairs (Knudsen 2005). Following the economic boycott imposed on the new Hamas cabinet, the social situation worsened dramatically. In the summer of 2006 an acute shortage of everything, from petrol to medicines to even basic food supplies, dominated the situation in the West Bank and Gaza Strip. This situation is aggravated by the fact that most public servants were not paid their salaries for several consecutive months with all the imagined repercussions of such a state of affairs.

A leading international think-tank, the International Crisis Group (ICG 2006: 32–33) argued that an economic boycott of Hamas would have a number of unwanted consequences. First, it would strengthen Hamas but weaken the population. It would also estrange Palestinians from Western donors and provoke inter-Palestinian tensions. Ultimately, a boycott would stop vital projects at the municipal level, reduce Hamas's accountability and reduce the Western countries' influence with the movement. 'Historically', claims the ICG, 'the more isolated the movement has been, the more radical' (ibid.: 37). If the ICG analysis were correct, the current aid embargo would not have the intended effect of forcing Hamas to accept the international community's terms but would isolate and radicalize it instead. In order to resolve the looming economic crisis, the Quartet (US, EU, Russia and the UN) looked for ways to bypass the Hamas government by routing aid-money through the office of the president (Mahmoud Abbas). This solution, officially termed a 'temporary mechanism', would avert the impending social crisis and solve the immediate economic shortages. However, it would also give a boost to the corruption and nepotism that characterized the PA under Fatah's rule, which was to some extent due to the fact that the PA was in part a client entity that encouraged illegal rent-seeking (Khan et al. 2004).

Reforming the Palestinian Authority

In the public and civil sector, the PA employs about a quarter of the labour force in the West Bank and Gaza Strip and is thus the major employer of Palestinians there. The salaries of government employees amount to US$ 115m per month (CFR 2005). Fatah's control of the PA made it a bastion of political patronage, which was used to bolster political support. 'Reforming' the PA and ending corruption has been Hamas's topmost policy and declared goal. In order to facilitate the restructuring of the PA, Hamas sought to include others, particularly Fatah, in the new cabinet. This strategy failed and the new cabinet was made up of Hamas's own representatives, independents and one Christian. Dismantling the PA – seen by many as a mere clientelist machine for Fatah – would nonetheless be a symbolic end of the Oslo process. Many observers have pointed to the irony that Hamas is now in charge of the political entity – the Palestinian Authority – that grew out of the Oslo Accords, which it strongly opposed.[10]

Hamas's election victory made it the official caretaker of the PA, yet within both Hamas and Fatah there were those who would have preferred to dismantle the PA, seeing it as a mere tool of the Israeli occupation. Dismantling the PA would force Israel, it was argued, to take direct control of the West Bank and Gaza, making Israel's de facto occupation clearly visible. Nonetheless, the struggle for control of the PA raised the prospects of a power struggle between Hamas and Fatah.

Hamas versus the PLO?

During the first years of Hamas's existence there was some friction, increasing over time, with the PLO, and Fatah in particular, which tried to include Hamas in its own nationalist folder (Milton-Edwards 1996: 197). Hamas consistently rejected the PLO's and Fatah's overtures, seeking instead to establish itself as a political alternative. The relationship between Hamas and the PLO reached an all-time low during the so-called Madrid process.[11] Nonetheless, Hamas's charter acknowledges the PLO as an 'ally, father, brother, relative, friend' (Hamas 1988: Article 27) and Hamas in the past avoided a military confrontation with Fatah. Under the leadership of Sheikh Yasin, Hamas strongly discouraged infighting between Palestinian political factions as this would only serve the interests of Israel and weaken the Palestinian quest for statehood.

Preceding Hamas's election victory in January 2006, there were signs that Fatah under Mahmoud Abbas's leadership was struggling to control its armed factions and suffered from internal factionalism. In December 2005, the split within Fatah became obvious when the jailed Fatah leader, Marwan Barghouti, launched his own election list, a move that posed a serious challenge to Fatah's so-called 'old guard'. Although Abbas managed to reconcile the party's factions and present a joint election list, Fatah was weakened, which is why Abbas and others within the movement made repeated attempts at postponing the elections, hoping that time would help the party regain its popularity (ICG 2006). In the meantime, Hamas grew stronger by the day and was able to fine-tune its electoral strategy.

The election results prompted an open confrontation between armed Fatah fighters and supporters of Hamas, with the conflict deepening in April 2006 when the new Hamas cabinet rejected the president's veto against forming a new security force under the command of Jamal Abu Samhadana.[12] The deployment of the 3,000-strong force in May 2006 caused a serious political and security crisis within the Palestinian Authority. The troops' build-up intensified the rivalry between Fatah and Hamas and led to clashes between their respective militia units in June 2006 (BBC News 2006a).

Amidst the ongoing aid embargo against the Hamas-led government and the calls for reform of the PA, political tension increased as well on this volatile 'third front' between Hamas and Fatah. As indicated above, Fatah was weakened by its election defeat – with the associated departure of clientelistic patronage through lost control of the PA; by internal factionalism, and by weakening control over militant groups and militias. During the spring and summer of 2006 the Hamas cabinet and the president's office were in frequent conflict, reflecting a continued power struggle. For one thing, President Mahmoud Abbas wanted the Hamas government to honour agreements with Israel signed by the PLO, but this was categorically rejected by the Hamas cabinet. In an attempt to force Hamas's hand, President Abbas announced plans for a referendum that would imply recognition of Israel and acceptance of a two-state solution as the basis for a peace agreement. Initially, the proposal was categorically rejected by Hamas's Foreign Minister Mahmoud Zahar. Following weeks of intense negotiations, the referendum was called off after Hamas and Fatah agreed on a joint document, popularly known as the 'Prisoners' Document', which, among other things, acknowledged a two-state solution to the conflict with Israel. Nonetheless, there remained a serious disagreement between Hamas and the president over their respective authorities and mandates and, by implication, over the question of who was the more 'authentic' representative of the Palestinian people. This situation was not likely to disappear, since the time has passed when one political party could dominate the Palestinian scene (Milton-Edwards and Crooke 2004: 309). Hamas did not accept the PLO as the sole representative of the Palestinian people, but the signing by Hamas and Fatah in June 2006 of the Prisoners' Document implied acknowledgement of the PLO as the sole representative and tied this to the call for its reform and democratization.

Israeli unilateralism

Israel's policies towards the PA have increasingly been unilateral, such as the pull-out ('disengagement') from Gaza, which was announced by Ariel Sharon in early 2005 and completed in mid-September the same year. Following in Sharon's footsteps, Prime Minister Ehud Olmert, leader of the Kadima party, announced plans to settle unilaterally the borders vis-à-vis the Palestinian Territories and to annex all of Jerusalem (the 'convergence' plan), drawing strong protest from both Hamas and President Abbas. If this strategy is implemented, it would derail the 'two-state solution', whereby the borders of a future Palestinian state would be settled through negotiation. Olmert has affirmed his plan unilaterally to settle the borders by 2008, if the Palestinians do not show willingness (whatever that means) to negotiate a final peace deal by the end of 2006 (BBC News 2006b). The Israeli government has been claiming since 2002 to be without a credible 'partner' in the peace negotiations. This claim to be lacking a 'Palestinian partner' is closely linked, some argue (Usher 2006b: 13), to the Israeli authorities' fiction that 'there is no Palestinian people'. In fact, the Israeli policy of unilateralism has gradually taken over with the tacit approval of the USA. Since the failed Camp David negotiations, there has been a gradual physical distancing from Palestinians, through a deliberate Israeli policy of separation, of control of movement of people and goods, and surveillance. The most visible and controversial result of this policy is the setting up of the Separation Wall, encircling areas of the West Bank, and the Gaza disengagement plan. This strategy has slowly eroded the foundations for a credible two-state solution to the Palestinian problem.

A Palestinian state with 'Provisional Borders'

Israel has never formally declared its support for a sovereign Palestinian state. Under the US-sponsored Road Map, Israel implicitly accepted a Palestinian state with provisional borders (PSPB), with the Palestinian Authority acting as a civilian administration. This was to be followed (in 2005) by 'final status negotiations' over 'borders, Jerusalem, refugees, settlements' leading to a permanent status agreement and a sovereign Palestinian state. Some analysts, however, argue that in return for accepting a provisional Palestinian state, Israel would seek an indefinite postponement of the final status negotiations or prolong the negotiation process to allow itself to complete its consolidation of sections of the West Bank, while turning the Palestinian territories into a vast 'municipality' (Usher 2006b: 23). Despite the fact that the original timetable for the Road Map has long passed and the political foundations withered, and many of the above-mentioned irreversible changes on the ground have become reality, the Road Map's two-state solution to the Palestinian problem is today the only peace scenario recognized by the UN, EU and the powerful supra-state groups, the G8 and the Quartet. [13]

Hamas's Charter would imply an outright rejection of the very idea of a two-state solution (Article 11, Hamas 1988). Hamas expressed the explicit goal of establishing an Islamic state on all of Mandatory Palestine. It has also insisted on its demand for an end to the Israeli occupation and withdrawal to the pre-1967 borders. However, the movement's policies have been more pragmatic and more nuanced than commonly acknowledged (ICG 2006). Hamas's leaders and founders, including the late Sheikh Yasin, have been vague about the question of whether they will accept the Israeli state (Gaess 2002).[14] Hamas co-founder, the late Ismail Abu Shanab, was more forthright in acknowledging that 'we cannot destroy Israel. The practical solution is for us to have a state alongside Israel' (Shanab cited in Gunning 2004: 61).

On several occasions, Hamas's most senior leaders (Yasin, Rantisi and others) have likewise supported 'interim solutions' that stopped short of the historic claim to all of Mandatory Palestine. In addition, senior Hamas representatives have ruled out neither amending the movement's charter nor direct negotiations with Israel (ICG 2006: 20). Hamas's increasing pragmatism on this question can be observed from the election manifesto of the 'Reform and Change' bloc that won the January 2006 elections. The election manifesto departed markedly from the Hamas Charter, proclaiming Palestine as an 'Arab and Islamic homeland' (text of manifesto reproduced in ICG 2006: 22). Nonetheless, the Hamas leadership has traditionally been split over accepting a negotiated solution to the conflict (and by implication accepting the Israeli state) that falls short of the historic claim to all of Palestine. Those belonging to the 'outside leadership' – represented by the Hamas leader Khaled Meshal – have been more reluctant to compromise over this issue than those living inside the Occupied Palestinian Territories. Irrespective of any internal disagreements, Hamas has offered – and kept – unilateral ceasefires since 2001. It has also offered a long-term truce (*hudna*) if Israel withdraws to the 1967 borders. This position was given official sanction in June 2006 with the ratification of the Prisoner's Document, where Hamas and Fatah jointly accepted a two-state solution to the conflict but left the question of official recognition of the state of Israel unresolved. In the current situation, it is not easy to see what more Hamas could have offered, short of agreeing to their own dismantlement (Milton-Edwards and Crooke 2004: 309). Moreover, Palestinians have in reality conceded giving up 78% of their ancestral homeland. The current stalemate is over the control of the 22% that is left – a piece of land that grows progressively smaller, cantonized and made discontinuous by Israeli settlements, bypass roads and the construction of a wall that runs inside the 1949 armistice line (Green Line), another instance of Israel's incremental land-grab on the West Bank.[15]

Israel versus Hamas

Historically, Israel was instrumental in Hamas's rise to power, giving official patronage to its predecessor, the Gaza-based Islamic Centre (al-Mujamma' al-Islami), hoping that it would emerge as a political alternative to the PLO, at the time the most significant military and political threat to the Israeli state. The honeymoon between the Israeli authorities and Hamas ended when Hamas carried out its first attack on civilians in 1994, making Hamas Israel's main target, with assassinations and reprisals against leaders and cadres, including the deportation of 415 leaders and activists to southern Lebanon in 1992 (ICG 2004: 8).[16] For the past decade, Israel's policy vis-à-vis Hamas has been one of hard-line rejection and targeted assassinations of leaders and cadres. Since mid-2001, Hamas has lost three of its founding members – Ismail Abu Shanab, Sheikh Ahmed Yasin and Abdel al-Aziz Rantisi – in addition to more than 300 cadres in Gaza and abroad.[17] The assassinations increased the popular support for Hamas which quickly recovered from the loss of its founders, although it became cautious about naming its new leaders publicly in an effort to protect their lives.[18]

Hamas is sometimes classified as a 'spoiler', a faction that can derail or 'spoil' a peace process (Stedman 1997). While 'limited' and 'greedy' spoilers can be either conditioned or co-opted to accept a peace deal, a 'total' spoiler defies such strategies, hence must be destroyed (ibid.). Israel's hard-line policies towards Hamas combined with targeted assassinations of its leaders are rooted in the conception of Hamas as a 'total spoiler'. A more nuanced analysis of Hamas's strategies shows that it is in fact a 'limited spoiler', whose use of suicide attacks has been carefully 'timed to coincide with major events in the peace process' (Kydd and Walter 2002: 263–4). Such attacks reduce the likelihood that peace agreements will be successful, especially where the parties to the conflict do not trust each other, as is the case in the Israeli-Palestinian conflict. Nonetheless, Hamas has on several occasions offered – and kept – unilateral ceasefires.

Tactical ceasefires?

Most Western governments follow a dual-engagement policy vis-à-vis Hamas: condemnation of the military wing and constructive engagement with the political wing. Israel, however, denies the distinction between the political and military wings and considers Hamas a single terrorist entity (Gunning 2004: 234).[19] As already stated, Israel views Hamas as a 'total spoiler' – an opponent that can neither be co-opted nor conditioned to accept a peace deal, hence must be destroyed. Consequently, Hamas's repeated offers of a ceasefire have not been reciprocated by the Israeli authorities; indeed it has been claimed that the authorities have purposely undermined them by killing senior Hamas leaders, even the most moderate ones, like Jamal Mansour in 2001.

Hamas's first official offer of a long-term truce (*hudna*) was made by Sheikh Yasin in the early 1990s and came after long deliberations within the movement.[20] The reason that offering a truce was so difficult was that it undermined the historical struggle against Israel which Hamas considered a religious obligation (Milton-Edwards and Crooke 2004: 299). Over the years, Hamas developed a more pragmatic attitude towards ceasefires, and since the early 1990s has been involved in about ten ceasefire initiatives. The latest official ceasefire was announced in June 2003 by Hamas and Islamic Jihad. The ceasefire was short-lived and terminated a few months later following the assassination of Hamas's founder Ismail Abu Shanab in August 2003. Nonetheless, Hamas has not carried out any suicide missions since the early months of 2005, up to the time of writing this chapter (July 2006), something that could be considered an undeclared ceasefire. However, unilateral ceasefires have largely been inconsequential for the conflict as a whole, partly due to the lack of ground rules and impartial monitoring (Milton-Edwards and Crooke 2004: 46). Another reason is the fact that historically 'offers of a truce by Hamas have emerged when the movement was weak or under pressure from the PA and Israel' (Malka 2005: 41).[21] For some, this means that targeted attacks, coupled with the credible threat of force, is the only way to moderate Hamas. Others claim that Hamas's offers of a truce are not a tactical weapon to win time and regroup, but an option legitimized and sanctified by religious belief and hence increasingly embraced by the organization (Milton-Edwards and Crooke 2004). Since 2003, Hamas has not only reduced its military activity, but its military capability has also been weakened (Hroub 2004). However, despite being subject to unprecedented political pressure from the 'international community' and under siege by Israel, Hamas has not suffered so far from organizational 'overextension' (Gunning 2004: 238). Thus, despite the loss of several of its leaders and cadres, Hamas has experienced neither internal factionalism nor defections. But there are two issues that have the potential for causing a rift within the organization because of differences within the Hamas leadership: the use of political violence (suicide bombs) and whether or not to accept the state of Israel.

Bargaining for a negotiated peace

Hamas was a vocal critic of the troubled Madrid process and never accepted the Oslo agreement. However, this does not mean that Hamas rejects a negotiated solution to the conflict. To the contrary, Hamas has appealed for international mediation and was ready for talks with Israel on the condition that Israel ends the occupation. The main obstacle is that the preconditions demanded for such negotiations – renunciation of violence, disarming, acceptance of Israel – are not acceptable to Hamas because non-compliance with these demands is the only major bargaining card for a 'belligerent' like Hamas (see Waage 2005, for a fuller explanation of this term). Giving the bargaining chips away at the outset, much like the PLO did during the Oslo Accords process, would leave Hamas without any clout in future multilateral negotiations (as envisaged by the Road Map). This is expressed by Hamas leader Khaled Meshal stating that 'negotiating without resistance leads to surrender but negotiating with resistance leads to peace (Meshal quoted in Malka 2005: 4). In such a situation, an alternative approach to Hamas would be to defer the main demands on the movement and establish a series of 'benchmarks' they must comply with in an effort to 'nudge' rather than force Hamas towards political integration (Malka 2005). At the moment there is no willingness among a significant segment of the international community, particularly the USA and Europe, to ease the demands on Hamas. The strategic options before the movement range from full compliance (accepting all of the international community's demands) to rejection of these demands, a move that could lead to resumption of armed resistance ('suicide bombings') and pre-emptive Israeli strikes and reprisals (Table 9.1). From the perspective of Hamas, the problem with full compliance is not only ideological, as it entails surrendering the historic claim to all of Mandatory Palestine, but also practical, as it will compromise its bargaining position vis-à-vis Israel, leaving it no leverage to ensure that the final peace deal (as envisaged in the Road Map) will be acceptable to Hamas or the Palestinians as a whole. Hamas must be in a position to have a say in negotiations regarding acceptable borders for the prospective state, and the refugee and Jerusalem issues.[22] This means that Hamas, like the PLO before it, is hard pressed between acceptance of preconditions that undermine its bargaining position and rejection of these terms, which will expose it to heavy-handed Israeli reprisals and continued international boycott.

During its first months in office, the new Hamas cabinet pursued a policy of 'non-compliance' where all the international community's demands were rejected, leading to an economic and political boycott as well as the targeted assassinations of Hamas cadres (Table 9.1). In an attempt to break the stalemate, Hamas could choose 'partial compliance', a strategy that neither compromises the main demands, nor provokes Israeli attacks or subjects the movement to reprisals (Table 9.1). In this scenario, the key demands on the movement are deferred (rather than rejected) within the context of a unilateral ceasefire. However, choosing partial compliance is made more difficult and less appealing by the fact that Israel has declared its intention to decide

TABLE 9.1 Bargaining for peace: choices before Hamas[1]

Conflict level	Option	Process	Bargaining position	Likely outcome of peace deal
Lowest	Full compliance	Resumption of Road Map process, formal negotiations, aid reinstated	Weak (no credible sanctions)[2]	Unacceptable (compromises historic claims)
	Partial compliance	Negotiations and dialogue, unilateral ceasefire, emergency aid reinstated	Weak	None (status quo)
	Non-compliance	Status quo: int. isolation, no aid, increasing poverty	None	Unilateral
	Rejection	Gradual worsening of situation, no aid, increased int. pressure, internal PA conflict	None	Unilateral
Highest	Resumption	Resumption of armed resistance (suicide bombings)	None (no credible military power)	None (military defeat)

Notes: 1. In these scenarios, the outcome is seen from the perspective of Hamas. 2. Assumes that Hamas unconditionally renounces violence.

unilaterally on its final borders. This, in turn, has serious consequences for selling a Hamas-brokered peace deal that implies abrogating the Right of Return to the Palestinian refugees, traditionally those least likely to concede to a two-state solution (Gunning 2004: 252).[23] This means that Hamas finds itself between a rock and a hard place, and none of the bargaining solutions outlined here would be acceptable to both Hamas and Israel. Without intervention from unaligned countries who could serve as brokers,[24] this leaves Hamas with the option of instituting a series of unilateral short-term strategies aimed at de-escalating the conflict, lifting the aid boycott and, over time, removing its terror-listing. This includes extending the current unconditional ceasefire, continuing the shuttle diplomacy to shore up political and economic support in the Middle East and abroad,[25] and restructuring the organization by separating its political and military wing (i.e., Izze-dine al-Qassam Brigades). There is no guarantee, however, that these measures would break the current stalemate. Moreover, restructuring the organization is also likely to be opposed from within Hamas.

Hamas, the internal challenge

It is widely acknowledged now that Hamas itself did not expect the sweeping victory it achieved. The initial expectation was that it would secure a formidable presence in the Palestinian Legislative Council, where it would enjoy the power to muster a strong veto on legislations and policies opposed by the organization and to pass legislation in line with its political and ideological commitments. Khaled Sulayman, a councillor from Jenin district, stated: 'we expected to do well, but not to such an extent where we exceeded 50%. Now anything more than 50% is a big achievement, but it can also become a headache for the movement'.[26]

In the days following the elections, two broad views were expressed within the movement. The first supported the forming of a government by allowing Hamas to occupy only second-tier ministerial seats, leaving crucial decision-making to Abbas – a government either of national unity or of technocrats that would be granted international accept-ability, and therefore financial support. It was speculated that, with such an arrangement, Hamas would be spared the pressure of dealing with Israel or recognizing its legitimacy, and would abide by agreements signed with Israel, or meet special conditions to secure the continued flow of outside aid. The second view favoured a full exercise of power by Hamas with the intention of reaping the fruits of its big victory. The idea of passing this unique opportunity of running ministries and other crucial governmental structures and bodies, in fact leaving its platform in other people's hands, was unthinkable to this group, especially at a time of increasing tension between Fatah and Hamas. This opinion maintains that it would be a betrayal of the trust placed in Hamas by its supporters, if it chose not to exercise full power of governance (Meshal's speech in Damascus on 28 January 2006).

By securing its big electoral victory, Hamas moved from the opposition movement into a ruling party and found itself face to face with a number of serious challenges. This shift necessitated an adjustment to the new reality of governance, rearranging and prioritizing the various issues of its agenda, and articulating the strategies to achieve them. Hamas needed to address all difficult issues facing the Palestinians and presented by the outside world in response to its victory. Among the issues are, first, Hamas's geographically scattered leadership, which poses additional difficulties for maintaining internal accord and cohesion. The internal differences are due to the distinct sets of conditions within which each section operates. The leadership in exile, represented by Meshal and the members of the politburo, which secures the resources, is more vulnerable to pressures from their host countries than the inside leadership. The inside leadership is more driven by the concerns of Palestinians living in Palestine and by the legacy of their mutual struggle with secular groups and factions against the occupation. Therefore, differences between Hamas and other factions within Palestine are generally expressed less dramatically.

A second challenge before Hamas is the need to make political and ideological adjustments in order to meet the expectations of the public, including those segments of the population who did not vote for it. There is also a need to develop a new discourse that does not alienate the important actors in the international community, particularly Europe and the United Nations. Linked to this problem is how to reconcile the movement's slogan, which states 'under occupation no law is above the law of resistance', with that articulated by the Palestinian Authority under Mahmoud Abbas, which says 'one authority, one law, and one gun'. The disagreement over this issue is linked to a great deal of constitutional and political ambiguity regarding the authority and mandate of the Fatah-controlled presidency and the Hamas cabinet. Such conditions do not help the movement in genuinely reconciling the tasks of national struggle and resistance on the one hand, with political engagement and internal reconstruction on the other.

Another challenge before Hamas is the relationship between Hamas and other political groups in Palestine over the role and status of the Palestine Liberation Organization, and how to develop a formula by which both bodies – the PA and the PLO – can cooperate in carrying out their respective mandates. A further problematic issue for Hamas is the stance adopted by the international community and the United Nations regarding the Palestinians' conflict with Israel. For example, Hamas strongly disagrees with the United Nations' weak response to Israeli violations and with the position taken by it that equates legitimate armed resistance with terrorism.

On the day-to-day level, Hamas has to deal with the hardships caused by the international aid boycott. Poverty, unemployment and social tension are likely to continue to rise and to pose challenges to Hamas's ability to govern. Although a large part of the population remains loyal to Hamas in the face of external pressures, it is possible that it will lessen its backing and support if hardships on the ground continue to mount.

In sum, Hamas is now obliged to deliver on its election promises and meet the people's expectations and demands for better services, security and economic development. Moreover, it must also demonstrate the merits of its brand of Islamism, which is the main theme in the organization's political and ideological charter. In order to deliver on these issues, Hamas would have to deal with the external pressures exerted by the US, Europe and some of the Arab states, and to articulate a clearer position regarding a number of difficult issues such as relations with other Palestinian groups, recognizing Israel, armed resistance and previously signed agreements with Israel.

Conclusion

In January 2006 Hamas scored a major political victory by trumping Fatah in the elections to the Palestinian Legislative Council (PLC). The first 100 days of the new Hamas cabinet were marked by international siege, a full aid boycott, and growing friction between the office of President Mahmoud Abbas (the head of Fatah), and the new Hamas cabinet. This left Hamas politically isolated, the president sidelined and the Palestinian populace sinking deeper into poverty and despair. By the summer of 2006, the Palestinian economy was reduced to shambles and the PA was bankrupt. Reforming the PA – Hamas's key election goal – is long overdue. Together, these conditions have paved the way for armed conflict between militia-groups aligned respectively with Fatah and Hamas in a context of weakening political control. With a majority of the seats in the PLC, Hamas nominally controls the Palestinian Authority, yet control of the PA remains disputed and is now a battlefield between forces loyal to Hamas and those loyal to President Abbas.

Hamas has in recent years undergone an incremental process of political integration, a process mostly ignored by the movement's foes and detractors. It has displayed political and tactical moderation, including keeping unilateral ceasefires until June 2006, abandoning the claim to all of Mandatory Palestine and accepting a two-state solution comprising the 1967 territories (Gaza and the West Bank with East Jerusalem). Hamas has not, however, complied with external pressures to abandon armed resistance, disarm and recognize Israel. The main reason for this is not only ideological, but strategic: complying with the demands would leave Hamas without any credible sanctions in the final-status negotiations that until now have been the only scenario for a lasting peace agreement. Hamas, therefore, is not opposed to negotiations with Israel, but cannot accept the preconditions for negotiations that would imply abrogating territorial, political and historic conditions to statehood. This is not because Hamas is a 'total spoiler', bent on breaking any peace deal with Israel, but because Hamas cannot accept a two-state solution that lacks popular legitimacy. By the same token, Israel considers itself better off with a unilateral security policy and a Separation Wall than with a full-fledged Palestinian state on its doorstep.

Israel has never formally declared its support for an independent sovereign Palestinian state, yet the two-state solution implied in the US sponsored Road Map is made contingent on Hamas's political acceptance of the state of Israel. Furthermore, despite the fact that the Road Map is politically dead, as are any other plans based on the Oslo formula, the international community has continued to base its policies vis-à-vis Hamas on this outmoded plan, using economic sanctions to force Hamas to comply with the demands on the movement: renouncing violence, disarming, accepting the state of Israel. At the same time, Israel has announced its intention to decide on its borders unilaterally, a plan that has received tacit backing from the US. The two-pronged strategy of sanctioning Hamas and rewarding Israel will ensure that the 'peace process' decays further amidst escalation of political violence, possibly marking the end of a two-state solution to the conflict.

Hamas is now deeply rooted in Palestinian society, well organized, well funded, disciplined and, so far, not tainted by corruption. The organization has come under increasing international pressure, but economic hardships and political isolation are likely to strengthen Hamas's popular support, not weaken it. Likewise the frequent attacks on Hamas leaders have not decapitated the movement, but increased its resolve.

As things stand, Hamas has the following three options: to step down from office and become a parliamentary opposition group (bearing in mind that such an action will be perceived by others as a defeat), to continue the current tense situation and confrontation with Fatah and other groups (which will weaken both Hamas and the opposition), or finally to reach a formula of national understanding that serves as thee basis for a national unity government. Through this last option, Hamas could perhaps deal more effectively with the deteriorating conditions on the ground and with the external pressures. By forming a national unity government, which requires a degree of flexibility over the complex differences between Hamas and others, the movement will be better placed to preserve its credibility and stay in power. More importantly, Palestinians will be, possibly, in a much better position not only to articulate a coherent and united perspective towards the two-state solution, but also to formulate the policies and strategies for this to materialise. This would also serve to weaken the political logic behind Israeli unilateralism that remains the major obstacle to a negotiated peace agreement.

Notes

1 This chapter has been prepared under a long-term collaborative agreement between the Chr. Michelsen Institute (CMI) and the Palestinian Institute for the Study of Democracy (Muwatin) funded by the Norwegian Agency for Development Co-operation (NORAD). It is a revised version of a paper presented to a joint CMI-Muwatin panel at the Wocmes2 conference in Amman, 11–16 June 2006.

2 'Hamas' ('zeal') is the Arabic acronym for 'Haraket al-Muqawama al-Islamiya', or Islamic Resistance Movement.

3 Note that the difference between votes cast for Hamas and Fatah was slim. Fatah's inordinate loss in the elections was due to the mixed electoral

system, combining a majority system (districts) and a system of proportional representation (lists). Hamas fielded only one candidate in the district elections, while Fatah fielded several. Dispersing the votes, Fatah lost several seats to Hamas.

4 Interview with Khaled Sulayman, conducted by Basem Ezbidi on 30 May 2006, in Ramallah.

5 Interview with Mahmoud Ramahi, conducted by Basem Ezbidi on 25 May 2006, in Ramallah.

6 Interview with Adnan Asfour, conducted by Basem Ezbidi on 6 July 2006, in Ramallah.

7 In the public and civil sector, the PA employs about 165,000 persons and is the major employer in the West Bank and Gaza. Assuming that each employee is the sole breadwinner for an average sized family of 6.37 persons (Sletten and Pedersen 2003: 57), about one million persons depend directly on the PA for their livelihoods.

8 The EU itself contributes about USD 300 million, with an additional 300m. coming from the member states (ICG 2006: 31).

9 This means that the international community pays the costs of the Israeli occupation. Under international law Israel is responsible for the welfare of those under occupation (Usher 2006b: 19).

10 Hamas was a vocal opponent of the Madrid process and the Oslo Accords, in line with the organization's rejection of negotiated settlements that fell short of a full Israeli withdrawal from the West Bank (Knudsen 2005)

11 The Madrid Process was mired with problems and was followed by the secret back-door negotiations that led to the signing of the Oslo Accords (Waage 2002).

12 In June 2006 Samhadana was killed by an Israeli targeted air strike in Rafah (Gaza Strip).

13 The Group of Eight (G8) consists of Canada, France, Germany, Italy, Japan, the United Kingdom, the United States of America and the Russian Federation.

14 In addition to reflecting a deliberate policy of political ambiguity, it is also borne out of a religiously defined right to conceal (Ar. *taqiyya*) beliefs or views that could harm Muslims (Abu-Amr 1997: 244–5).

15 The International Court of Justice (ICJ) ruled in July 2005 that the Wall breaches international law and should be dismantled. Yet the Israeli Supreme Court has defended the legality of the Wall.

16 Extra-judicial assassinations have not been confined to Hamas members but have included members of other political factions as well.

17 In September 1997, there was an ill-fated assassination attempt on Khaled Meshal, then head of the Hamas Politburo in Amman, by two Mossad agents. The failed attack forced Israel to release the imprisoned Sheikh Yasin in a deal brokered by King Hussein of Jordan.

18 For Hamas's policy of 'undisclosed leadership', see Hroub (2004: 31).

19 Israeli sources dispute Hamas's claim to separate political and military wings. This chapter assumes that there is such a separation (see Gunning 2004: 236).

20 It is important to differentiate between a long-term truce (*hudna*) and a short-term (or interim) ceasefire (*tahdi'ya*) (Malka 2005). Hamas's offer of a long-term truce is conditioned on an Israeli withdrawal to the 1967-borders. Ceasefires carry no political obligations but are meant to reduce tensions and de-escalate the conflict.

21 The latest official ceasefire offer from Hamas and Islamic Jihad came in June 2003, shortly after the twin assassinations of Yasin and Rantisi.

22 This scenario is comparable to the situation faced by the late President Yassir Arafat when, in 2000, he declined to sign the Camp David Accords (insisting on the peace of the brave) despite strong US pressure (Usher 2006: 16–17).

23 Opinion polls carried out after Hamas's election victory, show that Palestinian refugees in Lebanon overwhelmingly support the organization's stance of not recognizing Israel as well as martyrdom (suicide) operations (*Daily Star* 4/4 2006).

24 Norway is an unaligned country that is not bound by the the EU's and the US's terror-listing of Hamas and has traditionally had a very close relationship with Israel (Waage 2000). The Oslo 'backchannel' built close personal links between Norwegian diplomats and the PLO (Waage 2002) but did not develop comparable contacts with Palestinian Islamist groups.

25 After being sworn in, members of the new Hamas cabinet actively pursued this strategy, but with limited success, since most Western governments are either bound by the EU's terror-listing of Hamas or weary of stepping out of line with an international agenda that is supported by the US and the EU. Israel in July 2006, in a response to Hamas's capture of an Israeli soldier, arrested and jailed a number of Hamas ministers and PLC members in the West Bank.

26 Interview with Hamas legislator Khaled Sulayman, conducted by Basem Ezbidi, 30 May 2006, in Ramallah.

References

Abu-Amr, Z. (1997) 'Shaykh Ahmad Yasin and the origins of Hamas', in R. S. Appleby (ed.), *Spokesmen for the Despised: Fundamentalist Leaders of the Middle East*, Chicago: University of Chicago Press.

Agha, H and R. Malley (2006) 'Hamas: The Perils of Power', *New York Review of Books*, 9 March 2006.

BBC News (2006a) 'Rival Gaza forces exchange fire', 19 May 2006, http://news.bbc.co.uk/2/hi/middle_east/4996186.stm

— (2006b) 'Israel warns Hamas over borders', 10 May 2006, http://news.bbc.co.uk/2/hi/middle_east/4757399.stm.

CFR (2005) 'Hamas and the shrinking PA budget', 21 April 2006, Council of Foreign Relations (CFR), http://www.cfr.org/publication/10499/.

Daily Star (2006) 'Survey analyzes impact of Hamas victory in Lebanon', 4 April 2006, http://www.dailystar.com.lb/article.asp?edition_id=1&categ_id=2&article_id=23495

Gaess, R. (2002) 'Interviews from Gaza: What Hamas wants' (Abd al-Aziz

Rantisi, Sheikh Ahmed Yassin, Ismail Abu Shanab, Mahmoud al-Zahar), *Middle East Policy* 9 (4): 102–21.

Gunning, J. (2004) 'Peace with Hamas? The transforming potential of political participation', *International Affairs* 80 (2).

Hamas (1988) 'The Covenant of the Islamic Resistance Movement', 18 August 1988, www.yale.edu/lawweb/avalon/mideast/hamas.htm.

Hilal, J. (2006) 'Hamas's rise as charted in the polls, 1994–2005', *Journal of Palestine Studies* 35 (4): 6–19.

Hroub, K. (2004) 'Hamas after Sheikh Yasin and Rantisi', *Journal of Palestine Studies* 33 (4): 21–38.

ICG (2004) 'Dealing With Hamas', Amman, Brussels: International Crisis Group, *Middle East Report*, No. 21, www.icg.org//library/documents/ middle_east___north_africa/21_dealing_with_hamas.pdf.

— (2006) 'Enter Hamas: The Challenges of Political Integration', Brussels, Amman: International Crisis Group, *Middle East Report*, No. 49, 18 January 2006.

Khan, M. H., G. Giacaman, and I. Amundsen (2004) *State Formation in Palestine : Viability and Governance During a Social Transformation*, London: RoutledgeCurzon.

Knudsen, A. (2005) 'Crescent and sword: The Palestinian Hamas', *Third World Quarterly*, 26, 8, 1373–88.

Kydd, A., and B. F. Walter (2002) 'Sabotaging the peace: the politics of extremist violence', *International Organization*, 56 (2): 263–96.

Malka, H. (2005) 'Forcing choices: Testing the transformation of Hamas', *The Washington Quarterly*, 28 (4):37–54.

MFA (2005) *St. prp. nr. 1 (2005–2006): For budsjettåret 2006*, Oslo: Utenriksdepartementet (Ministry of Foreign Affairs, MFA).

Milton-Edwards, B., and A. Crooke (2004) 'Waving, not drowning: Strategic dimensions of ceasefires and Islamic movements', *Security Dialogue*, 35 (3): 295–310.

Milton-Edwards, B. (1996) *Islamic Politics in Palestine*, London: I.B. Tauris.

Milton-Edwards, B., and A. Crooke (2004) 'Elusive ingredient: Hamas and the peace process', *Journal of Palestine Studies*, 33 (4): 39-52.

Sletten, P. and J. Pedersen (2003) *Coping with Conflict: Palestinian Communities Two Years into the Intifada*, Oslo: FAFO Report, No. 408, www.fafo.no/pub/rapp/408/408.pdf.

Stedman, S. (1997) 'Spoiler problems in peace processes', *International Security*, 22 (2): 7–17.

US Department of State (2003) 'A Performance-based Roadmap to a Permanent Two-state Solution to the Israeli-Palestinian Conflict', 30 April 2003, www.state.gov/r/pa/prs/ps/2003/20062.htm.

Usher, G. (2006a) 'Hamas risen', *Middle East Report*, No. 238, Spring 2006.

— (2006b) 'The wall and the dismemberment of Palestine', *Race & Class*, 47 (3): 9-30.

Waage, H. H. (2000) 'How Norway Became One of Israel's Best Friends', *Journal of Peace Research* 37 (2):189–211.

— (2002) 'Explaining the Oslo backchannel: Norway's political past in the Middle East', *Middle East Journal*, 56 (4): 597–615.

— (2005) 'Norway's role in the Middle East peace talks: between a strong state and a weak belligerent', *Journal of Palestine Studies*, 34 (4): 6–24.

10 | Searching for a solution

SHARIF S. ELMUSA

Introduction

The current approaches to resolving the Israeli-Palestinian conflict have led to an impasse, and the conflict that has lasted more than a century looks set to continue for two main reasons. First, the chances for a viable Palestinian state in the West Bank and Gaza, as many observers agree, are slim, owing to the area's tattered geography and shrunken space. A rump state under Israeli tutelage is emerging instead – a collection of Palestinian 'bantustans'. Second, Israel's rejection of the Right of Return of the Palestinian refugees means that East Jordanian and Palestinian tensions would continue in Jordan.[1] In Israel, too, Palestinian-Jewish antagonism would continue because of the failure to resolve the Palestinian problem satisfactorily and because Israel insists on being an exclusively Jewish state, not a state for all its citizens. A dynamic Palestinian state in the West Bank and Gaza could encourage the Palestinians to press for greater political power, thereby exacerbating national and ethnic disputes in Israel and in Jordan.

If a durable peace is ever to materialize, we need to probe fresh possibilities, explore the roads not taken. These must be grounded in the principles of equality and reciprocity rather than on the dictates of power. This chapter proposes two alternatives, one exclusionary and the second inclusive: a revival of the 1947 UN partition plan and a single bi-national state in Israel, the West Bank and Gaza, and Jordan. The plan would avail the Palestinians of a sufficiently large territory for accommodating those refugees who wish to return. It also would afford them the sentimental space that they associate with *Palestine*, and that they might be willing to accept as a substitute for returning to their historic homeland – a state in the West Bank and Gaza alone does not fulfill these conditions. Under the plan, Israel would become almost totally Jewish, as the Zionists have always wanted it to be. Jordan would give its Palestinian citizens the option of returning to the Palestinian state, or of staying in Jordan without extra-territorial loyalties, or the two states could join in some form of federation.

A bi-national state in the territories of Israel, Jordan, Gaza and the West Bank – which we refer to for convenience as Greater Palestine – may be attractive for the Palestinians, as it would re-unite them after being dispersed. Objections, however, have been raised from Palestinian quarters; and Israeli Jews or East Jordanians may well prefer to remain the dominant groups in their own states. So, part of the burden of this chapter is to inquire into the plan's potential merits for the three protagonists. Such a state in principle is similar to the bi-national state between the Mediterranean Sea and the Jordan river, which has been advocated for many years. It is superior to the smaller state, or so I try to demonstrate, particularly by rendering the refugee problem one of movement within a single larger state.

What I am presenting here are propositions, in the sense that propositions are uncertain, yet serve to question positions that have been taken in spite of the dead end they have led to. Such propositions may sound heretical, but they can open the door to fresh thinking and in time might appear more plausible. The multi-ethnic state in particular could lead to unforeseen associations and complexities among the antagonists that are richer than those prevailing under the reductionism of the hegemony of single nationalities or ethnicities. It may sound utopian to many, but, as Russell Jacoby wisely observes, twentieth-century wars and massacres were the product of ethnocentricity and beliefs in racial and national superiority, not of calls for equality, cooperation and pluralism (Jacoby 2005).

Two notes are in order, one on terminology and the second on sources. I employ the concept of a 'bi-national' state to refer to a state comprising Arabs and Jews. This applies whether the state is only in Gaza and the West Bank and Israel or in Greater Palestine. I do not use the concept to refer to present-day Israel, although its citizens are chiefly Jews and Arabs. The word 'Arabs' in the context of Greater Palestine refers to both Jordanians and Palestinians. The reason for these seemingly idiosyncratic usages is that the people of Jordan, whether East Jordanian or of Palestinian origin, think of themselves as Arabs, in the broad sense of belonging to the Arab nation. As such, they would be categorized as ethnic groups in Jordan. Distinctions, I hope, will be clear from the context. It should also be borne in mind that both the Jordanian and Palestinian populations include other sub-ethnic minorities, like the Chechens and Armenians. Parallel statements may also be made about the Jewish population of Israel.

The Arab-Israel conflict has engendered a huge literature, and sources can only be selective. My arguments for a bi-national state in Greater Palestine are largely a critical engagement with exchanges on the two-state versus bi-national state solutions that appeared in three forums: *The Boston Review*,[2] *The New York Review of Books*[3] and *The Arab World Geographer (AWG)*.[4] The chapter expands on two essays I wrote for *Al-Ahram Weekly* and the *AWG* (Elmusa 2005 and 2006) and from which I quote here.

The end of a Palestinian state

The end of a Palestinian state has a twofold meaning. The first is that Israel's shredding of the Palestinian territory has rendered a viable Palestinian state in the West Bank and Gaza a remote possibility. The second is that even if it were to become a reality, such a state would fall far short of resolving the conflict because it has become perfectly clear that Israel rejects the Right of Return of the Palestinian refugees. The area is too small, comprising only slightly more than one-fifth of historic Palestine, and cannot take in many refugees. The Palestinian population in the West Bank and Gaza alone is nearing 3.8 million, and will double in the next 25 years or so. Even today Gaza, with its estimated 1.4 million inhabitants and paltry 365 square kilometers, suffers from overcrowdedness.

The Palestinians are a fairly homogenous national group, possessing a key political prerequisite for establishing a state of their own. In spite of Israel's effort to splinter them into ever-expanding categories – Christians, Druze, Muslims, Gazans, Jerusalemites, Jerichoites, residents of areas A, B or C, displaced persons and refugees[5] the Palestinians share a strong sense of common identity, solidified in their long defence against the Zionist and Israeli onslaught. Although the Palestine Liberation Organization has failed to realize its goal of creating a Palestinian state, it was able to promote a sense of Palestinian nationhood among the dispersed communities.

Equally, the Palestinians have accumulated rich political experience and developed, under adverse circumstances, civil-society and para-state institutions that, imperfect as they are, could form the institutional nucleus of a viable state. The high level of participation in the most recent presidential and legislative elections,[6] and the spirited yet orderly manner in which they were conducted all compellingly attest to their ability and readiness to form a political state. The Palestinians would not be a state trying to forge a nation of a multiplicity of identities (as is often the case), a state-nation, as it were, but a nation fashioning a state. What excludes the possibility of a viable state is the fragmented and vulnerable geography that Israel has left them with (See, among others: Aruri 2005, Elmusa 2005, Falah 2005, Moughrabi 2005, Sayigh 2005, and Yiftachel 2005.)

Fragmentation and severe restrictions on the mobility of people and goods have turned the Palestinian economy into a series of micro-economies attached to the Israeli economy. Control over international ports prevents direct linkage of Palestinian markets to Arab and international markets, except through Israeli mediation. A Palestinian state thus would be missing a critical component of statehood: a unified national market joined directly to external markets. A viable state cannot evolve without such a market.

Why did Israel force the Palestinians into this corner? Why did it keep expanding the settlements and building the bypass roads after Oslo? Why did it continue its tight control over the international ports and impede the movement of goods to and from Jordan? Why did it refuse to build a safe passage between Gaza and the West Bank? Why did it, in the pre-Oslo negotiations in Washington, DC, stubbornly refuse to demarcate the borders of the settlements and agree to a functional role over them, as the Palestinian delegation headed by Dr Haidar Abd Al-Shafi had consistently demanded? There is only one explanation: Israel has never seriously entertained the idea of a viable, sovereign Palestinian state (see, for example, Abed 1990).

Forget about the 'generous offer' of Prime Minister Ehud Barak to President Yassir Arafat at Camp David in July 2000; for there was no genuine state proposed, only disconnected fragments, only more land to be taken by Israel, and only the establishment of Israel as the virtual gatekeeper of the borders of any Palestinian state. Today, both Labour and Kadima are unified in a coalition government whose plans promise to leave the Palestinians in a much worse position than at Camp David.

Stubborn demography

Even if a viable Palestinian state were to come to fruition, Israel's rejection of the Right of Return will almost assuredly not bring peace. A few statistics help put the matter in perspective. There are today more than eight million Palestinians in Greater Palestine: 1.4 million in Israel (20% of the total), 1.4 million in Gaza, 2.4 million in the West Bank and 3.6 million in Jordan.[7] In 30 years or so, they will double to 16 million, not counting the relatively large concentrations of refugees in Lebanon and Syria. At a time when the advocacy of democracy has become a political mantra in the region, it is historically retrograde that the people who constitute the majority in Greater Palestine remain subject to dispossession by Israel and sub-citizens in Jordan. If the last century of strife has taught us anything, it is that they will fight fiercely for a state in which they are equal citizens.

The Palestinian demographic presence throughout the territory of Greater Palestine could have a double effect. Because the Palestinians would prefer to live in a unified state, they would constitute an integrative force in this territory; yet, because neither Israel nor Jordan have been able to find political arrangements that would satisfy Palestinian political ambitions, they would continue to be viewed as a source of instability and suspicion in both states.

Demography matters. In countries where aggrieved nationalities are concentrated in one area, we observe a centrifugal pressure towards secession or at least a demand for autonomy. The splitting of Czechoslovakia and Cyprus exemplify this conclusion. Quebec in Canada, the Basque region in Spain, and Kurdistan in Iraq and Turkey are further illustrations. Where ethnicities are more evenly spread and intermingled, only democratic accommodation can begin to tackle social tensions; South Africa stands out. Yet, in a third situation where the same nationality exists in two separate states, re-unification may be sought. Witness the two Germanys, North and South Korea, Mainland China and Taiwan. In Greater Palestine the 'demographic effect' is mixed. The diffusion of the Palestinian communities throughout the territory is a unifying factor, although their prolonged isolation from each other seeded the formation of distinct identities. The Jewish and East Jordanian concentration west and east of the Jordan river, in contrast, pulls in the opposite direction – separation. But of course, each will have in their midst a large number of Palestinians, and in their very neighbourhood could have a state full of them (more on the likely positions of Israel and Jordan below).

Although the Hashemite monarchy offered the Palestinians citizenship soon after the West Bank was annexed in the early 1950s, thereby acquiring the West Bank and helping to obliterate 'Palestine' from the map, it has failed to make them equal partners. East Jordanians,

215

in turn, continue to fear a Palestinian takeover. The recent scare in Jordan caused by the news leak that two top Israeli military commanders predicted the demise of the Hashemite regime is indicative of the ethnically induced volatility of Jordanian politics (Harel 2006).

In addition to the Palestinians in Jordan, there would be the Palestinians who are Israeli citizens but unable to overcome their third-class citizenship status in a state that insists on being a 'Jewish state'. Israel has kept its Palestinian citizens an ethnicity apart, a third-class collective, a politically powerless Other. This is an outcome of the very ideology of Zionism, which sought the establishment of a Jewish home in Palestine, oblivious to, and often ready to shove out and aside, the Palestinian indigenous population. As Oren Yiftachel succinctly writes, 'Zionism remains a deeply ethnocentric movement, premised on belief in its "historic right" over the entire "promised homeland" and the Othering of the Palestinians' (Yiftachel 2005: 10). The uncompromising ethnocentricity of Zionism constrains Israel from coming to terms with its own Palestinian citizens and with the refugees (Yiftachel 2005). It is not an exaggeration to say that Zionism was always obsessed with demography, picturing the Palestinians as a 'demographic problem' or more melodramatically as a 'demographic bomb'. Thus the unilateral withdrawal from Gaza on the eve of Ariel Sharon's incapacitation in January 2006 was explained as aiming to preserve a Jewish majority. The same alibi is given for the projected withdrawal from parts of the West Bank, under the overly technical name, 'realignment and convergence', perhaps to blunt criticism from Israeli opponents and mask the politics of land seizure. Palestinian citizens of Israel can hence look forward to being a subordinated minority for a long time.

In Greater Palestine we thus have not only the Palestinian predicament; there are also Jewish and East Jordanian dilemmas – for the presence of a Palestinian majority confronts both Jordan and Israel, and will continue to do so, with a central question of how to co-exist with this majority. Both the Jordanian regime and Israel have been apprehensive that a viable Palestinian state would only embolden their Palestinian citizens to press them for fundamental political concessions. That apprehension explains why they have never genuinely contemplated allowing such a state to emerge.

Alternatives

The cul-de-sac of a Palestinian state can be circumvented in two ways: by the resuscitation of the UN 1947 partition plan or by beginning to work toward creating a bi-national state in Greater Palestine. Objections can be easily stacked up against each idea. I will engage those that have been voiced, anticipate others, and perhaps raise more questions than offer answers!

1. Forward to the 1947 UN Partition Plan? The partition plan proposed the division of Palestine into two states, 'Jewish' and 'Arab', with what must be described as gerrymandered boundaries (United Nations 1947). It allocated to the Jews 55% of the area of the territory of British Mandate Palestine, even though they were a minority owning only about 6% of the land. The Jews seemingly agreed to it, for it realized their long quest for a state, and it was spatially divided in their favour. Their formal endorsement did not necessarily mean they were going to be content with those boundaries, and they left their options open for expansion, as suggested, for example, by Baruch Kimmerling (Kimmerling 1983). The Palestinians rejected the plan, insisting on preserving the unity of their homeland. Communal violence erupted, and on 15 May 1948 Israel declared itself a state. The Arab armies intervened to save the day, but miserably failed. The war enabled Israel to occupy approximately an additional 23% more land than was allotted to it under the plan. In 1949 the Arab states and Israel signed an armistice agreement, leaving the conquered territory under Israeli control. The Palestinians experienced what they call the Nakba, catastrophe, epitomized by the expulsion of the majority of the population to the neighbouring Arab states. What was left of Palestine was split two ways: Gaza, under Egyptian administration, and the West Bank, annexed to Jordan. The rest is history.

Could a plan that was unacceptable to the Palestinians in 1947 be revived now? It would be too obvious to say that Israel was built on the idea of recreating an imagined, biblical Israel, and that the time that has elapsed since 1947 is minuscule by comparison. Further, the partition plan is the only UN resolution that designates borders for the said Jewish state. The subsequent borders of Israel, including those of the 1949 armistice lines and of the aftermath of the 1967 war, were the result of conquest. Israel itself never defined borders for itself, a tactic that allowed it to expand and retreat according to circumstances.

It was a major political error for the Palestinians not to insist in their negotiations with the Israelis that led to Oslo on tabling the plan at least as an opening position. Once they had commenced from the 1967 borders, they were bound to look intransigent if they did not make compromises within that area: which is exactly what they were accused of after the failure of the Camp David negotiations in 2000.

Implementation of the partition plan would entail Israel giving back the 23% of Palestine it acquired in the 1948 war. From a Palestinian perspective, this would double the size of a state in the West Bank and Gaza. The actual borders of a new partition do not have to correspond to the lines identified by the plan. The two states could be consolidated, each in one part of Palestine, the Palestinians in the eastern and the northernmost areas. The criteria of division would be: near equality in the land area, access to the Mediterranean and Red Seas and mutual strategic vulnerability or, more positively, strategically secure terrain. The enlargement of the land area would provide room for the Palestinian refugees who wish to return. The consolidated area would include the region where the Palestinian citizens of Israel are concentrated. Access to the Mediterranean serves instrumental and existential objectives in that Palestinians associate Palestine with cities like Acre, Haifa, Jaffa and Jerusalem. It is possible to supplant Gaza with areas in the north. Gaza is militarily indefensible, as its population has bitterly learned.

Crucially, a part of the Galilee was to be a segment of the Palestinian state, including the cities of Acre and Safad. Israeli analysts occasionally floated the idea of incorporating the parts of the Galilee – where the Palestinian citizens of Israel are concentrated – into a West Bank and Gaza state. So this should not be objectionable to the Israelis. A port on the Red Sea is significant as the centre of the world economy progressively shifts to Asia. It provides a sea link with Egypt, Saudi Arabia and Yemen. Israelis in large numbers spend their holidays in Egypt's Red Sea resorts. It would be truly ironic to deny the Palestinians the same privilege in an Arab country. In short, a Palestinian state could start from Haifa and arc northward and eastward, follow nearly the borders of the West Bank and continue along Wadi Araba, and terminate on the Red Sea.

It is easy to find fault in such a map; this is merely an illustration. What matters are the criteria on which it is based.[8]

For Israel, reversion to the partition plan involves a loss of land, but it is the share that was acquired by war. It would be giving it back rather than giving it up. A Palestinian state according to the map I have outlined has the virtue of limiting Israel's frontiers with Arab states to those with Palestine and Egypt only, thereby reducing the probability of conflict. By incorporating its Arab citizens in a Palestinian state – a desire hinted at by Israeli analysts and which has public encouragement – Israel becomes as nearly purely Jewish as politics could ever allow. In return for the land it cedes, it achieves an end to the conflict with the Palestinians, lower probability of wars breaking out with its neighbours and, above all, the Jewishness it has craved. This is the kind of trade-off Israel needs to decide on if it wants to realize enduring peace: ethnic purity versus land. To ask for both is to invite eternal strife.

For Jordan, the main advantage of implementing the partition plan is that it allows a large number of Palestinian refugees to leave Jordan for their new state. The East Jordanians would then be in a position to demand from those Palestinians choosing to stay behind loyalty as citizens of Jordan. This does not shut the door to some form of integration between the Palestinian and Jordanian states.

The revival of the partition plan would, I think, find broad support among the Palestinians and Jordanians. Israel, which is not satisfied with the 1967 boundaries, would oppose it. Israel can do so chiefly because of its greater power. How long will this opposition last?

2. *A Bi-national state in Greater Palestine?* Bi-nationalism was the Palestinian approach to resolving the conflict with the Israelis, until the PLO adopted unambiguously the two-state strategy in 1988. Fatah adopted bi-nationalism in the late 1960s. The adoption was brief, without much deliberation on the institutional modalities and without identifying steps by which it could be achieved or what it would mean for its military and political tactics. The idea was played out to an international audience in 1974 in the famous speech by Yassir Arafat, head of the PLO, before the UN General Assembly. What Arafat called for, in a nutshell, was the de-Zionization of Israel. The reaction of Israel and its supporters was prompt and unequivocally negative: secular bi-nationalism was a ruse for the destruction of the Jewish state. Bi-nationalism lay dormant afterwards, except among some stalwart activists. It was sometimes used as a scarecrow by the supporters of the two-state solution to frighten Israeli expansionists that more land acquisition would entail bi-nationalism by default (e.g. Qureia 2004).

Recently, seeing that what was emerging was an even worse form of South African apartheid, some have begun to renew the proposal of a bi-national Israeli-Palestinian state.

The proposal for a bi-nationalism that includes Jordan is fundamentally the same as the more limited Israel/Palestine idea; it differs from it in that it stretches the geography of the state, offering an opportunity to address the refugees' Right of Return. Bi-nationalism has been contested from Palestinian and Israeli perpectives, and cannot be expected to find ready acceptance among East Jordanians.

The contestation of bi-nationalism comes in three forms. Critics contend that there is a lack of public backing for the idea on both sides of the divide and that its advocates have failed to systematize it into a programme. Then there are specifically Zionist criticisms and nationalist Palestinian ones, although both are very much intertwined. Zionists attack bi-nationalism because they want a Jewish state, which in turn is predicated upon a supposition that Jews would become persecuted in a state in which Arabs are the majority. Palestinian opposition centres on the disparity of power resources between the two communities and fear that Palestinian identity would be overwhelmed and distanced from its Arab tributaries.

Defenders of bi-nationalism are faulted for not delving into the details and translating the idea into a programme (Lustick 2002, Tamari 2002). This is a valid, though not insurmountable, charge. Some advocates have already attempted to clarify political and legal concepts necessary for governance, as well as difficulties that would be confronted in the formation of such a state and some problems need to be confronted head on. Ian Lustick, even though he prefers two states, is aware how the Palestinians and Israelis might drift into a bi-national state without having thought about it. Lama Abu-Odeh, a lawyer, advises that United States federalism be taken seriously as a model, coupled with a legal strategy for the Palestinians in pursuing their goals. Segal sketches an outline for a bi-national confederation. There are two widely divergent recommendations, suggesting a need for further dialogue among the advocates to bridge the gap. Lustick brings up the salient land question. The bulk of land in Israel is state land, and the best of it is technically owned by the Jewish National Fund, as was the case before the establishment of the Israeli state. This political-legal regime discriminates against the Palestinians' ability to buy land and farm in places of their own choosing. Attempts to refashion the land regime would be met with fierce resistance from Zionists.

The land question is a good reminder that in fact many issues that need to be considered in a bi-national state have already been raised because Israel insists on being a Jewish state, not a state of all it citizens, 30% of whom are not Jews.[9] So, one important site for detail is the struggle and writings of the Israeli-Palestinians (see, for example, *Middle East Report Online* 1999). Another site is South Africa, where similar conditions of power asymmetry exist.[10] Such examples could help determine the feasibility of such a demanding political project.

Critics of bi-nationalism stress the lack of public support for the idea, among both Israeli Jews and Palestinians. Public opinion surveys in Israel indicate that only a small minority of Jewish Israelis think it is a good option (Newman 2005, Reuveny 2005). The finding hardly comes as a surprise, since Jews are the privileged citizens under the status quo. On the other hand the assertion, by Lustick and Salim Tamari, that the Palestinians themselves do not desire a bi-national state is more problematic.

It could be said that the Palestinian opposition to the 1947 UN partition scheme was less for wanting to expel the Jews and more for their unwillingness to watch their homeland divided. The PLO inherited this position in its early years. Its shift to the two-state position was based on what was thought to be a pragmatic realization that bi-nationalism was not on the cards because of Israel's vehement refusal, as noted above. Does this mean that if suddenly Israel changed its mind and offered the Palestinians a partnership in a joint state, they would refuse? It is highly unlikely. At any rate, this may be something worth further investigation.

What is particularly new on the scene is the rise of Hamas, the Islamic resistance movement. Whereas Fatah could promote secular bi-nationalism without many ideologial contradictions, it would be a thorny task for Hamas to do likewise. This organization functions within an Islamist ideological *cum* Palestinian nationalist frame. In Egypt the Muslim Brothers have not unequivocally accepted that non-Muslims are entitled to full citizenship rights and responsibilities. Hamas itself does not have any recognizable political theorists, but since it won the elections it seems to have recognized the special situation of Palestine and has not, for example, fully pushed for an Islamist socio-cultural agenda. It is conceivable, within an open-minded Islamic

221

outlook that updates the widely-recognized notions of the 'People of the Book', and sees that Arabs and Jews are the progeny of Abraham, to agree to a state based on civic citizenship. Be that as it may, the religious political revival among Palestinians and Israelis cannot be separated from the ongoing conflict, and it is not unreasonable to anticipate that this would abate under conditions of peace and prosperity. Hizbullah has accepted a multi-ethnic formula in Lebanon, and is currently represented by 14 members in the Parliament and two in the cabinet. Could not Hamas do the same in Palestine?

Whatever the Palestinian attitude towards a bi-national state might be, a few Israelis have warmed to the idea. Apart from Zionist discourse, the advocates of bi-nationalism have not succeeded in placing it on the political agenda. It may also be that circumstances have so far been unpropitious. Lack of public support is insufficient to discredit the concept: public opinion is not immutable. It is easier in the climate of hostility to call for the separation of the combatants than to persuade them to live together amicably, even if they already are living together.

The Zionist objection to bi-nationalism is strikingly simple. It centres on the wish to keep Israel a 'Jewish state' (Karsh 2003, Newman 2005). A Jewish state in this lexicon is a state of all the Jews anywhere in the world, and not a state of all of its citizens. At the hub of this doctrine is that Jews alone have the right to 'return' to Israel, whereas the Palestinian refugees do not. As Gabriel Piterberg put it: 'what structurally defines the nature of the Israeli state is the return of Jews and the non-return of Arabs to Palestine. If this dynamic of return/ non-return were to disappear, the Zionist state would lose its identity' (Piterberg 2001).

Yet, Efraim Karsh chides the Palestinians for insisting on the Right of Return of the refugees because it would threaten the demographic predominance of the Jews.

The idea of a Jewish state does not comport with the evolution of international norms for state legitimacy. Since World War II 'international normative criteria for state legitimacy has [sic] shifted from racial and ethnic criteria to a civil-territorial principle ... by the end of the century ethnocracy has fallen into disrepute' (Tilley 2005). One of the key factors for the shift was that the war itself and the devastation it wreaked, including the Holocaust, were the product of 'organic' ideas of nationalism and the purported superiority of certain races over others. Civic nationalism has not won universal allegiance, and essentialist nationalism persists, but the advocacy of diversity and multiculturalism have made the defense of organic nationalist states that much harder. Zionists often confuse categories, by alleging that Israel is as Jewish as France is French. But, as Tony Judt points out, the argument in the case of France is circular: 'France is the state of all the French; all French persons are by definition citizens of France; and all citizens of France are ... French' (Judt 2003b). The equivalent proposition for Israel is: Israel is the state of all the Jews; all Jewish persons are by definition citizens of Israel; and all citizens of Israel are ... Jews. The third part of the proposition is clearly empirically wrong; thus the assertion that Israel is as Jewish as France is French cannot be sustained.

Another Zionist complementary position is that Jews cannot agree to become a minority because they would be persecuted by an Arab majority, as was indicated earlier. Jews are a minority in many places, especially in the United States, which provides Israel much by way of economic, military and diplomatic sustenance. Rationalization of the necessity for a Jewish majority in Israel requires that the Arabs be pictured darkly, as bent on the annihilation of the Jews and as culturally incapable of forming democratic, pluralistic systems.[11] But, as Robert Blecher demonstrates, pro-Israel intellectuals in the United States made an about-face with regard to the possibility of democracy in Iraq between the first and second Gulf wars. In 1991 they held that democracy was not possible in Arab countries so as to justify not going into Iraq, only to reverse their position in 2002–2003 on the eve of the invasion of that country (Blecher 2002). This U-turn was not mediated by theoretical deliberation in either case, but by political expediency. Commentators like Karsh and Abraham Foxman must acknowledge that if Arabs cannot deliver equity to the Jews, the same is true of Jews towards the Arab minority in Israel. If the assertion is that only Jews are capable of being democratic and egalitarian, surely this implies a belief in ethnic supremacy.

It is not irrelevant to recall here that Arabs and Jews had a history of rich cultural co-production, as Ammiel Alcalay has admirably shown (Alcalay 1993). This is not to say that relations between Arabs and Jews were always sweetness and light, only to note that a fruitful and creative partnership had once been forged between the two peoples. Arab and Muslim tolerance, apart from historical relations with Jews, is very much evident in the fantastic array of ethnicities, with their temples and shrines, with their languages, with their sacred and profane texts.

That some are fighting each other is in no small part owed to the legacy of Britain and France that so arbitrarily shredded the region into numerous states in order to prolong their colonial rule. This legacy of fragmentation is what must be reversed; nationalistic and ethnic retrenchment is hardly the way to do it.

New concepts and practices have emerged in the last fifty years that foster coexistence among heterogeneous groups. DNA analysis is gradually revealing that ethnic purity anywhere is fiction, and it would be interesting if a census of Palestinians and Jews included genetic testing to determine their respective ancestry. Even without the aid of biology, Tony Judt writes:

> Israel itself is a multicultural society in all but name; yet it remains distinctive among democratic states in its resort to ethnoreligious criteria with which to denominate and rank its citizens ... it is Jewish *state* in which one community – Jews – is set above others, in an age when that sort of state has no place. [Emphasis in the original] (Judt 2003a)

An interesting twist here is that the international endorsement of a Palestinian state, especially in the recent document known as the Road Map, specifies that a Palestinian state must be a non-ethnic democracy, 'a practicing democracy based on tolerance and liberty' (United Nations 2003). It does not demand the same of Israel, either out of sheer obliviousness to the fate of the Palestinian citizens of Israel or erroneously assuming that Israel is already practicing that brand of democracy.

Disapproval from a Palestinian perspective is a mirror image of the Zionist one; except that it is the oppressed who are projected as the potential losers of bi-nationalism. The skewed initial power distribution, according to Tamari, would impede the Palestinians from having a fair access to material and institutional resources. It would also threaten their national Arab identity. Tamari judges bi-nationalism as 'counterproductive and escapist'.

It is necessary at the outset to distinguish bi-nationalism from the reason that impelled the PLO to switch positions in favour of two states. The PLO's shift, as mentioned earlier, stemmed from its assessment of the *infeasibility* of such a state, owing to Israel's rejection. The PLO in fact had to explain to the Palestinians how it was giving up the bulk of their homeland, and so initially the two-state position was forwarded as *barnamij marhali*, a transitional programme. It still insisted on the

Right of Return and did not specify the territory of the Palestinian state; nevertheless, it was clear that what was meant was the West Bank and Gaza. Tamari's dissatisfaction, on the other hand, is premised not on the infeasibility, but on the *undesirability*, of a bi-national state. There is a big difference between the two rationales; the one leaves the possibility for bi-nationalism contingent on Israel's consent, whereas the second forecloses it altogether. A key corollary of the *undesirability* of a bi-national state is that it would be better for the Palestinian refugees to waive their Right of Return.

The power gap, whether economic, military or educational, among the two populations is undeniably wide. Nor is a separate Palestinian state going to change the balance of power in the foreseeable future: witness the massive Israeli assault on Gaza and Lebanon in summer 2006, ostensibly as retaliation against the capture of one Israeli soldier by Hamas and two by Hizbullah. Power disparity has also spawned cases of the classic cognitive duality of the colonized perceiving themselves as inferior to the colonizers. This permeates the daily level of conversation, expressed in admiring comments of how well *al-Yahud* (Jews) do things compared to the lousy ways of the Arabs. The resistance and nationalist and Islamist cultural revival, analogous to those of many national liberation movements, lend countervailing influence. The colonial, superiority–inferiority inheritance is versatile, however, and has persisted on both sides of the divide, as the copious post-colonial literature amply demonstrates. So what is required is an in-depth understanding of the 'constructions' of 'Israel' and 'Israeli' in Palestinian culture, of how the effects of oppression and resistance play out in the cognitive map of the Palestinians under Israeli rule, and then ways of combating these.

The two-state solution itself does not necessarily mean separation and reduction of dependence on Israel. Palestinians from all social strata – workers, merchants, intellectuals, professionals – were eager for close relations with Israel. Dependency is bad for some, beneficial for others. Even if delinking of economic and other ties with Israel and reorienation toward the Arab region were possible, the economies of Arab countries themselves, like Jordan and Egypt, would be more hitched with Israel's. Israel, in contrast, has been able to connect with the global economy and to import labour from East Europe and Asia, and, owing to the collapse of the Arab economic boycott after Oslo, is much more prepared for delinking than the Palestinian state would be. This in part explains the confidence with which it is pursuing a unilateral pullback.

Under bi-nationalism the imbalance of power could be expected to last for a long time. This would be similar to the situation in South Africa, although the 'gap' perhaps is (or at least used to be) narrower between the Palestinians and Israelis than between the blacks and whites of South Africa. Yet the African National Congress chose pluralism. To be sure, the jury is still out on that country's bold experiment, and we do not know if it will be possible for the blacks and whites to co-exist, and whether whites will accept being part of the society in which the majority is black and in which they are no longer the 'ruling class.' Bi-nationalism is not without risks; but it is hard to see how the outcome could be worse than what has happened so far.

The foregoing concerns are all entangled with the complex subject of identity. It is not necessary to have to accept the infinite fluidity of identity as portrayed in some postmodern writings, which Abu-Odeh seems to espouse, to allow room for the construction and malleability of identity. Nor will the two communities be compelled to forfeit their national identities. On the other hand, the worldwide ethnic 'involution' may suggest that identity has become fixed. This development is, perhaps, a consequence of the weakening of political identity – political in the sense of asking what type of society one wants to live in. It is a culmination of histories in which power and status have often been apportioned along ethnic lines rendering ethnicity a catalyst of various manifestations of identity. But it is not the last word on identity. So one core question here is whether in a bi-national state Arabs and Jews would negotiate strategic issues as individuals or as national collectives. Abu-Odeh endorses the former approach, Segal the latter. Tamari, on the other hand, hypothesizes that Palestinians cannot achieve parity, whether as a community or as individuals.

It may be that questions about resources, such as land and other core issues, could be negotiated or struggled for communally. Then, as the correlation between ethnicity and distribution grows weaker, negotiations could be assumed by individuals or corporate bodies (i.e. unions or syndicates) across national lines. Many aspects of culture and lifestyle are not ethnically specific, and numerous factors could ameliorate the Palestinian or Arab-Jewish dichotomy. The elite of both sides often leads a 'westernized' life, and the culture of the Jewish Ashkenazi resembles Arab culture in many of its expressions. Of significance to the sustainability of Palestinian culture is the fact that the state would be surrounded by Arab countries. Even so, conjecturing the course of social and cultural change in such a state is not easy, and decisions have to be made with imperfect information.

That may help explain why the two sides are caught up in a curious paradox: if the Palestinians are going to be the losers, why don't the Israelis find bi-nationalism appealing? Conversely, if Zionist demography-mongers and the scales of power would tip in favour of the Palestinians because of their greater numbers, why do the Palestinian frown on it? Could it be that the objection to bi-nationalism lies in this space between mutual fears of the unknown? Could these topics (with the prospect of never-ending fighting as a background) be a place where proponents of bi-nationalism need to make an intervention?

Both Lustick and Tamari leave out two large segments of the Palestinian population, the Palestinian citizens of Israel and the refugees, an omission that raises doubts about their postulates. If bi-nationalism is unhealthy for the Palestinians who hold Israeli citizenship, they would be expected to favour incorporation in a Palestinian state. Yet only a small fraction of them seems inclined to do so. How can their reluctance be explained? Is it a case of 'false consciousness?' Would they prefer a bi-national state that includes other Palestinians as well?

As for the refugees, Lustick's and Tamari's reasoning implies that they should not necessarily expect the Right of Return. This, albeit unwittingly, comes perilously close to the Zionist position, that 'any return by the refugees ... was an *objective* impossibility, rather than an eventuality that the state itself was resolved at any cost to block' (Piterberg 2002, emphasis added). Israeli practices such as the razing of villages and towns, thereby radically altering the pre-1948 landscape, were intended precisely to discourage any idea of return. Whether the forecasts about the injurious consequences of power disparity are true or not, if they are taken at face value by the refugees they will add another form of objective impossibility to the arithmetic of the Right of Return.

Superior space and opportunities in a bi-national state in Greater Palestine A bi-national state in Greater Palestine conceptually resembles a similar state in Israel and the West Bank and Gaza. Practically, by including Jordan, it raises further questions, especially for Jordanians, while at the same time offering superior opportunities.

Such an expanded state is large enough for everybody; no one has to be squeezed out. It allows people to move into places where their hearts or their pockets feel at home. The question of the return of the Palestinian refugees in Jordan becomes a matter of normal movement within a country. With a decrease in competition for space, the Palestinian refugees in Syria and Lebanon would be given the option of finding a home in the proposed state. It is reasonable to expect that the refugees who choose to return would opt for the urban centres, and whether the villages still exist or not would not constitute an objective impossibility. The Palestinian Right of Return for the major refugee clusters thus can be resolved as regards residence, identity and political status, rendering other aspects, such as compensation, easier to tackle. The inclusion of Jordan in a bi-national state would further mitigate the fears of Jewish cultural preponderance and the threat to the Arab dimension of their identity.

It may all be good for the Palestinians, but what of the East Jordanians? They might justifiably wonder what good a bi-national state would do them. A response might be that they are already embroiled, and there is the threat that Israel would expel more and more Palestinians to Jordan, further exacerbating the demographic imbalance against East Jordanians. Ariel Sharon's dictum 'Jordan is the Palestinian state' lurks behind many Israeli actions in the West Bank and Gaza. The Hashemites began their career on a high rhetorical note of pan-Arabism, which has diminished into the parochial and divisive 'Jordan first'. They and Zionism divided up Greater Palestine and undertook to suppress Palestinian nationalism. In the process, a deep Palestinian–East Jordanian cleavage evolved that kept the two peoples suspicious of each other (Lynch 2004). Palestinian hypernational displays in Jordan after the 1967 war and the Jordanian government's crackdown on the militias and political presence in 1970 were manifestations of these. Yet, considering their cultural affinity, they could eventually forge a common identity, although the example of Iraq must be borne in mind. The East Jordanians could gain in terms of recognition and status as well as economically from an expanded state. Being part of a state that encompasses such cities as Bethlehem, Nazareth and Jerusalem, which the late king Hussein used to call the spiritual capital of Jordan, the East Jordanians would acquire enhanced international prestige.

A single state in Greater Palestine means a large population and therefore a large market, highly desirable in today's extremely competitive world economy. The economic bonus could benefit all, Palestinians, East Jordanians and Israelis.

Conclusion

The peace-making effort has reached a strategic impasse. Israel rejects the Right of Return of the refugees. A viable West Bank and Gaza state is nowhere on the horizon. The Palestinians face the prospect of being forced to live in a rump state; of being ethnically cleansed, by slow haemorrhage or en masse, from the West Bank; of Gaza dissolving imperceptibly into populous Egypt and whatever remains of the West Bank reverting back to the control of the Hashemites. But they are already the largest national-ethnic group in Greater Palestine and, if they are not accommodated, they are likely to resist fiercely their fragmentation and disenfranchisement. Instability is likely to continue to loom over Jordan. Tensions between Arabs and Jews in Israel may not let up. Israel will continue to be perceived as an alien, crusader-state, a product of Western colonialism. Two 'new' proposals have been presented for avoiding these eventualities, both including a resolution of the issue of the Right of Return: the revival of the 1947 partition plan with consolidated boundaries, and a bi-national state in Greater Palestine. The fog of present hostilities makes a tolerant, inclusive political order hard to envisage; however, it is not impossible. It may sound utopian, but the wars and massacres of the 20th and 21st centuries have not been the result of the advocacy of pluralism and tolerance, but of nationalistic and ethnic bigotry and intolerance. Israel bears a special responsibility for whatever order emerges; the choices it makes will largely determine the course of the conflict.

Notes

1 The term 'East Jordanian' designates the holders of Jordanian citizenship from what was once called 'Transjordan' and later on became the East Bank of the pre-1967 Hashemite Kingdom of Jordan.

2 In this forum arguments for bi-nationalism are by Abu-Odeh (2002) who provided a lead piece and a response, Lustick (2002), and Segal (2002). Against are Karsh (2002), Lustick (2002), and Tamari (2002). Lustick strongly favours two states, but considers bi-nationalism because it might become unintentionally the default solution. Segal advocates a confederation, which he calls 'a species' of bi-nationalism. Quotes from or attribution to these authors throughout this chapter are from the preceding sources.

3 In this forum arguments for bi-nationalism are by Tony Judt (2003a, b) who provided a lead article and a response. Those against include Fox-

man (2003), and Walzer (2003). Quotes from or attribution to these authors throughout this chapter are from the preceding sources.

4 In this forum the main question is whether a Palestinian state in the West Bank and Gaza remains on the cards. Nonetheless some participants provide normative points of view. Those for bi-nationalism include Elmusa (2005) and Tilley (2005); those against include Newman (2005).

5 Some of these, like Druze and Muslims, are political distinctions that Israel makes for the time-honoured purpose of divide-and-rule. Others, like Jerusalemites, while having the same objective as the former, are also legal categories. Areas A, B and C were so designated by the Oslo Accords. Displaced persons are the refugees of the 1967 war.

6 The presidential elections were held in January 2005 and the legislative in January 2006.

7 This is based on the oft-cited ratio of the Palestinians as constituting 60% of that country's population. The figure for Israel is calculated from Israel's Central Bureau of Statistics; for Jordan, Gaza and the West Bank from the CIA database https://www.cia.gov/cia/publications/factbook/geos/is.html#People

8 Mandron (2001) also suggests a consolidated map, but he takes as his starting point the 1967 boundaries and focuses mainly on military matters.

9 Of these approximately 65% are Palestinians and 35% Russian immigrants.

10 See, for example, a recent article by Mbembe (2006). Mbembe worries about what he considers an ongoing polarization along ethnic lines, expressed in 'nativism' by South African populists and an unwillingness on the part of whites, especially the upper stratum, to get seriously engaged in the reconciliation project by sharing its wealth.

11 For example, Foxman (2003), and Karsh (2002). Yiftachel (2002) provides an insightful discussion of this prevalent attitude.

References

Abed, G. (1990) *The Economic Viability of a Palestinian State*, Washington, DC: Institute of Palestine Studies.

Abu-Odeh, L. (2002) 'The case for binationalism', *Boston Review*, December/January, http://bostonreview.net/BR26.6/abu-odeh.html

Alcalay, Ammiel (1993) *After Jews and Arabs: Remaking Levantine culture*, Minneapolis: University of Minnesota Press.

Aruri, Naseer H. (2005) 'US policy and the single state in Palestine', *The Arab World Geographer*, 8(3): 133–9.

Middle East Report Online (1999) 'Equal rights for Arabs in a Jewish state: A goal unrealizable' (interview with Azmi Bishara), December. http://www.merip.org/mero/mero121499.html

Blecher, Robert (2003) 'Free people will set the course of history: Intellectuals, democracy and American empire', *Middle East Report Online*, March. http://www.merip.org/mero/interventions/blecher_interv.html

— (2002) 'Living on the edge: The threat of "Transfer" in Israel and Palestine',

Middle East Report Online, 225 (Winter), http://www.merip.org/mer/
mer225/225_blecher.html

Elmusa, Sharif (2005) 'Greater Palestine: Matching demography, geography
and heart', *The Arab World Geographer*, 8 (3): 156–60.

— (2006) 'A greater Palestine?', *Al-Ahram Weekly*, 27 April–3 May, http://
weekly.ahram.org.eg/2006/792/re2.htm

Falah, Ghazi-Walid (2005) 'Geopolitics of "enclavisation" and the demise of a
two-state solution to the Israeli-Palestinian conflict', *Third World Quarterly*,
26 (8): 1341–72.

Foxman, Abraham (2003) 'An alternative future: An exchange', *New York
Review of Books*, 4 December, http://mafhoum.com/press6/169P3.html

Harel, Amos (2006) 'Israel fears harm to ties with Jordan due to comments by
IDF commander,' *Ha'aretz*, February 23.

Jacoby, Russell (2005) *Picture Imperfect: Utopian Thought for an Anti-utopian
Age*, New York: Columbia University Press.

Kimmerling, Baruch (1983) *Zionism and Territory: The Socio-Territorial
Dimensions of Zionist Politics*, Cambridge, MA: Schenkman Publishing
Company.

Judt, Tony (2003a) 'Israel: The Alternative', *New York Review of Books*,
23 October, www.nybooks.com/articles/16671.

— (2003b) 'An alternative future: An exchange', *New York Review of Books*,
4 December, http://mafhoum.com/press6/169P3.html

Lustick, Ian (2002) 'The cunning of history: A response to "The case of bi-
nationalism"', *Boston Review*, January.

Lynch, Marc (2004) 'No Jordan option', *Middle East Report Online*, 21 June,
http://www.merip.org/mero/mero062104.html

Mandron, Guy (2001) 'Redividing Palestine?', *New Left Review*, July/August:
61–9.

Mbembe, Achille (2006) 'South Africa's second coming: The Nongqawuse
syndrome', http://www.opendemocracy.net/democracy-Africa_democracy/
southafrica_succession_3649.jsp

Middle East Report Online (1999) 'Equal rights for Arabs in a Jewish state: A
goal unrealizable' (interview with Azmi Bishara), December, http://www.
merip.org/mero/mero121499.html

Moughrabi, Fouad (2005) 'Waiting for the barbarians: When Palestine becomes Finland', *The Arab World Geographer*, Vol. 8, No. 3, 130–32.

Newman, David (2005) 'There is no solution other than the two-state solution',
The Arab World Geographer, 8 (3): 153–5.

Piterberg, Gabriel (2001) 'Erasures', *New Left Review*, July/August: 31–46.

Qureia, Ahmad (2004) 'Israel's unilateral moves are pushing us toward a
one-state solution', *Ha'aretz*, 9 January.

Reuveny, Rafael (2005) 'The binational state and the colonial imperative:
The Israeli-Palestinian conflict in historical perspective', *The Arab World
Geographer*, 8 (3):109–17.

Sayigh, Yazid (2005) 'Closing window of opportunity for the two-state solution?', *The Arab World Geographer*, 8 (3): 122–124.

Segal, Jerome (2002) 'A binational confederation', *Boston Review*, January. http://bosyonreview.net/BR26.6/segal.html

Tamari, Salim (2002) 'The binationalist lure', *Boston Review*, January, http://bosyonreview.net/BR26.6/tamari.html

Tilley, Virginia (2005) 'From "Jewish state and Arab state" to "Israel and Palestine"? International norms, ethnocracy, and the two-state solution', *The Arab World Geographer*, 8 (3): 140–6.

United Nations (1947) Resolution 181 (II): Future Government of Palestine, http://daccessdds.un.org/doc/RESOLUTION/GEN/NR0/038/88/IMG/NR003888.pdf?OpenElement

— (2003) *A Performance-based Roadmap to a Permanent Two-State Solution to the Israeli-Palestinian Conflict*, www.un.org/media/main/roadmap122002.html

Walzer, Michael (2003) 'An alternative future: An exchange', *New York Review of Books*, 4 December, http://mafhoum.com/press6/169P3.html

Yiftachel, Oren (2005) 'Neither two states nor one: The disengagement and "creeping apartheid" in Israel/Palestine', *The Arab World Geographer*, 8 (3):125–129.

— (2002) 'The shrinking space of citizenship: Ethnocratic politics in Israel', *Middle East Report Online*, 223 (Summer). http://www.merip.org/mer/mer223/223_yiftachel.html

11 | Justice as the way forward

KARMA NABULSI

I cried when I saw one of the exiled Iraqi Kurds voting [for the Iraqi president]. I struggled in Lebanon and was imprisoned in Ansar camp, and in Al-Ramleh ... don't I have the right to vote to choose my president?[2]

Claims for the one-state or two-state solution can be seen in two ways by the Palestinian body politic. They can be seen to be ideological, and thus intrinsic, or tactical, and thus instrumental. Which claim is being asserted, and how the Palestinians in al-Shatat[1] view these claims, are intimately connected to two core principles that have defined the Palestinian struggle from its inception: self-determination for the Palestinian people, and the Right of Return as defined by United Nations' resolution 194 of 1948 (the return of those refugees who wish to do so to their original homes). The fundamental question that connects these two principles to the debate about a one-state or two-state solution is whether they are harmonious and conjoined to each other, or are incommensurable and in conflict with each other. Previously – the last time probably in 1988 at the Palestine National Council in Algiers – it was commonly understood that both of these principles were fundamental, and were, above all, inextricably linked to each other.

However, since the Oslo process began, we have seen the slow emergence of a Palestinian political discourse of a predominantly interest-based nature, which assumes that the two key principles of self-determination and the Right of Return are incompatible with each other rather than complementary. Indeed, the discourse customarily sets out these two principles in contrast to each other, and constructs the debate as being a stark and inevitable choice between self-determination and the Right of Return of refugees. In a variety of ways, this discourse has been exported to areas within the national movement. From the Geneva initiative to the Nusseibeh-Ayalon platform one can hear articulated the claim that there can be no independent Palestinian state while holding on to the Right of Return as set out in UN resolution 194.[3]

This formula of what is usually described as 'painful compromise' between two core principles worked its way into Palestinian political discourse at the level of the leadership in the early 1990s, and during the Oslo era was played out through the institutional structures that were created and elections that were held in the West Bank and Gaza after 1995. The design of these administrative structures fragmented the two constituencies; those in the West Bank and Gaza became separate political bodies from those living outside Palestine. Ultimately many Palestinians who campaigned for the Right of Return no longer saw this aim as achievable within a two-state framework. The institutional arrangements that helped strengthen this discourse also brought about a radical fragmentation not just among geographically disparate Palestinians, but also between different Palestinian classes, between Palestinian refugees and non-refugees, between Gaza and the West Bank, between those under occupation who lived in the cities and those living in the refugee camps, and between those who remain loyal to the old party structures within the historic national movement in exile, and the majority who do not. The Palestinians have been reduced to distinct interest groups pursuing different agendas, and are at this moment unable to deliberate as a single people in any real sense. Worse than that, they find it almost impossible to share common aspirations for the future, either through a one- or two-state solution, or any solution at all.

Through a set of meetings exploring the civic and political structures – past, current and future – that Palestinians possess in al-Shatat, one can chart the course and contours of the gradual destruction of political participation, and the feelings it evokes among Palestinians worldwide. This chapter will illustrate aspects of the nature of the fragmentation of the Palestinian people outside of historical Palestine, showing how this fracture fits in with appeals for a one- or two-state solution, as well as calls for the key constitutional principles of the Palestinian people, that of self determination and the Right of Return, restored to a single unified platform. It will do so by relying upon a new resource created by the Palestinian people themselves: transcripts of meetings held by Palestinians living in refugee camps and exile communities in over 100 meetings held in more than 26 countries outside the West Bank and Gaza Strip.[4] This narrative will rely upon

234

those who participated in these meetings to illustrate the main arguments presented here. It is based on the premise that only through relying upon a collective understanding of Palestinians everywhere can one begin to appreciate that the one-state and two-state solutions are very far removed from the priorities of action and discussion among Palestinians. Rather, these two core principles are understood as forming the basis of any collective platform, and there is a need for their renewed articulation in order that they be advanced. The Prisoners' Document signed in June 2006 by the factions illustrates this common understanding on Right of Return and right of self-determination in emphatic terms.[5]

Background to political fragmentation

How did a highly unified people become divided into competing interest groups? One key factor was in the way the Palestinians living outside Palestine accepted a representation of themselves that was constructed by the international community under the terms of the Madrid and Oslo peace processes. Although formally a people with the internationally recognized right of self determination and of return, at the start of the interim arrangements in the wake of the Oslo agreements of 1993, those in al-Shatat were described as 'Palestinian refugees', rather than a core element of the Palestinian decision-making body politic, and were made the subject of 'final status' negotiations. The issue was set aside for multilateral discussions. In a real sense, this separation suddenly put the civic and political status of millions of Palestinians into an existential limbo from which they have yet to emerge. Here is how one participant at a meeting in Germany expressed this sense of loss and betrayal:

> Concerning the PLO's policy – and as any Palestinian who lives outside Palestine and who doesn't have a framework other than the PLO – I must seek someone to represent me. Will it be the Jordanian system, or the so-and-so party, or the such-and-such organization? The PLO represents all Palestinian people outside Palestine. But when the PLO arrived at Oslo they leapt very high – a very high jump that went beyond our thinking – and the Palestinian people who live outside Palestine could no longer adjust to the propositions it made. As unions, we used to be very active here. But [the PLO] no longer needs people to criticize it and tell it that it is behaving in a way that doesn't

correspond with what the Palestinian people really want. Its main concern has always been to replace institutions that actually discuss things and object to things.[6]

By 2001 the Oslo process had broken down completely, no progress had been made on the refugee issue from its start, and the lack of attention and focus upon this issue had contributed to a huge impasse. What had been seen in 1993 as the core of the conflict – the rights of the 1948 refugees – had become, after seven years of neglect, the area where external pressure was brought to bear on the Palestinian political leadership to make concessions on the basic rights of refugees in order to advance negotiations with Israel, which was refusing even to discuss the issue of refugee rights. This sense of exclusion was frequently remarked upon by Palestinians from al-Shatat:

> What really concerns me is that they are negotiating without taking our opinions; they are negotiating in our absence, and as Palestinians, whether refugees or not, those who consider themselves refugees or not are negotiating in our name, as if we don't have an opinion and as if we are not concerned. Are they talking about the Right of Return *or* compensation, or compensation *and* the Right of Return? We don't know what they are negotiating about.[7]

This had the effect of increasing the feeling of exclusion and marginalization concerning the closed-door discussions and declared policy positions advanced in the international arena by various Palestinian actors, both official and semi-official, during the period leading up to 2000, and just after it. As one Palestinian in the USA noted:

> I see the core issue as being the responsibility which is upon ourselves, as a unified people who are not willing to sit by and watch a closed-door policy. We have to take action against that – we shouldn't sit by and watch the Palestinian representatives give away our rights without having our voice heard. Our voice must be heard.[8]

Yet this marginalization of Palestinians from participation in the process of decision-making through their national institutions, especially in exile, started long before that. It began with Israel's continual efforts since the late 1960s to weaken the national liberation movement by aiming its military attacks against Palestinian institutions and their personnel. These attempts escalated into the 1982 Israeli invasion of

Lebanon, where Israel sought to crush the PLO and its institutional infrastructure. The reasons for the failure of the two-state solution can only be understood within the historic context of Israeli policies and in reference to the Palestinian national movement's institutional history.

The PLO, the PNA, and the Palestinian refugees and exiles

The Palestine Liberation Organization (PLO), the umbrella institution within which the formerly broad-based popular movement operated, relied heavily for its active support from those Palestinian refugees in the Arab world who had been expelled from their homes in Palestine in 1948, in the Nakba (catastrophe). After earlier Palestinian uprisings for independence during the 1920s, 1930s, and during 1947–8, organized resistance was relaunched in the mid 1960s. By then Palestinians living in the refugee camps of Lebanon, Syria, Jordan (West Bank and East Bank), Gaza, Egypt, and exiles living in the Gulf would have waited for more than seventeen years for Israel to implement the United Nations resolution 194, which affirmed their right to return to the homes, cities, farms and villages whence they had been expelled.

The resumption of organized resistance was launched by the PLO factions which re-organized and reformulated the PLO after the June 1967 Arab-Israeli war. The PLO came to be recognized as the sole legitimate representative of Palestinians outside and inside Mandate Palestine in the mid 1970s:

> The PLO is the only legitimate representative, and this is not a marginal issue. It was recognized at the Rabat Summit first. There is an Arab consensus that the PLO is the only legitimate representative; this means that it is the political representative for the Palestinian people inside Palestine and also abroad.[9]

After enjoying a wave of political, diplomatic, and military successes in the late 1960s and 1970s – the PLO was recognized as the sole legitimate voice of the Palestinian people by the United Nations and the Arab League in 1974 – the PLO suffered a series of severe institutional, military, and political shocks: in Jordan in 1970, in Lebanon in 1982, and finally in the Gulf in the early 1990s. These shocks undercut what effective democratic mechanisms it had developed, and fractured the decision-making process through the national institutions built by the PLO and through collective platforms. The first of the fractures occurred when the PLO moved the remnants of its shattered institutional base from Lebanon to Tunis as a result of the 1982 Israeli invasion of Lebanon, after tens of thousands of civilians (Lebanese and Palestinians), cadres, and fighters of the movement had been killed. Much of its institutional infrastructure and popular base drawn from the 300,000 Palestinian refugees living in the camps there was shattered.

> We should rethink our relationship with the PLO. The relationship starts from top to bottom, but we, as Palestinian refugees, should think of the PLO as the representative legitimate authority, as we agreed. We are a part of this society, and we demand to rebuild the social, political, syndicate, media, medical, and legal structures of the PLO. Before the (1982) invasion, regardless of its factions, we used to see it as an organization which interacts with its people. But there were organisations, and there were trade unions, and labour federations.[10]

Another fracture between the 'inside' (that is Palestinians in the West Bank and Gaza) and 'outside' (in al-Shatat or Palestinians living outside Mandate Palestine and unable to return to any part of it) came when the core elite of the PLO's political institutions resettled in Gaza under the terms of the Oslo Accords after 1993. As a refugee in Jordan explained:

> The absence of the institution is the cause of the problem. There is no Palestinian institution that works for me as a human being, as a Palestinian citizen. I do exist, and the seed exists inside me – and either I water it to let it grow, or I forget it and it will wilt. Before the peace treaties [with Israel], Palestinian political parties were more effective, and we had a voice: we worked properly! We made our voice heard to the entire world. But the world now only hears the voice of the Palestinian president, and his prime minister. As a citizen, I no longer have a voice. His voice is enough. But before the peace process my voice was heard. If this peace will silence me then I don't want it![11]

Although the PLO continued to exist nominally as an overarching institution representing the voice of all Palestinians, its leadership was transposed into the temporary institutions of the Palestinian Authority (PA), an entity created through negotiations with Israel, and which was an administrative arm of the PLO. Many Palestinians no longer felt represented by the PA:

There are two parties here. Those of us who are outside feel that the Authority does not care about them, and only cares about the Palestinians inside Palestine. The other party is the Palestinians in al-Shatat who feel somewhat lost. Who are we? The Authority is busy with itself and its institutions, and the big question is: who represents the Palestinians in al-Shatat?[12]

As the PA was responsible only for Palestinians inside the West Bank and Gaza (although UNRWA continued to provide social and economic welfare to the refugees there), this created an important disjunction in the representation of Palestinians who live outside:

> The PLO used to represent all Palestinian political factions ... in the United Arab Emirates we had a women's union, a students' union, a workers' union, an engineers' union and a writers' union. These unions had headquarters and they were effective. But when the PLO was marginalized these unions stopped working. It was not the state which decided to end these unions: it was our decision. The Palestinian Authority is now negotiating on the West Bank and Gaza, and on the rights of the Palestinians, and their goal is to negotiate as the Palestinian Authority and not as the PLO.[13]

The PLO had previously operated in a far closer relationship with the associations and civil society in the refugee camps outside the West Bank and Gaza. This is how one participant at a meeting in Frankfurt put it:

> As for our conditions as a community, all unions and federations and committees that existed in the community were destroyed after the Oslo agreements. You can say that they have deserted us. The PLO deserted the Students' Union, the Labour Union, the Women's Union, and the Workers' Trade Union's Federation. There were a lot of unions, and they were all working under the PLO on the media level and on the leadership level. The members of the PLO came from people who work abroad. After the Oslo agreements, all these unions were destroyed, and the PLO deserted all of the unions and federations. And people lost confidence in the PLO – not as a representative, but as a channel of communication and as a process of connection that no longer exists.[14]

This chasm was to damage severely the associational structures of the unions and other exile groups that were part of the fabric of Palestinian political and civil society in al-Shatat, especially given that the majority of the Palestinian people were living outside occupied Palestine. A Palestinian in London summarized this sentiment after an extensive discussion on the issue at a public meeting of Palestinians organized by the Association of the Palestinian Community in the United Kingdom:

> So it seems everyone has reached a conclusion – albeit an emotional one. This result, that the PLO is the only legitimate representative of the Palestinian people, is nearly taken for granted. I personally have doubts about this issue at the present time. Is the PLO really still the only legitimate representative for the Palestinian people? I think that this question is important, and a very important one in this meeting when it is asked within this framework; when we wonder when was the PLO the only legitimate representative for the Palestinian people? And why it might not still be so?
>
> I say that the PLO was the only legitimate representative for the Palestinian people when the voice of the Palestinian student, worker, peasant, and woman, was heard, wherever they were, whether the student was in Dakar, Moscow, or London; his voice was automatically heard by the Executive Committee of the PLO through very organized union structures and frameworks; when the opinion and attitude of the Palestinian peasant in any village was conveyed to the Palestinian National Council, and then to the Palestinian Central Council, then to the Palestinian Executive Committee, in a totally democratic and coherent way.
>
> So there were seven representatives in the Palestinian National Council for the students' union, and ten for the labour union, and fifteen for the women's union, and so on. Consequently, the decision was issued by the Legislative Council, which was adopted by the PLO's Executive Committee, that it was a democratic representative for all the Palestinian sections. Back then, we were able to say that the Palestinian decision that was issued by the PLO was the only legitimate representative for the Palestinian people.
>
> What happened now? The PLO is what is left in a framework that has been completely emptied of any content; a non-legitimate National Council; a non-legitimate unelected Executive Committee; and a union structure that had been dissolved by a decision from inside the PLO

which resulted in the absence of the students', labour, and women's unions. Thus free democratic self-expression is totally absent in the opinion of the Palestinian sectors.[15]

Historically since 1948, Palestinians had always resisted attempts to separate the 'outside' from the 'inside', and since the Israeli occupation of the West Bank and Gaza in 1967, when Israel tried to establish an alternative leadership to the PLO through the 'Village Leagues'. Instead, almost all politically active Palestinians living under military occupation within the 1967 borders (22% of historic Palestine) became, if they were not already, after 1965 (when Fatah began its armed struggle), members of the underground movements that made up the PLO, such as Fatah, the Popular Front for the Liberation of Palestine, and the Democratic Front for the Liberation of Palestine, and this connected the inside with the outside. With the establishment of the PA, this vibrant collective political activity was destroyed, leaving Palestinians from the outside with an increasing feeling of helplessness:

> The biggest thing that I need to emphasize here as a Palestinian is the marginalization of the PLO. We, as Palestinians, actually had a structure that represented us. And now what we have is the Authority, and as I said before it does not represent all the Palestinians. I am speaking structurally – at least the PLO previously included political movements and labour unions, so that we were able to connect with each other. Where are things going for Palestinians in the world? Right now it feels as if we are foreigners, in each country – we began disintegrating after the Authority came in … just watching, without any connection and without any respect. To me, structurally, that is the biggest flaw that we are facing.[16]

Therefore the migration of much of the official apparatus of the PLO into the occupied Palestinian territories in 1994 had a number of compelling consequences: it fractured the links between Palestinians inside and outside the occupied territories, seriously weakened political representation of Palestinians living outside, and created new cleavages. These points came up repeatedly in the course of the different meetings.

> The PLO was marginalized after establishing the National Authority in the West Bank and Gaza. Why? We know that the PLO includes all the factions inside and outside Palestine, like those in Lebanon, and

it also includes the camps. The party or the organization that won is Fatah, and it agreed to introduce the Authority through the Oslo agreements. Of course, the process of establishing the Authority was not correct, because it assumed the task of political representation instead of the PLO, and in the name of all the Palestinians inside and outside, and it assumed also the task of making deals and devising political solutions. The PNC has not met for years, I think for the past 20 years, and the PLO's institutions have not been renewed or activated. The last meeting was held when Clinton came ... and it had one goal, which was to abandon the Right of Return.[17]

The impact of the Oslo Process on Palestinian refugees and exiles

The most important factor in the marginalization of the Palestinians' ability to determine their future collectively was in the terms of the structure and procedures of the Oslo agreement itself.

The PA represents only the Palestinians *inside* Palestine. So this means that we shouldn't neglect the PLO simply because [the PA] did. There is a programme in the PLO which demands the Right of Return. If we neglect the PLO and do not demand to reform it, it's like neglecting our rights, especially our right to return, and we will no longer have a political representative who will defend this right. The suggestion is very specific, which is to revive the PLO's institutions on the basis of political foundations. This is a Palestinian popular demand for those who live outside and those who live *inside* Palestine: the two groups can't be separated. These are the common demands of the Palestinian people.[18]

The abrupt obstruction of Palestinians' ability to both discuss and reach common goals, and the establishment into formal structures of disenfranchisement can best be illustrated by the elections in the West Bank and Gaza. The most enduring damage to the integrity of the Palestinian body politic between inside and outside Palestine came as a direct result of the elections by which the Palestinian Legislative Council (PLC) was established in the West Bank and Gaza in 1996. Instead of enhancing democracy and representation, these elections further fragmented the Palestinian people as a whole, excluding as they did all Palestinians outside the territories from their process. Refugees felt particularly disenfranchised as a result:

Among the demands they spoke of on the political level, according to the [Civitas] project, is the role of Palestinians in decision-making; the decisions which are taken on the international level. Palestinian decisions are taken either by the Palestinian representative, the PLO, or by the Palestinian Authority. But the Palestinian refugee is totally forgotten.[19]

This institutional change occurred without a simultaneous process occurring within the Palestine National Council, the Palestinian parliament-in-exile, through which the Palestinians exiled in 1948 have been connected to the PLO since its creation. Many participants emphasized the need to revitalize the PLO:

It is well known that the Palestinian Authority represents only and exclusively the Palestinian people who live inside [the West Bank and Gaza Strip]. The PLO represents the largest sector of the Palestinian people who live in different countries. Therefore I think in order to exert pressure on the Palestinian negotiators, as well as the other party to the conflict, it is very important to activate the PLO's role. This is because it includes all sectors of the Palestinian people, not only the Palestinians inside.[20]

Although, under the terms of the PLO/PA arrangements, the PLC holds a percentage of the seats within the Palestine National Council, there were no simultaneous elections to this larger, more historically legitimate body (the PLO), which represents the majority of refugees. The last elections, although bringing in a platform closer to the interests of many Palestinian people outside, still reconfirmed this division and different status. This separation was keenly perceived by Palestinians from the outside:

Here, there is some sort of confusion between the Palestinian Authority and the PLO. We think that the PA represents our Palestinian brothers who elected it, this is our opinion. We don't want to elect the Authority, but the PLO. The PLO is our only legitimate representative, and if there is an election to be conducted for someone to represent us, we want people to represent us in the Palestinian National Council not in the Legislative Council which represents people in the Gaza Strip and the West Bank.[21]

The development of civil society inside the West Bank and Gaza Strip excluded the Palestinians outside

The enhancing of civil society structures and funding of NGOs inside the West Bank and Gaza further intensified a perceived division between Palestinians inside and outside: those inside received considerable international funding, whilst the political and civic aspirations and needs of those living outside the Palestinian territories were ignored, neglected, and even rejected; at best they were classified as objects of humanitarian relief. As a Palestinian in Baghdad saw it, Palestinians in Iraq no longer had any representation:

> I am pretty pessimistic. I have no relations with the PLO, I haven't even entered the Embassy in its old or its new building at Al-Saadoun Street, except once. To speak frankly, when you enter the Embassy you feel you are a stranger, as if you weren't a member of the Palestinian community in this country. And they start asking questions like: Where are you going? What do you want? Who do you want to see?[22]

This exclusion means denying Palestinians residing outside the West Bank and Gaza the most elementary right to help shape the key constitutional and political institutions of a future state that belongs to them as much as to those residing inside occupied Palestine. Many Palestinians felt betrayed by the PLO:

> Ever since the Palestinian leadership was established in Palestine, the PLO turned its back on the Palestinians abroad as if we were not Palestinians. They didn't even take our opinions in the Palestinian elections.[23]

The shape of political and civic society outside the West Bank and Gaza

The current inability of the Palestinians outside to organize themselves comes from the collapse of the political system there, and their connection to the almost defunct PLO.

> The PLO is absent and it doesn't know anything about the needs and rights of the refugees. There are no effective federations. The conditions of the camp are very poor. There are no youth centres to organize our youth and educate them... We demand the rebuilding of the PLO. Those initiatives, from the Geneva Accords to the Dead Sea meeting, triggered a frustrated reaction from refugee circles ... the Right of Return cannot be revoked, and the PLO must be reactivated.[24]

The weakening of the PLO institutions, the mainstream party Fatah, and other smaller factions, had been going on for some years, especially outside the West Bank and Gaza Strip. Over the last five years, different spheres of power came to be located outside Palestine, with several competing for sole legitimacy and leadership. After the death of Yassir Arafat (who was simultaneously the elected head of the PA, the head of the PLO, and the elected head of Fatah) in November 2004, any semblance of unity inside the various PLO institutions and the party systems collapsed entirely, and this has played itself out with some force since Arafat's death. A Palestinian from the United Arab Emirates commented:

> All talk of forming an independent committee in this country is meaningless. We tried that when the PLO was still a strong organization, but now it is marginalized. The Palestinian Authority represents the Palestinians who are in the West Bank and Gaza, while the PLO represents all Palestinians ... The PLO had established institutions, popular institutions, women's unions, students' unions, and unions for all social sectors. These ... used to contact them, and they had a joint programme for every community, and a general programme for all Palestinians. The PLO organizations are now marginalized.[25]

There were several types of organization and associational structures in exile before 1993, and new formations have developed in the past decade. The relocation of the PLO leadership to the West Bank and Gaza was accompanied by a withdrawal of its attention, representation, funding, and other vital civic and political support to the vast network of unions, associations, communities, and party activists outside occupied Palestine. No progress was being made throughout the 1990s in negotiations with Israel or host countries on the main issues relating to Palestinian refugees: their rights, their urgent concerns, their lack of any legal status or civic or social rights in many host countries, from Egypt to Iraq to Lebanon to Yemen – yet the entire focus remained on the Palestinians who lived inside West Bank and Gaza. The tiers and webs of connection between civic and political structures on the national level began to dissolve, as these associations, activists, and factions became sidelined and ignored.

> For me it's normal; I have the right to return to my land ... I live in exile and don't know the [PLC] candidates, but we follow the news of

Palestine, and we follow everything that happens in Palestine. And the issue is not about judging a person as good or bad if I don't live in this country. It is true that we are distanced from what they are bargaining over. They are bargaining over the Right of Return for the refugees. We don't live in Palestine, and someone else is electing the person who will be negotiating in our name. I went to many places for the purpose of filling in an application, and in every place I went I was told that 'my opinion doesn't count'.[26]

The Right of Return movement developed in strength from the mid-1990s for a number of reasons. Primary among these was the exclusion, since the creation of the PA, of Palestinians outside from the political framework of decision-making, and concerns about the tenor and track Palestinian negotiators were taking. There was an accompanying sense that along with their exclusion, this issue of crucial importance to refugees was being quietly dropped under international pressure (although it remained an official PLO position). As a participant from Yemen noted:

I shall start with the PLO and the need to restore its dignity on the basis that it is the only legitimate representative of the Palestinian people. We have felt that its institutions have been dismantled, and that some of its representatives don't represent us any more ... We know ourselves more than they do. We don't want a passport or an identity card. Things shouldn't be as they are now. I have the right, as a Palestinian, to vote in order to choose the person who will represent me, so that I can guarantee that the rights of the Palestinian people, endorsed by United Nations' resolutions, will not be lost or renounced, especially the Right of Return to our country and properties.[27]

The civic landscape of Palestinian refugee and al-Shatat communities in each host country consists of a range of small institutions, clubs, charities, associations, newsletters, and other bodies, each representing a different faction or political party, many emerging for a season or a year to hold one or two events or publications before ceasing to be active in anything but name. In many of the communities, Palestinians have not come together in an institutional or collective form for many years, if ever, except in some places on religious holidays and for social events.

With the disintegration of the PLO institutions in exile, many Palestinians had abandoned the framework of the PLO to work in single-issue political movements, or in Islamic organizations, and sought to consolidate their own political positions and views. As the loss of representation increased, many saw the national institutions of the PLO as increasingly corrupt and ineffective, and many new and emerging civic groups and individuals believed it was not worth strengthening or restoring them, nor putting time into any mobilizing towards this endeavour, especially as the PLO itself was seen to have abandoned its constituents. One participant at a meeting in Denmark put it quite simply:

> The PLO office doesn't want you! The PA doesn't want you! Our rights have been lost since the time of the Nakba until now. We have lived 40 years in Lebanon, and no one ever considered taking our voice into account![28]

Islamic and some smaller political parties operated outside the PA in the occupied Palestinian territories and outside the PLO. Many of these see no incentive to engage in a mobilization process to strengthen the PLO's grassroots base through a reconnection between the mass of the people and its representatives in order to frame a collective platform.

> If one wants the connection to be with the PLO, we then demand the PLO to adhere to its National Charter, in order to exist as the only legitimate representative of the Palestinian people. And since there are initiatives designed to convey our voice to the Authority, we demand the Authority define its standing in respect of the basics. The Palestinian people in the host countries and the camps want to return to an entirely freed Palestine.[29]

Others abandoned the framework of the PLO yet remain informed by the need for a unifying framework, and a huge range of these types of institutions were competing for supremacy. In North America, most of the younger generation knew nothing of the PLO nor had even heard of the existence of the PNC, and associated the PA with recent corruption stories and with abandoning stands that reflected the Palestinian people's views.

> Listening to this discussion, I conclude that the problem is not about people, it is about the PLO's institutions. Some people don't trust the

PLO. Let us be outspoken here: there is corruption in the PLO. Also by not representing all the spectrums and different forces, it has resulted in separating people from the PLO.[30]

Others from Lebanon and Palestine, resident in the USA, were either involved in the remnants of the smaller political organizations, or were independently organized into small, sometimes very active institutions. However the majority were organized through religious associations or family and municipal clubs and associations, and Arab-American associations. What also became apparent is that the civic life of Palestinian refugees and exiles is highly constrained by the older national associational structures that had largely collapsed in practice, but had not yet been replaced. This leaves a highly conservative method and style of politics dominating both political and civic spheres in exile. Equally, the inherited practices from the national liberation movement means some very small groups of leaders saw themselves as the vanguard, and thus entitled to take decisions on behalf of the people they claimed to represent. The political environment and constraints of host countries where these political elites lived played a pivotal role in their position and their dominance in Palestinian political life. This perversion of the political process was commented upon by a participant at a meeting in Berlin:

> I am one of those who participated in the elections, and in unions and federations, until I had had enough. There weren't fair elections in any of these federations and institutions. And we were told who will be members in the administrative body. In short, names would come from the top; the so-and-so organization wants to assign such-and-such from Fatah or the Democratic Front or Popular Front. The names are dictated to us, and we remain as false witnesses.[31]

Articulating a unifying mechanism to achieve a common platform on a one-state or two-state solution

The delinking of al-Shatat Palestinians from the framework of collective deliberation, after the Madrid and Oslo processes, has meant that it has become nearly impossible to discuss a claim for a platform, collective endeavour, or common goal in the Palestinian political field. Indeed without a unifying umbrella to operate and debate issues relevant to Palestinian destiny, agendas and intellectual debates could only serve to increase fragmentation. Without having a framework to enfranchise the millions of voiceless and powerless Palestinians now unable to make their own contributions to such issues, the task for intellectuals and others in a privileged position is to assist in making one. Individuals and groups could start to look for ways of reconnecting and restructuring the body politic to serve them, facilitating a process that strengthens and gives primacy to the role of the collective and popular Palestinian agendas in forging national direction.

First, as a Palestinian refugee, I have the right – and we all have the right – to participate in the legislative, municipal, and presidential elections that were conducted. If you want to know how, I can point to Iraq as an example. Iraq was invaded two years ago, yet all the refugees from all over the world went to the embassies in the countries where they live and voted like everyone else. And I, as a member in the PLO who belongs to the PLO office here, have the legal right to have an embassy in Lebanon, to be able to vote through it, and to express my own opinion, because expressing personal opinions is one sort of democracy; it is participatory or popular sovereignty, the rule of people by people.[32]

However, a small illustration from a recent study demonstrates that Palestinians in refugee camps and exile communities have increasingly recognized that the work of reconnecting Palestinians wherever they live must be given priority, and that task must be implemented before any common platform can be hammered out with regard to overall political strategies on a future solution or model. This is how a Palestinian participant at a meeting in the United Arab Emirates put it:

Palestinians are dispersed in the Arab countries with no authority to unite them, and we don't look after each other, and we don't have coordinated forums: everyone works on his own and for his own interests. I wish that we could have a group to represent us in the UAE or in Palestinian forums so that our voice could be heard by the PLO, which we don't know except through the press. No one from the PLO ever comes to visit us in this country, although they come and go without bothering to invite the Palestinian community. I have been working in this country for twenty-five years, and I have never seen any representative from the PLO and not one of them ever invited the Palestinian community. We don't represent the Palestinian community which includes the worker and the machinist, so how should we convey this

249

to them and how should we meet with them and show them that we are educated? In any case, they don't care about us. I am from Yafa [Jaffa], but the Palestinians and the Arabs gave me nationality as a Gaza citizen, so they would say this is not a Palestinian, he's from Gaza. I think this is our fault, we should feel that we are valuable and we should unite as Palestinians, then we can ask the others to give us our rights.[33]

This sentiment was echoed by Palestinians in every meeting that was held by activists seeking to register what Palestinians in exile are looking for: the means to achieve a common platform, rather than a platform itself.

> The [PLO] was absent and frozen in the last period. The institutions of the PLO should be activated so that all the Palestinian communities abroad can have a political role in the National Council and in the PLO; not only a voice and support, but also participating in the decision-making process. Therefore our democratic representation is aimed at participating politically in the struggle, so that we can have a voice and real participation, not only in Italy, but also in other areas of the Arab world. We have 5 million Palestinians, which is greater than the number of Palestinians in Palestine, and they are a pillar of support for the Palestinian national project, and they should be represented in the national Palestinian decision. But our opinion was not taken regarding Oslo and other agreements. We should have a common Palestinian position so that all the Palestinian factions agree on it, even if each retains its particularities. There should be a common and agreed programme and this programme should be implemented outside and inside. This is achieved by democratic representation.[34]

The implications of these expressions are profound. First, none of the current assertions, claims, or arguments in favour of either a one-state or a two-state strategy by political groups, intellectuals, and rights-based organizations can have any real meaning until there is a method to incorporate these claims within a deliberative discussion that is understood and agreed upon by all sectors of society – inside and outside Palestine. At the moment there is no collective process to ensure that all voices are heard, or to understand how many, or where, we are, or how to measure the size of the constituencies, weigh them, or give particular arguments a place in the overall deliberation about what the Palestinian people want, and then work towards the common goal of a recognized platform.

There is an important and powerful role for advocacy by Palestinian individuals, activists, academics, and intellectuals speaking on behalf of a people, especially one that is so disenfranchised. But such advocacy cannot replace the fundamental right of a people speaking for itself. When the latter right cannot be practised by millions of people, the former becomes an elitist rather than a popular enterprise, and lacks popular legitimacy. The path towards national reconstruction and the twin goals of self-determination and the Right of Return are essential underpinnings which can legitimize either a one-state or a two-state solution.

Notes

1 The term al-Shatat is used throughout. The closest translation for it in English is 'diaspora'. Diaspora however is inadequate and, worse, eludes the nature of the Palestinian dispersal since 1947. Neither the use of the term diaspora, nor that of 'refugees' is sufficient to capture the totality of the current Palestinian dispersal, and the different legal statuses recognized under international law. There are several million refugees in both occupied Palestine and exile (as well as internally displaced inside the Green Line). Until such a time as there is a solution to the conflict, the outside Palestinians do not yet constitute a diaspora. In defining it thus, one could undermine the various existing legal, political, and civic statuses of the several million Palestinians who live outside historic Palestine.

2 Participant, public meeting, London, United Kingdom (3 July 2005). Unpublished draft of Report: 'Foundations and Directions: Civitas', Oxford University, Alden Press, 2006.

3 The details of the Geneva initiative can be found at http://www.geneva-accord.org. Details of the Nusseibeh-Ayalon plan ('The People's Voice') can be found at http://www.mifkad.org.il/en/principles.asp

4 Meetings were held inside Palestine as well, but they are not drawn upon for this chapter. The Civitas project, facilitated at Nuffield College, Oxford, helped coordinate meetings run and convened by Palestinian activists in countries across the Middle East, Europe, and the Americas from January to September 2005. The transcripts of these meetings are translated into English, and the Report is published (in September 2006) in both the original Arabic, and in English. The extracts used here is from the English draft of the Report, which can also be found online.

5 The full text of the National Conciliation Document of the Prisoners, known as the Prisoners' Document, can be found at http://www.jmcc.org/documents/prisoners2.htm. It was first signed on 11 May 2006; a second version appeared on 28 June 2006, signed by the leaderships of all the main

factions currently in Israeli prisons. There were some reservations on certain points made by Islamic Jihad.

6 Participant, syndicate group meeting, Frankfurt, Germany (24 April 2005).

7 Participant, public meeting, Montreal, Canada (3 July 2005).

8 Participant, public meeting, Detroit, Michigan, United States (28 June 2005).

9 Participant, activist meeting, Athens, Greece (6 May 2005).

10 Participant, public meeting for disabled persons, Beirut, Lebanon (15 May 2005).

11 Participant, women's preparatory meeting, Amman, Jordan (30 August 2005).

12 Participant, women's meeting, Athens, Greece (16 April 2005).

13 Participant, public meeting, Sharjah, United Arab Emirates (17 November 2005).

14 Participant, syndicate group meeting, Frankfurt, Germany (24 April 2005).

15 Participant, public meeting, London, United Kingdom (3 July 2005).

16 Participant, public meeting, Detroit, Michigan, USA. (28 June 2005).

17 Participant, public meeting, Padua, Italy (8 October 2005).

18 Participant, activists' meeting, Athens, Greece (6 May 2005).

19 Participant, public meeting, Khartoum, Sudan (7 June 2005).

20 (Participant, public meeting, Dammam, Saudi Arabia (5 October 2005).

21 Participant, worker's meeting, Beddawi camp, Lebanon. (7 April 2005).

22 Participant, syndicate meeting, the shelter of Al-Salam Neighbourhood (Al-Tobaji), Baghdad, Iraq (14 May 2005).

23 Participant, preparatory Meeting, Amman, Jordan (26 July 2004).

24 Participant, preparatory workshop, Jaramana camp, Syria (1 June 2005).

25 Participant, public meeting, Sharjah, United Arab Emirates (17 November 2005).

26 Participant, women's preparatory meeting, Amman, Jordan (30 August 2005).

27 Participant, public meeting, Yemen (20 April 2005).

28 Participant, public meeting, Koge, Denmark (18 March 2005).

29 Participant, public meeting, Vlaardigen, Netherlands (31 March 2005).

30 Participant, workers' meeting, Shatila camp, Lebanon (15 April 2005).

31 Participant, syndicate meeting, Berlin, Germany (June 25, 2005).

32 Participant, students' meeting, Wavel Camp, Lebanon (10 April 2005).

33 Participant, public meeting, Sharjah, United Arab Emirates (17 November 2005).

34 Participant, public meeting, Padua, Italy (8 October 2005).

Index

Negev, judaization of, 49
neo-conservatives in USA, 10, 105,
    107, 115, 117
Netanyahu, Benjamin, 72
'New' Middle East, 10–11
Nitseret Elit, 50
Nixon, Richard M., 103
non-governmental organizations
    (NGOs), role of, 133–4
Nusseibeh-Ayalon platform, 53, 233

occupied territories, legal status of,
    81, 86, 87
occupied territory, definition of, 83
Olmert, Ehud, 12, 52, 55–6, 58, 61, 63,
    72, 91, 92, 186, 195
one-state solution, 20, 35, 185, 186;
    Islamic, 181–6 *see also* bi-national
    state
Oslo Accords, 3, 5, 39–40, 48, 53, 71,
    77, 81, 87, 89, 100, 104, 111, 130,
    131, 132, 138, 154, 168, 169, 172,
    175, 189, 190, 238, 242; failure
    of, 10, 236; historic implications
    of, 85–7; impact on Palestinians,
    242–3; opposed by Hamas, 193,
    199; Oslo II, 85–6; resentment at,
    191
Ottoman Empire, 1, 30, 34; Palestine
    within, 32–3

Palestine: as last colonial issue, 1–29;
    definition of, 33; dependence
    on Israel, 124, 140, 214, 225;
    development plans, 133–4
Palestine Conciliation Commission,
    37
Palestine Liberation Organization
    (PLO), 4, 20, 76, 87, 90, 91, 123,
    130, 168, 176, 185, 186, 190,
    197, 204, 213, 235, 237–42;
    absence of, 249, 250; adopts
    two-state strategy, 219, 224; as
    sole representative of Palestinian
    people, 92–3, 237, 240, 246, 247;
    emergence of, 37–8; freezing of
    institutions, 5; marginalization
    of, 241–2; moves to Tunis, 238;
    political hegemony of, 188 (end
    of, 190); portrayed as terrorist,
    103; recognition of Israel, 77,
    83; recognized by Israel, 39, 71,

84; relations with Hamas, 193–5;
    rentier relationship, 4; revival of,
    17, 22, 244; secular culture of, 7;
    shift to two-state solution, 221;
    weakening of, 245, 247
Palestine National Charter, 88
Palestine National Congress, 35
Palestine National Council (PNC), 76,
    88, 89, 233, 240; failure to meet,
    242; institutional change in, 243
Palestinian Authority (PA), 5, 53, 64,
    80, 86, 99, 104, 106, 109, 111,
    140, 160, 171, 173, 175, 188, 196,
    203, 204; approach to WBGS
    economy, 133, 134–6; as employer,
    193; cutting of funds to, 178;
    dependence on external donors,
    90; dismantlement of, 193;
    establishment of, 90, 123, 130;
    facilitated by Israel, 59; failure of,
    113; felt to be unrepresentative,
    238; financial obligations of,
    191–3; nature and structure
    of, 131–3; opposed by Hamas,
    168–9; reform of, 193, 205; secret
    accounts of, 134; withering of,
    16–17
Palestinian economy: Israeli dom-
    inance of, 158; weakness of, 192
Palestinian Legislative Council (PLC),
    75, 91, 137
Palestinian refugees, 38, 41, 200, 212,
    219; organisational forms of, 248;
    repatriation of, 37; right of return,
    3, 10, 11, 18, 40, 43, 45, 72, 85, 92,
    100, 110, 160, 163, 202, 211, 213,
    214, 218, 220, 227, 228, 233–4,
    236, 242, 244, 245–6, 251 (rejected
    by Israel, 229; waiving of, 225);
    status of, 80
Palestinian state, 41, 44, 138, 219;
    and Hamas, 188–210; building
    of, 87–90, 106; defined by Israel,
    144; Israel's position on, 18, 205;
    limited nature of, 114; recognition
    of, 111; stripped of meaning,
    42–3; viability of, 123–43, 160, 186,
    213–14
Palestinian Telecommunication
    Company, 136
Palestinians: as homogeneous
    national group, 213;